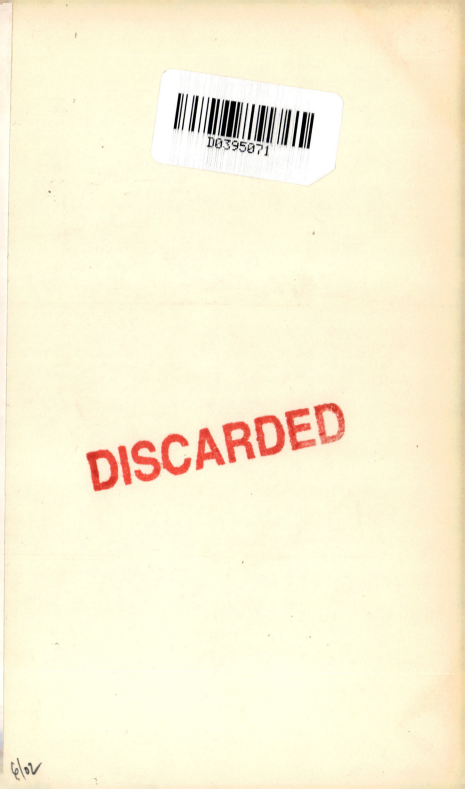

6/02

AMERICAN WRITING
in the TWENTIETH CENTURY

THE LIBRARY OF CONGRESS SERIES
IN AMERICAN CIVILIZATION
edited by Ralph Henry Gabriel

AMERICAN WRITING
in the TWENTIETH CENTURY

WILLARD THORP

HARVARD UNIVERSITY PRESS
CAMBRIDGE, MASSACHUSETTS — 1960

Library of Congress Catalog Card Number 59–14739
Printed in the United States of America

Preface

THIS is a favorable moment for telling the story of America's accomplishment in literature in this century. Beginning about 1912 and continuing through the second World War a new generation of writers brought about an extraordinary renaissance in fiction, poetry, the drama, and criticism. Only once before, in the 1840's and 1850's, had there been in America a literary achievement of this magnitude. What Emerson, Thoreau, Hawthorne, Melville, and Whitman produced in those years was equaled nearly a century later by the contributions of Robinson, Frost, O'Neill, Willa Cather, Hemingway, Faulkner, and a score of other writers only slightly less distinguished.

Time may prove this second renaissance even more impressive than the first. Certainly its scope is greater. There were no dramatists in the first group and only one poet of stature, Whitman. Before the 1920's only a few American writers had received much acclaim abroad — Cooper everywhere in Europe, Poe and Whitman in France, Mark Twain in England. Our writers in this century have made American literature a part of world literature. It was symptomatic that in 1930, when this second renaissance was approaching its apogee, Sinclair Lewis should be the first American to win the Nobel Prize in literature. Since then it has been awarded to O'Neill (1936), Pearl Buck (1938), T. S. Eliot (1948) — who had become a British subject in 1927 — Faulkner (1950), and Hemingway (1954). American works are now a staple in the foreign bookmart. On the bookstalls of Paris, Munich, and Rome volumes with such strangely familiar titles as *La Route au Tobac, Le Bruit et la Fureur, Mord im Dom,* and *Tenera è la notte* greet the wondering eyes of American tourists. Europeans may fear lest Coca-Cola cause the downfall of their civilization, but European critics have little but praise for modern American literature. Typical of their judgments is what André Gide said in *Interviews Imaginaires* (written during the second World War): "There is no contemporary literature that arouses my curiosity more than that of the United States. . . . All these new American novelists are seized and held like children by the present moment, by the here and now; they are far from books and free from the ratiocinations, the preoccupations, the feelings of remorse that darken and complicate our old world."

Already much of the writing produced between 1900 and 1950 can be viewed in perspective. Much of it, indeed, seems to have been written a long time ago. The giants of the earlier years — Edith Wharton, Willa Cather, Lewis, Robinson, O'Neill — have departed, each leaving a large body of writing (an *oeuvre,* as the French say) which can now be objectively assessed. The works of many of this giant race who are still writing — Eliot, Dos Passos, Hemingway, Faulkner — are certain to stand as land marks in the American literary scene. With the abrupt changes in the mood of the nation, caused by two World Wars and a depression, literary movements were often short-lived. New attitudes and forms gave way quickly under the pressures of the time. The battle over free verse just before the first World War, the moral crusade of the humanist critics in the late 1920's, the "socialist realism" of the proletarian novelists of the 1930's now have the look of skirmishes fought in a far-off time.

The lull in American writing since the second World

War has also given perspective to what went before in this century. Much of the prose and verse of the younger writers seems uncertain of direction, a continuation of the work of their elders rather than a new departure. The only major writer to achieve wide recognition in the 1950's was James Gould Cozzens whose war novel, *Guard of Honor,* won a Pulitzer Prize in 1949 and whose *By Love Possessed* deserved the award in 1958. But Cozzens belongs to the generation of Hemingway and Fitzgerald. Popular success came to him late. Because there has been, in more than a decade, little that is experimental in technique or markedly new in content, the writers of this century's renaissance stand out in strong relief against the literary pallor of these later years.

The literary situation in the 1950's resembles in some ways — though this observation should not be pressed too hard — that which obtained fifty years ago. Poetry has again lost favor with publishers and readers. The stage, in bondage to the theatrical unions and Broadway real-estate owners, is once more concerned chiefly with box-office success, as it was in the days of Belasco. What creative vitality there has been on Broadway in the 1950's came to it largely from the small off-Broadway theaters where imaginative directors, actors, and designers either got their start or, if already established, were afforded a chance to experiment. But the off-Broadway movement produced no new playwright. Once again the novel has crowded other literary forms. The term best seller came into general use around 1910 and from that time on the biggest best sellers have generally been novels. But a popular novel today reaches an audience unimaginable in 1910. In the hope (often realized) that his novel will have an audience of millions waiting for it, the author and his publisher write into their contract clauses protecting a multitude of subsidiary rights — book club, digest, radio, movie, television, soft-cover reprint. In this welter of popular fiction old patterns are discernable. The religious novel is in vogue again (in 1913 *The Inside of the Cup*; in 1950 *The Cardinal*); and so is the costume romance (*Alice of Old Vincennes* in 1900; *Giant* in 1952).

Whether the wheel has come full circle and we are once more in a waiting period when most reading is "hammock reading," as they called it in 1910; whether another literary renaissance is just ahead of us, time will tell.

The plan of this book is simple. In the main the unfolding story of American writing in this century is told chronologically, though there is a topical arrangement as well. In Chapter One ("The Age of Innocence") the chief stress is on the novels of the period from 1900 to 1914 since little poetry or drama of importance was written during those years. The second chapter ("New Voices") describes the renaissance in poetry and fiction which took place between 1912 and 1922. The subject of Chapter Three will be clear at once from the title: "Dramatic Interlude, 1915–1940." Two chapters are then devoted to the many novelists of distinction who began to publish after the First World War. To give these chapters coherence and shape they are organized thematically: Chapter Four being called "Caste and Class in the Novel, 1920–1950" and Chapter Five, "The Persistence of Naturalism in the Novel." In each of these chapters there is a backward glance to the earlier years of the century. Chapter Six, "Make It New: Poetry, 1920–1950," parallels these two chapters on the novelists.

During this half-century span there were several regional movements in our literature. Of these the most influential and long-lived was the "Southern Renaissance," which is the subject of Chapter Seven. Because throughout this period critical writing kept pace with the work of the novelists, poets, and dramatists, it seemed appropriate to devote the concluding chapter ("Off to the Critical Wars") to the critics who praised or dissented from, but in any event analyzed and debated, the new writing season by season.

I should like to call attention to another principle of organization. In a survey of this kind the author and the reader must move rapidly from writer to writer and from one work to another. There is too little space for leisurely criticism and evaluation. To overcome this handicap in some degree, I have concluded each chapter with a several-page consideration of at least one outstanding writer whose work is representative of the period or theme under discussion. It has thus been possible to introduce critical surveys of the work of Edith Wharton, E. A. Robinson, Robert Frost, Willa Cather, Eugene O'Neill, John Dos Passos, Ernest Hemingway, Wallace Stevens, William Faulkner, and T. S. Eliot.

Princeton, New Jersey   *Willard Thorp*

CONTENTS

AMERICAN WRITING
in the TWENTIETH CENTURY

ONE

The Age of Innocence

I

WHEN Edith Wharton in 1920 turned back to the days of her childhood to write about New York's social elite in the 1870's, she called her novel *The Age of Innocence.* The title epitomizes quite as well the period when she was doing her best writing, the years between 1900 and 1914. Parents had no reason to be apprehensive about the books their children withdrew from the public library when the best-sellers, during one three-year period (1901–1903), were *Graustark, Mrs. Wiggs of the Cabbage Patch, The Virginian, The Little Shepherd of Kingdom Come, The Call of the Wild,* and *Rebecca of Sunnybrook Farm.* The mood in the novels of the day is buoyant and optimistic. Virility always weds purity in the last chapter, after the mean and cynical characters have been thoroughly disposed of. Human relationships are a simple black and white. No hero or heroine is permitted to indulge in introspection, because to look inward was considered morbid. Freud was uncovering the unconscious in Vienna but Americans did not discover Freud until just before the Germans occupied Belgium. The occasional voice which objected to this diet of literary treacle was readily silenced. Thus Mrs. Gene Stratton-Porter told off a minister of the gospel who called her *Laddie* "molasses fiction":

What a wonderful compliment! All the world loves sweets.

1

. . . Molasses is more necessary to the happiness of human and beast than vinegar, and over-indulgence in it is not nearly so harmful to the system. I am a molasses person myself. . . . So are most of my friends — all of them who are happy, as a matter of fact. . . . Forever the acid of life will have to be doled out by those who have enough in their systems to be accustomed to it. God gave me a taste for sweets and the sales of the books I write prove that a few other people are similar to me in this.[1]

How is one to account for this mood of optimism, though toward the end of the period the "acid of life" was beginning to sour the molasses? What was happening in literature was decidedly at variance with the social changes of the Progressive Era, a period marked by the growth of the power of labor, the reform of municipal politics, the regulation of the giant trusts, and the demand for an end to the pillaging of our national resources.

It must be remembered that this was also the age of the "full dinner pail." The panic of 1907 was a banker's panic and lasted less than a year. It scarcely affected the fundamental prosperity of the country. The wounds of the Civil War had been healed. Old sectional differences and animosities were disappearing. A new national pride was engendered by our gaudy victory over Spain. A short war and a merry one, it had lasted long enough to produce a crop of heroes who belonged to the entire nation—Rowan who carried the message to Garcia, Commodore Dewey ("You may fire when ready, Gridley"), and Theodore Roosevelt. The War had also brought into being a new empire for Americans to rejoice in. We were at last a world power, as T. R.'s deeds and words when he became President constantly reminded us.

Roosevelt embodied the new nationalism. Though an easterner and an aristocrat, he loved the wild west and fired his countrymen with enthusiasm for it. (His enormously popular *Winning of the West* could be bought in a paper-covered edition for a quarter.) Southerners did not forget that his mother was born in Georgia and that his uncles had fought for the Confederacy. McKinley permitted the Spanish American War to take place, but T. R. was so much its foremost hero that Mr. Dooley thought his book about the Rough Riders should have been called "Alone in Cubia." As President, he shook the big stick at Japan and Russia, Germany and England, as well as Colombia and little Santo Domingo.

The nationalism of the Rooseveltian era bursts out in the fiction of the day, often in unexpected places. Those who read John Fox, Jr.'s *The Little Shepherd of Kingdom Come* many years ago probably have vague recollections of the "Kingdom" as belonging to God. Not at all. What young Major Chad Buford, a hero in the Union Army, dreams of at the War's end is something quite different. His ambitions are Rooseveltian before the event.

In his breast still burned the spirit that had led his race to the land, had wrenched it from savage and from King, had made it the high temple of Liberty for the worship of free men — the Kingdom Come for the oppressed of the earth — and, himself the unconscious Shepherd of that Spirit, he was going to help carry its ideals across a continent west-ward to another sea and on — who knows — to the gates of the rising sun.

II

By 1900 the strength of the New England tradition, on the wane for thirty years, was at last played out. There were no new luminaries to occupy the chairs in Boston's Saturday Club, once reserved for Emerson and Parkman and their peers. The passing of the great age was lamented — in New England at least. "We are freshly convinced," wrote a reviewer in the *Atlantic* in 1900, "that the Puritan vein and the transcendental vein are worked out. . . . The life of the Northeastern states is too settled, circumscribed, and safe, it has been too long fat and 'set', and prosperous, to afford the best of dramatic material. If Spain had had the will or the power to bombard the cities of the New England seaboard in the summer of 1898, we might have had some strong novels of New England life in the next generation."

When Thomas Bailey Aldrich assumed the editorship of the *Atlantic* in 1881, he brought gentility with him. He and his friends R. H. Stoddard and E. C. Stedman were bent on upholding the Ideal in literature. They despised naturalism (an abominable Gaulish invention of Zola and Flaubert) and fought to keep American letters free from its taint. If American life was daily growing more corrupt because the commercial spirit was everywhere rampant and all kinds of dangerous foreigners were pouring through our "unguarded gates," literature could still be the preserver of the True and the Beautiful. When danger threatened, the Genteel Spirit did not hesitate to act. Even W. D. Howells, champion of realism in fiction, raised his voice in protest when Gorki docked at New York with a woman who was not his wife. The "dean" of drama critics, William Winter (known along Broadway as "Weeping Willie"), was still denouncing Ibsen, Wilde, and Shaw as late as 1906. (In this same year children were forbidden to borrow *Huckleberry Finn* at the Brooklyn Public Library.) Early in 1907 the season's performances of *Salomé* were stopped at the Metropolitan Opera House.

The sway of the Genteel Tradition might have been shortened if death or other calamities had not silenced a remarkable group of younger writers who had made names for themselves by 1900 in spite of the strength and frankness of their work. Stephen Crane was only twenty-eight when he died in that year, leaving behind him one novel which is a classic, *The Red Badge of Courage* (1895), a handful of impressionistic free-verse poems, *The Black*

Riders (1895), and three or four short stories which show no mark of time. Frank Norris died at thirty-two, two years after Crane. The brutality of his *McTeague* (1899) and the socialistic undertone heard in the first half of *The Octopus* (1901) were forgiven because he was at heart a romancer and so knew how to reach a large public. Ambrose Bierce, whose Civil War stories, published in the nineties, were the first to tell about battle as the men in blue and gray had known it, lived on into the Age of Innocence (the date of his death is not known), but he had grown so disgusted with American life that he signed off with *The Shadow on the Dial* (1909), a collection of devasting essays on the America of his time. Three years earlier readers had distinctly not been amused by such Menckenian definitions as these in his *Devil's Dictionary*:

Christian, *n.* One who follows the teachings of Christ in so far as they are not inconsistent with a life of sin.

Flesh, *n.* The Second Person of the Secular Trinity.

Senate, *n.* A body of elderly gentlemen charged with high duties and misdemeanors.

Death and disillusionment were not the only disasters which deprived Americans of writing suited to the new century. Neglect was another. Several authors whose careers began in this period were compelled to struggle for years against indifference or hostility before they could make their way. The case of Theodore Dreiser is the most spectacular. Frank Norris, a reader for Doubleday, accepted his first novel, *Sister Carrie*, a truthful account of a country girl who "goes wrong" in Chicago but climbs over the two men in her life to success on the stage. The novel was printed in 1900 but never issued by the publishers because someone behind the scenes ordered the edition to the warehouse. (Dreiser suspected that his censor was Mrs. Doubleday.) As a result of this traumatic experience Dreiser suffered a breakdown and did not venture another novel until *Jennie Gerhardt* (1911). In 1915 he was in trouble again when his publishers withdrew *The "Genius"* under threat of prosecution by the New York Society for the Suppression of Vice. Few American writers have absorbed so much abuse from critics and self-appointed censors.

Two of the best poets of this century, Robinson and Frost, had to persist for years in the face of almost utter neglect. Robinson's first volume, *The Torrent and the Night Before* (1896), was overlooked by the reviewers. Though *Captain Craig* (1902) had the endorsement of Theodore Roosevelt, whose approbation could usually make a writer, it fared no better. Robert Frost met similar discouragement. In 1912 he gave up and sailed for England where his genius was fostered by a group of sympathetic writers. When he returned to American in 1915 he brought with him his first two volumes of verse and an English reputation founded on them.

III

When the new century opened, readers had their noses in historical novels. Three best sellers in 1899 had been Charles Major's *When Knighthood was in Flower*, Winston Churchill's *Richard Carvel*, and P. L. Ford's *Janice Meredith*. In 1900 they were joined by Mary Johnston's *To Have and to Hold* and Maurice Thompson's *Alice of Old Vincennes*, to make up half of the items on the list of best-selling fiction. Though this vogue for stories about the American past (the most popular themes were the Revolution, the Civil War, and pioneering days) persisted only a half-dozen years, it forms a distinct episode in our literary history. How strongly the current was flowing in this direction can be seen from the fact that several novelists who had little talent for historical fiction turned aside to have a try at it. In 1901 Sarah Orne Jewett published *The Tory Lover* and in 1902 Ellen Glasgow was ready with *The Battle-Ground*. Tarkington became popular over night with his second novel, *Monsieur Beaucaire* (1900), set in eighteenth century England.

Americans have been fond of historical novels since Cooper wrote *The Spy* (1821) in emulation of Scott, but these historical romances of the decade 1900–1910 are discernibly the product of the time in which they were written. The new nationalism breathes through them and many noble words are spoken about the destiny of the nation. The Civil War novels (many of them written by southerners) conclude with the reunion of brothers or lovers who had chosen opposite sides in the conflict. Frequently the benign shade of Lincoln looks down upon these reconciliations, as on the last page of Churchill's *The Crisis* when a northern soldier and his southern sweetheart are at last in each other's arms.

In the morning came to them the news of Abraham Lincoln's death. And the same thought was in both their hearts, who had known him as it was given to few to know him. How he had lived in sorrow; how he had died a martyr on the very day of Christ's death upon the cross. And they believed that Abraham Lincoln gave his life for his country even as Christ gave his for the world.

And so must we believe that God has reserved for this Nation a destiny high upon the earth.

Some of these romances have become subclassics and are still read by adults as well as children.[2] As pictures of the American past they are more trustworthy than their Hollywood offspring, notwithstanding the huge sums spent on "research" by the studios. Paul Leicester Ford was a respectable historian and though in his *Janice Meredith* the Americans seem to be fighting the British in order that the heroine may wed dashing Jack Brereton, the details of the battles at Princeton and Yorktown are authentic. Winston Churchill, deservedly the most popular of these romancers, was painstaking with his facts. Each of his three historical novels (*Richard Carvel, The Crisis, The*

Crossing) ends with an "Afterword" which states the patriotic lesson he was trying to teach and just where he had departed from history in order to make his plot come out right.

Quite as popular as these historical romances and like them in belonging to a tradition in American writing while evincing the new spirit of the times, were the novels about the far west. The west has meant many things to Americans — Eldorado, free land, escape from family and creditors, big game, fabulous wealth from mines, herds, and lumber. In 1900 it was beginning to mean something new: a land of vanishing glory. The great open spaces which once belonged to the future were suddenly a part of history. Owen Wister, whose *The Virginian: A Horseman of the Plains* (1902) was the most popular of the new westerns, makes the point dramatically in his prefatory note "To the Reader." Because his novel presents Wyoming between 1874 and 1890, it is, he says, a "colonial romance." Wyoming in those years was a colony as "wild as was Virginia one hundred years earlier."

Had you left New York or San Francisco at ten o'clock this morning, by noon the day after to-morrow you could step out at Cheyenne. There you would stand at the heart of the world that is the subject of my picture, yet you would look around you in vain for the reality. It is a vanished world. No journeys, save those which memory can take, will bring you to it now. The mountains are there, far and shining, and the sunlight, and the infinite earth, and the air that seems forever the true fountain of youth, — but where is the buffalo, and the wild antelope, and where the horseman with his pasturing thousands? So like its old self does the sage-brush seem when revisited, that you wait for the horseman to appear.

But he will never come again. He rides in his historic yesterday. You will no more see him gallop out of the unchanging silence than you will see Columbus on the unchanging sea come sailing from Palos with his caravels.

From the earliest days Americans were eager for news from the west. Those who were setting forth on the Oregon or Santa Fé trails wanted accounts which would tell them how to survive deserts and Indians and deep snow in the mountain passes. For those who stayed home, the recorded journeys into the plains and mountains (many of them written by well-known authors) gave added color: Irving's *A Tour on the Prairies* (1835), for example, Parkman's *Oregon Trail* (1849), and Bayard Taylor's *El Dorado* (1850). Only gradually did the west invade fiction as the eastern publishers discovered Bret Harte, Mark Twain, and Helen Hunt Jackson. The west flourished, of course, in hundreds of dime novels but most of the hacks who poured them out did not know a lariat from a land office. Along with the sins of New York and the sufferings of near-white girls sold into slavery, the west was part of their stock-in-trade.

The authors of this new western fiction knew the scenes and people they were writing about. Stewart Edward White had lived among lumberjacks, rivermen, and miners from Michigan to California. Emerson Hough had practiced law in Whiteoaks, New Mexico, when it was "half cow-town and half mining camp," but soon turned to writing about the west for various magazines. He had published his authentic *The Story of the Cowboy* (1897) — a great favorite of Theodore Roosevelt's — before he began to put his knowledge and experience of the west into fiction.[3] Owen Wister, Philadelphia born and Harvard educated, had lived long enough in Wyoming to know whom he could safely clap on the shoulder and salute as "you old son-of-a —— ," with or without a smile. Zane Grey had not seen the west until he wrote his third novel but he learned fast. His vast audience — over nineteen million copies of his sixty-three novels have been sold — accepted his west as authentic because he provided plenty of shooting, hard riding, and brutality.

In the first decade of the new century the writers of western fiction traveled with the pioneers all the way from the trans-Alleghenies to the Chilikoot Pass in Alaska. Churchill celebrated the settling of Kentucky and the campaign of George Rogers Clark "which gave the Republic Ohio, Indiana, and Illinois" (*The Crossing*, 1904). Hough wrote about land speculation in the Louisiana Territory (*The Mississippi Bubble*, 1902) and the Oregon boundary dispute (*54–40 or Fight*, 1909). White covered the last of the logging years in Michigan's Upper Peninsula (*The Blazed Trail*, 1902) and the gold rush in the Black Hills of South Dakota in the early 1890's (*The Claim Jumpers*, 1901). Jack London turned his experiences in the Alaska gold strike into frontier fiction (*Burning Daylight*, 1900).

Probably the best of the westerns — certainly the one which is chiefly remembered today — is Wister's *The Virginian*, a best seller in 1902. At first glance it is hard to see why it has captivated so many readers. The hero never seems to work at his job as foreman of the cow-punchers and most of the steers on Judge Henry's ranch were added by the illustrator. A few Indians lurk along the Bow Leg trail. There is an off-stage vigilante lynching, and of course the hero has finally to shoot it out with Trampas, the foul-mouthed villain. Essentially it is a love story with a trickle of action and a handsome backdrop — "open land and woodland, pines and sage-brush, all silent and grave and lustrous in the sunshine." No doubt it is the love story which made the novel so appealing. The girl, a schoolteacher from Vermont, at first thinks this lanky, soft-spoken southerner who persists in trying to marry her is impossibly crude and ignorant. But after she has taught him some Shakespeare and Browning (he balks at Jane Austen) and saved him from death by a bullet wound, she comes to see how wise and tender he is, and yields. In addition to the love story, there is the homely wisdom of the Virginian, akin to that of Wescott's David Harum and Bacheller's Eben Holden. In *The Virginian*, too, representatives of the three great sections of America are shown at their best. New Englanders could be proud of sweet and spunky Molly Wood, southerners of the manly Virginian, and westerners of Judge Henry who explains the law of the range to Molly and so persuades her to say Yes to her lover. There is also the fact, not to be denied, that *The Virginian* is well written.

The "westerns," one of America's gifts to the world, still lead a vigorous life in the movies and comic books and drugstore fiction. Now and then an excellent one comes along — Walter Van Tilburg Clark's *The Ox-bow Incident* (1940), for example — to prove that the love of the west and the knowledge of it shown by Wister and White and Hough have not abated.

IV

The downpour of historical novels and westerns in the first years of the century, steady and heavy as it was, could not match the deluge of family novels. As farm and village lost population to the cities, as the divorce rate increased alarmingly and the news of birth control got around, Americans wanted to be assured by the novelists that life was still wholesome among the plain people of the back country.[4] The domestic novel had long been a favorite, as the careers of Louisa May Alcott and Susan Warner abundantly prove, but now reports were coming in from all over the land that the American home was safe. Month after month this good news arrived — from northern New York (*Eben Holden*, 1900), the state of Maine (*Rebecca of Sunnybrook Farm*, 1903), the Cumberland mountains

(*The Little Shepherd of Kingdom Come*, 1903), the Ozarks (*The Shepherd of the Hills*, 1907), Indiana (*The Girl of the Limberlost*, 1909), and Vermont (*Pollyanna*, 1913). All of these novels were fabulous best sellers.

The craze may have been set off in 1901 by Alice Hegan Rice's *Mrs. Wiggs of the Cabbage Patch*, for it was on the best-seller list for two years while the presses worked overtime to produce 40,000 copies a month. Though the setting is a slum in Louisville rather than a farm or a village, in every other respect her story provided the model — the widowed mother whom no hardship defeats, her brave little brood of five who prosper on poverty and good works, and the modest bonanza at the end. When Mrs. Wiggs says, "Looks like ever'thing in the world comes right, if we jes' wait long enough," she speaks the moral of all these family novels. One additional subtheme was soon added. In the center of the stage is a cheery little girl — Rebecca or Pollyanna or Molly Make-Believe — whose inexhaustible optimism sets a wonderful example to her elders. Nothing gets her down, neither family poverty nor drudgery nor life in an orphan asylum nor loneliness when she is adopted by strangers.

The most literate version of the type, Irving Bacheller's *Eben Holden*, should be singled out because he crowded into it just about everything which readers of novels wanted in 1900. The orphan hero is a Vermont boy who is rescued and cared for by salty-tongued Eben (the David Harum type). After many hardships they find refuge with a kindly farm family in the St. Lawrence valley. The boy grows up (Eben always at his side), goes to college, and then on to the big city (New York, of course) to become a journalist. Horace Greeley befriends him and introduces him to several great men. He fights in the Civil War (emerging as a hero), meets and talks with Mr. Lincoln, marries his childhood sweetheart, and becomes a success in politics.

The inevitable words about the virtues of country life are put in the mouth of Horace Greeley.

"I like the country best," said he, when I had finished, "because there I see more truth in things. Here the lie has many forms — unique, varied, ingenious. The rouge and powder on the lady's cheek — they are lies, both of them; the baronial and ducal crests are lies and the fools who use them are liars; the people who soak themselves in rum have nothing but lies in their heads; the multitude who live by their wits and the lack of them in others — they are all liars; the many who imagine a vain thing and pretend to be what they are not — liars every one of them. It is bound to be so in the great cities, and it is a mark of decay. . . . For truth you've got to get back into the woods. You can find men there a good deal as God made them — genuine, strong and simple."

Eben Holden is a family novel, a Civil War novel, a success novel rolled into one. There are also pioneers in it though their trek has not been a long one. Bacheller's Preface is a tribute to the hardy woodchoppers who came west, out of Vermont, to found homes in the Adirondack wilderness. "Far from the centers of life their amusements, their humors, their religion, their folk lore, their views of things had in them the flavor of the timber lands, the simplicity of childhood. Every son was nurtured in the love of honor and industry, and the hope of sometime being president."

Were these novels which celebrated the strong past of America, in the deeds of her great men, in the self-reliance of the pioneers, and in the simple goodness of the plain people, mere escape literature, written to make a nation both proud and happy? Most of them were, but occasionally one hears undertones of regret for things vanished and anxiety about things to come. Would the new generation be worthy of its heritage? Some of the novelists had their doubts. White admired the "picturesque spectacle of energies running riot" in pioneer days, but he warned his readers that though the power was still in evidence, in the new days of trusts and monopolies it had gone beyond "its proper application." In his historical novels Churchill was given to prescient little homilies like these dying words of Judge Whipple in *The Crisis* (1901). He is speaking to young Stephen Brice, a Civil War hero who had been an aide to Lincoln.

> "In the days gone by our fathers worked for the good of the people, and they had no thought of gain. A time is coming when we shall need that blood and that bone in this Republic. Wealth not yet dreamed of will flow out of this land, and the waters of it will rot all save the pure, and corrupt all save the incorruptible. Half-tried men will go down before that flood. You and those like you will remember how your fathers governed, — strongly, sternly, justly. It was so that they governed themselves. Be vigilant. Serve your city, serve your state, but above all serve your country."

v

As if in corroboration of these prophecies of eventual disaster the novels of the "muckrakers" and their allies began to appear in the middle of the first decade. They were the immediate outgrowth of the muckraking journalism that flourished between 1902 and 1911. In his *Autobiography* (1931) Lincoln Steffens claims that the article which touched off this journalistic assault on corruption in business and politics was his "Tweed Days in St. Louis," which appeared in *McClure's Magazine* for October 1902.[5] Steffens was not long in possession of the field, though his *The Shame of the Cities* (1904) was the most impressively documented of the muckraking works which soon crowded the magazines and publishers' lists. In the same year Ida Tarbell's two-volume *History of the Standard Oil Company* hastened John D. Rockefeller into expiatory philanthropy. The muckrakers took credit for the reforms which followed their airing, in 1905 and 1906, of scandals in the life-insurance companies. They went on to expose timber frauds in Oregon, the patent medicine racket, the buying of labor leaders in the building trades, and many other ills of American life.

In their forays they spared neither men nor institutions. David Graham Phillips dared accuse United States Senators of high crimes in his "The Treason of the Senate," serialized in the *Cosmopolitan* in 1906. The iniquities of New York's richest congregation were laid bare in Charles Edward Russell's "Trinity Church: a Riddle of Riches." (Old Trinity owned some of the worst slums and bordelloes in the city.) Corrupt senators, political bosses, and mayors, rebate-accepting railroad officials, and venal insurance company presidents attempted to answer back or fled the country, depending on their degree of guilt. No company executive would ever again dare to repeat William Vanderbilt's famous sneer, "The public be damned."

At the height of this fervor for reform by exposure President Roosevelt called on the journalists to beware of sensationalism. His reference to Bunyan's man with the muckrake, made in a speech at the Gridiron Club in 1906, gave the crusade its name.

It is because I feel that there should be no rest in the endless war against the forces of evil that I ask that the war be conducted with sanity, as with resolution. The men with muckrakes are often indispensable to the well-being of society, but only if they know when to stop raking the muck, and to look upward to the celestial crown above them, to the crown of worthy endeavor.

The muckraking novelists explored as many depraved areas in American life as the journalists. The case histories found in Russell's *Lawless Wealth* (1908) and Gustavus Myers' *History of the Great American Fortunes* (1910) were paralleled in the careers of such fictional pirates of finance as Matthew Blacklock in Phillips' *The Deluge*

(1905) and the hero of Robert Barr's *The Speculations of John Steele* (1905). The crimes of the insurance companies, the prosecution of which made Charles Evans Hughes Governor of New York, gave Phillips his materials for *Light-Fingered Gentry* (1907). In *Mr. Crewe's Career* (1907) — one of the best sellers among the muckraking novels — Churchill showed how the "United Northeastern Railroads" bribed governors and legislators. Brand Whitlock, in *The Turn of the Balance* (1907), asserted that in modern America there was one law for the poor and another for the rich. In *The Jungle*, a best seller in 1906, Upton Sinclair disclosed the filthy conditions in Chicago's meat-packing plants. He intended his novel as a plea for Socialism, but his thesis made no converts to the cause. Instead, after gagging on paragraphs like the following, readers cleared their throats and demanded a national meat-inspection law.

There were those who made the tins for the canned-meat; and their hands, too, were a maze of cuts, and each cut represented a chance for blood-poisoning. Some worked at the stamping-machines, and it was very seldom that one could work long there at the pace that was set, and not give out and forget himself, and have a part of his hand chopped off. There were the "hoisters," as they were called, whose task it was to press the lever which lifted the dead cattle off the floor. They ran along upon a rafter, peering down through the damp and the steam; and as old Durham's architects had not built the killing-room for the convenience of the hoisters, at every few feet they would have to stoop under a beam, say four feet above the one they ran on; which got them into the habit of stooping, so that in a few years they would be walking like chimpanzees. Worst of any, however, were the fertilizer-men, and those who served in the cooking-rooms. These people could not be shown to the visitor, — for the odor of a fertilizer-man would scare any ordinary visitor at a hundred yards, and as for the other men, who worked in tank-rooms full of steam, and in some of which there were open vats near the level of the floor, their peculiar trouble was that they fell into the vats;

and when they were fished out, there was never enough of them left to be worth exhibiting, — sometimes they would be overlooked for days, till all but the bones of them had gone out to the world as Durham's Pure Leaf Lard!

The muckraking novelists in no sense formed a "school." Phillips was the only one who began his career as a muckraking journalist. The others had various personal reasons for anger at the degradation of American life. Churchill abandoned the writing of historical romances as a direct consequence of his experiences in the New Hampshire legislature. Brand Whitlock, who served as a reform mayor of Toledo from 1905 to 1913, had an even closer view of political chicanery. His liberalism was also fostered by his admiration for Altgeld of Illinois, the Governor who had dared to pardon three of the anarchists convicted of inciting the Haymarket Riot. It was his conversion to Socialism that impelled Upton Sinclair to pick up the muckrake and started him on his long career as a propagandist in fiction. In 1905 he helped Jack London organize the Intercollegiate Socialist Society. *The Jungle*, which he was working on at the time, had been commissioned by the Socialist weekly, *Appeal to Reason*, in which it was serialized.

The muckraking novels are better social documents than literature. Their authors were too angry and too intent on reform by disclosure to pay much attention to the probabilities of plot and the intricacies of character. But their contribution to American life was not negligible. The muckraking journalists and historians turned a strong light on long-standing abuses of political and economic power. The novelists, by disseminating their findings, helped to bring Americans face to face with the social problems of the new century.

After the shock and anger had worn itself out, another kind of fiction, influenced to some extent by the novels of the muckrakers, began to appear. It is deeply concerned with the social ills of the twentieth century, but it looks behind the corruption in big business, seeking to discover what had gone wrong with American social morality. For sensationalism it substitutes analysis and reflection. It was less preoccupied with the schemes of the malefactors than with the effect of their conspiracies on the individual and on the institutions of marriage (Phillips' *The Hungry Heart*, 1909), the family (Robert Herrick's *Together*, 1908), and religion (Churchill's *The Inside of the Cup*, 1913). The chief aim of these "problem" novelists was to explore the extent of the corruption caused by the era's lust for money and power. They recognized that the new century had brought with it problems with which an older, simpler morality could not cope. Yet some of them took as their standards the individualistic ethics of Emerson or the aesthetic utopianism of William Morris. Some had read Veblen. Though they were called "reform novelists," reform meant to them not coercive legislation, but the conversion of the individual to decency and integrity.

The novelist who followed this line undeviatingly throughout his long career was Robert Herrick (1868–1938). He came to Chicago in 1893 to teach literature and composition in the faculty which William Rainey Harper had gathered for the recently established University of Chicago. In this city of his exile Herrick found the acquisitive society in all its ruthlessness and naked greed: "hunger and sorrow and sordid misery . . . the brutal rich, the brutalized poor; the stupid good, the pedantic, the foolish — all, all that made the waking world." He was both appalled and fascinated by the spectacle. Occasionally he sends his characters farther west in search of new worlds to conquer, or to Europe for culture, or to New England to heal their broken spirits and recover their moral sense, but Chicago is the focus of their life, as it was for him.

Whatever the moral dilemmas in his novels — and Herrick covered an astonishing number of them — his theme is always the same, the gradual corruption of the individual by greed. Like Sinclair Lewis later on, he admired businessmen who were builders and not despoilers, and professional men — especially doctors and architects — because they were healers and makers. Yet few of his heroes escape moral defeat. They are ruined by ambitious wives who do not appreciate their idealism or they make the fatal first mistake of getting in on a good thing.

Herrick is the best of the problem novelists. Yet, except in *The Memoirs of an American Citizen* (1905) he never touched greatness. His distaste is usually too evident, and so is his moralism. Unlike Dreiser, who was drawn to the Chicago buccaneers as by a magnet, Herrick seldom makes us sense their hunger for power. Nor could he provide the solutions to the enigmatic moral situations he explored.

VI

The work of one novelist — Edith Wharton (1862–1937) — stands far above the earnest mediocrity of Phillips, Churchill, and Herrick. Because Mrs. Wharton's later novels were a falling off from her earlier achievement — the turning point came when her *Glimpses of the Moon* (1922) was serialized in *The Pictorial Review* — her reputation with the critics declined in the last fifteen years of her life. But now that it seems no longer necessary to call her a snob and a Francophile or to make the inevitable comparisons between her work and that of Henry James, we can be certain that four or five of her novels are a clear mirror of the age and will hold a permanent place in our literature. There is no doubt about *The House of Mirth* (1905), a sensation in 1905 and 1906, *Ethan Frome* (1911), *The Custom of the Country* (1913), and *The Age of Innocence* (1920). Some would add *The Reef* (1912).

One book, *The Valley of Decision* (1902), has been undeservedly forgotten. It has been dismissed as a tour de force, and it is that certainly, with its elaborate recreation of the poverty and pageantry in the ducal courts of Italy on the eve of the French Revolution; but it is also a warm and human story and in its leading character, Odo, Duke of Pianura, we see one of the first of a long line of Wharton heroes whose idealism is crippled because they make the compromises which their society demands of them.

Though Mrs. Wharton was isolated from middle-class life in America and from contact with other writers — first by her social position and later by her expatriation in France — her career as a novelist resembles in important respects that of the other fiction-writers of her generation. When the vogue of the historical novel was at its height, she wrote *The Valley of Decision*. In *The Fruit of the Tree* (1907), after doing a little hasty research in the textile mills at Adams, Massachusetts, she tried her hand at a novel of social reform in which noble words are spoken about the hardships and aspirations of mill-workers in New England. She soon found her *métier* in the "problem" novel, in the sense in which the term was used in the first years of the century. In barest outline the plots of many of her stories suggest ethical situations which Churchill and Phillips might have handled: a third husband discovers that his wife expects him to make a place in their life for his predecessors ("The Other Two," 1904); the heroine of *The House of Mirth*, Lily Bart, unmarried at twenty-nine and in search of a husband with money, sinks lower and lower in the New York society she cannot forsake until the only way out of her unhappiness is an overdose of chloral; Ethan Frome, desperately in love and seeking escape from his nagging wife by suicide, succeeds only in crippling himself and the woman he loves and so condemning the three of them to a lifetime of shared misery.

In her early and best work Mrs. Wharton's themes are not in the least "got up." She found them in the lives of the people of her set or, in the case of *Ethan Frome*, in New England where she spent her summers. (After the first World War they were suggested to her by the derangements of a changing society in which she had little real interest.) But there are other reasons why her early novels stand out in the crowd. For one thing, she was a stylist and her rightness of tone contrasts with the awkwardness of Dreiser, the flashiness of Phillips, and the archness of O. Henry. She could also adapt her style to her story. *The Valley of Decision* renders without strain and with an astonishing authenticity the decadent life of the Italian ducal courts. In *Ethan Frome*, once she has dropped overboard her needless and rather too fastidious narrator, the story of three lives on a barren farm in the Berkshires is told with the simplicity this rural tragedy required.

It was inevitable that Mrs. Wharton should become a master of satire, a mode which, strangely enough, none of the problem novelists adopted. Though she disdained many of the conventions and attitudes of the old New York society, the paralyzing effects of which she had escaped by becoming a writer, she never ceased to admire the matriarchs of Washington Square and Madison Avenue who, in her girlhood, had ruled their families down to the remotest cousin. From such a union of disdain and admiration satire is born. Her two finest novels which deal with the society she knew from the inside are in part satirical — *The House of Mirth* and *The Age of Innocence*. Disdain is in the ascendant in the first and admiration in the second. She reserved her sharpest satirical weapons for Undine Spragg, the "new woman" of *The Custom of the Country* (1913). No other American would write such vigorous satire until Sinclair Lewis came on the scene.

Recently arrived from Apex City and with a world to

conquer, Undine marries Ralph Marvell in order that the right New York doors may open to her. But she soon discovers that she has "given herself to the exclusive and the dowdy when the future belonged to the strong and promiscuous." She blunders through an affair and two more marriages only to be stopped before an ineluctable goal. The novel concludes on a superbly ironic note. Just before the grandest party she has ever given, Undine learns that Jim Driscoll — "that pitiful nonentity" — has been made ambassador to England. Her newest ambition is to be an ambassador's wife, but her husband tells her that divorcées are never received at court.

. But under all the dazzle a tiny black cloud remained. She had learned that there was something she could never get, something that neither beauty nor influence nor millions could ever buy her. She could never be an Ambassador's wife; and as she advanced to welcome her first guests she said to herself that it was the one part she was really made for.

One of Mrs. Wharton's greatest assets as a novelist was her love of detail and her accuracy in using it. When she was not writing fiction she was putting together books about country houses in Europe and America and accounts of her travels. From her stored-up memories of cities, rooms, opera houses, gardens, cathedrals, streets, clothes, vehicles she could summon any detail she needed. Much of the charm of *The Age of Innocence* (1920) derives from its pictures of fashionable New York life in the 1870's. As in this passage, she can always be trusted as an eyewitness to the way her characters lived.

"In my youth," Miss Jackson rejoined, "it was considered vulgar to dress in the newest fashions; and Amy Sillerton has always told me that in Boston the rule was to put away one's Paris dresses for two years. Old Mrs. Baxter Pennilow, who did everything handsomely, used to import twelve a year, two velvet, two satin, two silk, and the other six of poplin and the finest cashmere. It was a standing order, and as she was ill for two years before she died they found forty-eight Worth dresses that had never been taken out of tissue paper; and when the girls left off their mourning they were able to wear the first lot at the Symphony concerts without looking in advance of the fashion."

In the final analysis, what raises Mrs. Wharton's novels far above the level of American fiction of her time is her adherence to Henry James's faith in "the perfect dependence of the 'moral' sense of a work of art on the amount of felt life concerned in producing it." In her best work her judgment of life was capable of resolving the moral dilemmas she requires her characters to face. What happened, unfortunately, in the novels after *The Age of Innocence* was, as Blake Nevius says, that her "own moral sensibility [became] progressively inadequate to the demands made upon it by her subjects." [6] Unlike Willa Cather, who retreated from the materialistic twenties into the pastel shades of history and thus salvaged her art, Mrs. Wharton tried to face the new age which she disliked as much as Miss Cather did. It was too much for her. Where she had once been compassionate or ironic she now became mawkish or petulant.

At last we realize how well she understood her earlier characters and the swirling currents of their time — and hers. It has been usual, for example, to say that there is little real love in her fiction. Yet, as Louis Auchincloss has said, "hers was not a world where romance was apt to flourish." The point of *The Custom of the Country* is that Undine Spragg is incapable of love. In *The Age of Innocence* love is stifled by the characters themselves.

Edmund Wilson offers an important corrective to another idea which flourished too long. Mrs. Wharton's women are so much stronger than her men that she seems at times to be expressing an ill-concealed feminism, the result, some said, of her marriage which ended in divorce.

Mr. Wilson has found the real reason for the intentional weakness of Amherst in *The Fruit of the Tree* and Darrow in *The Reef*. Her not-so-heroic heroes, these idealists whose impulses are thwarted, are "made helpless by a commercial civilization." But if she understood this "new" American man, she could not admire him.

She never ceased to resent him because he had failed to stand up to the temptations and threats of that civilization and because he had not been strong enough to save from that moneyed world, in which it was even easier for a woman than for a man to be caught, a woman, courageous herself, whom he might have, whom he should have, loved.[7]

Standing aloof from her time, knowing less at firsthand about the corrupters of the age of innocence than Phillips or Herrick, she understood its dilemmas better than they did, because she was a greater artist.

TWO

New Voices

THE YEARS between 1912 and 1922 in American literature stand out so clearly that it almost seems as if the writers whose work characterizes the decade had kept in mind the convenience of future literary historians. By 1917 it was ·evident that something like a revolution in both form and content had taken place. Critics, editors, publishers, as well as the writers themselves, were very much aware of what was happening. "New" was the word for it — the new poetry, the new novel, the new drama — and there was rejoicing in all quarters that in this new literature American culture had at last come of age.

Looking back on the fervor of these years, we can see that the brave hopes were justified. A mere listing, year by year, of a few of the landmarks proves that the mediocrity of the first decade of the century had been left behind. In October 1912 the first issue of *Poetry: A Magazine of Verse* appeared. It was planned with such foresight that it is still enjoying good health nearly a half century later. Willa Cather's first novel in the vein which would be peculiarly her own, *O Pioneers!*, arrived in 1913. In the same year Vachel Lindsay's famous "General William Booth Enters into Heaven" was out in book form. Frost's *North of Boston*, his second volume but the first to evince his characteristic rhythms and subjects, was published in 1914. In 1915 Edgar Lee Masters, who had been writing since the late nineties, published *Spoon River Anthology*, the one book of his which is certain to endure. The year 1916 was especially memorable. E. A. Robinson published the volume in which he later believed he had reached his peak, *The Man Against the Sky*. The realism of Carl Sandburg's *Chicago Poems* delighted some Chicagoans and disgusted others. (If this was the "new" poetry they wanted none of it.) Eugene O'Neill's *Bound East for Cardiff* was also of that vintage year. In 1917 Joseph Hergesheimer's *The Three Black Pennys* drew apt comparisons with the work of Bennett and Galsworthy. In the same year Edna St. Vincent Millay's "Renascence" was the title-poem in the first collection of her verse. In 1918 admirers of Booth Tarkington found a new seriousness in his *The Magnificent Ambersons*. In 1918, too, the leading critic among the new writers, Van Wyck Brooks, published his *Letters and Leadership* in which he urged the poets and novelists to seize the initiative in organizing the "higher life" in America. In 1919 James Branch Cabell's *Jurgen* found for him the wide audience he had been seeking for fifteen years. In the same year Sherwood Anderson's *Winesburg, Ohio* (his fourth book) indicated the arrival of another major writer. In 1920 F. Scott Fitzgerald's *This Side of Paradise* inaugurated the jazz age, while Sinclair Lewis, in *Main Street*, was putting his stethoscope to small-town life in the middle west. The voice of the new Bohemians was heard in Floyd Dell's *The Briary-Bush* in 1921.

By 1922 there were signs that the era of the "new" literature had come to an end. Followers of *avant garde* writing in that year were struggling to make sense of T. S. Eliot's *The Waste Land* and were puzzling over the ironies of E. E. Cummings' *The Enormous Room*. If they had

contrived to smuggle out of Paris a copy of Joyce's
Ulysses, its tell-tale blue-paper binding disguised in a plain
wrapper, they were arguing about such technical matters
as the stream of consciousness method and the literary
uses of myth.

Before this remarkable decade was half over several
volumes appeared proclaiming what had been accomplished
and attempting to define what gave the movement its dis-
tinctiveness. One of the most revealing of these appraisals
is Lloyd Morris' *The Young Idea: An Anthology of Opinions Concerning the Spirit and Aims of Contemporary
American Literature*. Of the more than twenty writers
who responded to Morris' questions, only four were pessimistic about the movement. (E. A. Robinson was one of
them.) The rest were certain that a revolution had oc-
curred, particularly in poetry. The new spirit was a "revolt
against Victorian pruderies and reticences." The "voice of
youth" could be heard in it. America was at last discovering
itself in literature and the new writers fortunately possessed the "virile freedom of the Elizabethans." Summing
up the opinions he had collected, Morris noted that the
basis of the movement was "a determination to express a
reaction to experience in terms of the thought and feeling
of our own time and country."

Remembering that the "new" literature came to fruition
during the first World War, one is surprised at the exuberance and optimism most of these writers exhibited and at
the hopeful tone of the commentators. Then one remembers that the critics as well as the poets and novelists were
living in the afterglow of the progressive movement and
that many of them were infected with Wilson's New
Freedom. As for the War, it was still seen as a crusade to
make the world safe for democracy until the dire consequences of the peace began to appear. It would be the

writers of the next generation — Dos Passos, Hemingway, Cummings — who would turn in revulsion from Wilsonian idealism.

The years between 1890 and 1912 have been aptly named the "twilight interval" of American poetry. Reviewers and publishers conspired to suppress all but the most conventional and innocuous verse. In favor with magazine editors were the folksy Hoosier poems of James Whitcomb Riley, the open-road Bohemianism of Bliss Carman and Richard Hovey, and the neat stanzas of Clinton Scollard. Some of the women poets of the day — Louise Imogen Guiney and Lizette Reese, in particular — were careful artists but the impulse of their poetry was literary. Around the turn of the century a false dawn momentarily lighted up the gloom of the twilight interval. Stephen Crane's free-verse experiments in *War is Kind* (1899) showed great promise but Crane died at twenty-eight in the year after the book's publication. Death took others of this generation who might have reformed the state of poetry: George Cabot Lodge at thirty-six, in 1909; William Vaughn Moody at forty-one, in 1910; and Trumbull Stickney — the most gifted of these three Harvard friends — at thirty, in 1904. Two poets of this generation who eventually made their way to fame, Frost and Robinson, persisted in the face of constant rebuffs. The popular enthusiasm for poetry after 1912 helped to provide them with a public. Thus by accident they took their place among the "new" poets who marched under the banners of Harriet Monroe (1860–1936) and Amy Lowell (1874–1925), fuglemen of the procession.

II

As soon as the first issue of *Poetry* was off the press Miss Monroe's little magazine became the rallying point of the new movement in verse. She assured her subscribers that *Poetry* would be "a refuge, a green isle in the sea, where Beauty may plant her gardens, and Truth, austere revealer of joy and sorrow, of hidden delights and despairs, may follow her brave quest unafraid." Some of the contributions she received hardly conformed to her standards of Beauty and Truth, but she had promised that *Poetry* would belong to no clique and that its sole standard would be quality. She kept her word. During the first three years she printed poems by such diverse practitioners as William Butler Yeats, Ezra Pound, Vachel Lindsay, D. H. Lawrence, T. S. Eliot, Edgar Lee Masters, Wallace Stevens, Robert Frost, and Marianne Moore. In begging money from Chicago businessmen for her venture she had told them that there was a public for poetry in America and that there were many excellent poets who could find no outlet for their work. The success of *Poetry* proved she had read the situation correctly.

The aims of *Poetry*, as they evolved, might have been very different if Ezra Pound had not moved in before the doors were open. In the first issue it was announced that "such of his poetic work as receives magazine publication in America will appear exclusively in *Poetry*." In the second issue he consents to "act as foreign correspondent of *Poetry*, keeping its readers informed of the present interests of the art in England, France and elsewhere." As Miss Monroe later acknowledged, in her autobiography, *A Poet's Life*, she thought Pound the best critic of poetry living and also the greatest teacher of it. His "acid touch on weak spots" in the conduct of *Poetry*, as well as the sheaves of new verse (his own and that of his friends) which he sent across the Atlantic, gave the magazine an admirably cosmopolitan tone.

The first poem in the fourth issue of *Poetry*, "General William Booth Enters into Heaven," pulled into Miss Monroe's orbit one of the most gifted and certainly the most eccentric of the new poets, Vachel Lindsay (1879–1931). The fame of this poem — Miss Monroe always considered it the finest first appearance in the magazine — did much to distract Lindsay from the course he had already planned for himself when a student at Hiram College. Born to parents who were devout followers of Alexander Campbell, founder of the Disciples of Christ denomination, Lindsay's ambitions were dominated by the Campbellite vision of the earth as a vast field of struggle between good and evil forces and the belief that Jesus will soon come to the aid of Christians in their contest against the "potentates" and make his cause triumphant. To the redemptive and millenarian strain in the Campbellite theology Lindsay added his own gospel of beauty. Every village and city in America might be transformed if only a prophet would arise in each to persuade parents that all children were called to be artists and craftsmen. Lindsay's ambition was to effect this great transformation in at least one city, preferably his native Springfield, Illinois. But Springfield was not listening; the "legions of angels" needed for the work failed to sign up. Yet Lindsay persisted through the years in trying to translate his vision of a "nation transformed" into poems which would move men to follow his gleam. Unfortunately these vision poems are so chaotic that even a willing reader cannot find any sure landmarks in them, as he can in the difficult cosmic geography of Yeats's Byzantium or Blake's Jerusalem.

In another kind of poetry Lindsay excelled. He called it "the higher vaudeville," and soon audiences all over the country were paying him well to recite it. With eyes closed and head thrown back, he chanted and whispered "The Congo" and thundered "General William Booth" from so many platforms that he came to loathe both the poems and his performance of them. At the same time he exulted in the fervent response he evoked. This might be one way to win America to the gospel of beauty.

Though Lindsay travelled thousands of miles through America, first as the "vagabond poet," literally trading rhymes for bread, and later as the "higher vaudeville" artist, he knew little about the nation he longed to redeem from ugliness and sin. At two points he did make contact and at these points his most successful poems were touched into life. Vision-haunted himself, he understood the American visionaries: Alexander Campbell, Mary Baker Eddy, John Brown, Johnny Appleseed, and Bryan — "gigantic troubadour, speaking like a siege gun." He was also sensitive, as no poet had been, to the characteristic American rhythms, to the throb of the college "locomotive," to jazz syncopations, and camp-meeting revival shouts. For the twenty or so poems of this kind which audiences demanded to hear over and over again Lindsay invented a rhythmic pattern which he used with great versatility: a four-stress line in which the dominant foot is often the paeon (four syllables, one long and three short). With this simple instrument he could conjure up the cakewalk strut of the Negroes in "The Congo," of the "*calm*-horn, *balm*-horn, *psalm*-horn" toots of the autos streaming down the Santa Fé trail. He used the line for comedy, bathos, excitement. He could also use it with quiet power at the end of "Bryan, Bryan, Bryan, Bryan":

> Where is that boy, that Heaven-born Bryan,
> That Homer Bryan, who sang from the West?
> Gone to join the shadows with Altgeld the Eagle,
> Where the kings and the slaves and the troubadours rest.

In 1935 Edgar Lee Masters (1869–1950) wrote a perceptive biography of his friend Lindsay. They had come from the same down-state region of Illinois and they became famous as poets in the new movement within a year of each other. There the similarities end. Lindsay was an idealist whose life touched America only fitfully. The Masters of *Spoon River Anthology* (1915) was a man of the world, a successful lawyer, and a lover of many women. His knowledge of people made him a realist who was capable of penetrating the lives of the weak of will, the strong of arm, the clown, the boozer, the fighter, the tender of heart, the simple soul, the loud, the proud, and the happy ones who lay sleeping under their gravestones on "the Hill" above Spoon River.

Masters once asserted that these two hundred and fourteen poems were written under a spell of such intense "clairvoyance and clairaudience" that he lost all sense of time and was pulled back to the real world only when twilight came. It is likely that the poems were composed in a few months (probably between March 1914 and January 1915) but their period of gestation was much longer, almost as long, indeed, as Masters' life up to that time.

Masters' boyhood days in Petersburg and Lewistown were not happy. His family was poor and though he respected the political liberalism of his father, he was determined not to follow him in submitting to the hypocrisies of small-town life. He read law in his father's office but as soon as he could he made his escape to Chicago. One positive thing he took with him, a passion for literature, stimulated by a year of study at Knox College where his admiration for Shelley, Herbert Spencer, and Swinburne earned him the name of "Atheist." As a young lawyer in Chicago, Masters attached himself to the widestepping "Press Club crowd," several members of which knew as much about the seamy side of village life as he did.

Between 1898 and 1911 Masters published eleven books, chiefly verse and verse plays. Though their themes betrayed his extreme democratic idealism, their style was self-consciously literary. External forces were needed to precipitate the one story Masters had to tell. His friend William Marion Reedy, editor of a Henry George weekly in St. Louis, *Reedy's Mirror,* started the reaction in 1909 when he gave Masters a copy of the *Greek Anthology* and so put into his mind the idea of creating a series of verse epitaphs. His friendship with Dreiser inspired him to speak with the "sceptical daring" which he admired in the novelist's work. Finally there was the influence of the free-verse writers in *Poetry,* Sandburg in particular. The immediate impulse to the writing of the *Spoon River Anthology* was a visit of Masters' mother in May 1914. As they gossiped about the old days, he resolved to put on paper the "characters interlocked by fate" he had known as a boy and to give them a chance to speak in self-defense from the grave.

There is some evidence that Masters intended to line up his characters in a series of contrasted and interrelated epitaphs but inspiration took over and blurred the plot. It is well that it did, for in the completed work it is the individual lives which stand out rather than the pattern Spoon River imposed on them, driving some to drink and suicide, some to the world beyond the village, permitting happiness to a few.

Of the works produced by the new poets *Spoon River Anthology* made the deepest impression and the volume was reprinted many times during the next twenty years. Possibly its most immediate effect was the touching off of the "revolt from the village" which preoccupied many of the novelists of the time. Spoon River was the first village to have its veil of decency removed but Sherwood Anderson's Winesburg and Sinclair Lewis' Gopher Prairie soon suffered the same exposure.

In April 1914 Masters wrote to Dreiser: "Next Monday I am going for a tramp to the sand dunes with a Swede

bard. He is a new find and I think has the right fire."
The "Swede bard" was Carl Sandburg whose "Chicago" —

> Hog Butcher for the World
> Tool Maker, Stacker of Wheat

had stirred the anger of genteel Chicagoans when *Poetry* printed it with eight other poems of his in the issue for March 1914.

The son of a Swedish immigrant who settled in Galesburg, Illinois, Sandburg (b. 1878) had come the long way round to reach the offices of *Poetry* and fame. He had blacked the boots of county politicians in a Galesburg barber shop, worked as a railroad section hand and a farm laborer, served in the army during the Spanish American War, studied for a time at Lombard College, worked as an organizer for the Social Democratic party. Before he settled down to newspaper work in Chicago in 1912 (his profession for the next twenty years) he had wandered over much of the middle west, listening to the people talk, learning their ballads and their folksay.

By 1916 Sandburg had accumulated enough poems to fill a volume. Mrs. Henderson, assistant editor of *Poetry*, persuaded the firm of Holt to take it, a venture it soon had reason to be proud of. Few volumes of American verse have stirred up so much controversy as *Chicago Poems*, but it found readers as well as detractors. Soon "Chicago," "The Harbor," "To a Contemporary Bunk-shooter" were known even to schoolchildren. The six-line "Fog" was so often reprinted that Alexander Woollcott remarked that it had earned more per word in royalties than any other poem of its time.

In his subsequent volumes of verse Sandburg's themes and style changed little. His best poems are short, vivid impressions of persons or places formed in the free-verse mode he never abandoned. Though Sandburg made little technical progress as a poet, his faith in the people, in their ability to endure and come through, remained strong through the years. He wrote his best testament to them in *The People, Yes* (1936), a collection of American folk sayings set off by poems in praise of the collective wisdom of his countrymen.

> In the darkness with a bundle of grief
>   the people march.
> In the night, and overhead a shovel of stars for
>   keeps, the people march:
>   "Where to? what next?"

Sandburg found the subject best suited to his talents and his democratic faith when, in 1919, he began his six-volume biography of Lincoln, completed twenty years later. The Lincoln it reveals is the Lincoln who spoke to the hearts of the people through the barriers set up by reluctant generals and partisan politicians.

III

While Miss Monroe in Chicago was efficiently building *Poetry* into a magazine with an international reputation, Amy Lowell of Boston was forwarding the new movement in a floodlighted campaign of which America has never seen the like. A cousin of James Russell Lowell and a sister of the president of Harvard, Miss Lowell was equipped for her task with her family's money and prestige, the ability to compel publishers to do her bidding, and a platform manner as impressive as her physical bulk. Once she got her hands on the new movement, she moulded it as she wished; then, through reviews, appearances before women's clubs, and her influential *Tendencies in Modern American Poetry* (1917), she proceeded to establish her version as the only true account.

Ezra Pound, who helped educate Miss Monroe as an editor, played an important role in the conversion of Miss Lowell to the new poetry. Their association was brief — from July 1913 to midsummer of the next year. Inevitably two such opinionated individuals quarreled and went their separate ways. For Pound their alliance was only one episode in a long career of preparing "ultimate affronts to / Human redundancies." For Miss Lowell the experience was arresting and decisive. Shortly after they met in London, Pound remarked to Robert Frost: "When I get through with that girl she'll think she was born in free-verse."

When Pound dispatriated himself in England in 1908 he was taken up at once by Yeats and Ford Madox Ford as an American "original," a likely successor to James McNeill Whistler. He even talked like Whistler and like him he was an expert in the gentle art of making enemies — and friends. In no time at all he was discovering promising young poets and formulating new artistic creeds. One of the first of his enthusiasms was Imagism, a theory of poetry which he set about promoting with his usual energy.

The concepts which made up the doctrine of Imagism were developed by a group of Soho poets who gathered around T. E. Hulme, a Cambridge amateur philosopher. He believed that the romanticism of Victorian poetry represented the decadent stage of the vicious humanism which had dominated Western thought for three centuries. The cure needed was a new kind of poetry, terse, strong, purged of all extraneous emotion and didactic comment on cosmic problems. The poets in the group, F. S. Flint, Richard Aldington, and the Americans, Pound and Hilda Doolittle, experimented with the compressed Japanese forms, the *tanka* (thirty-one syllables in five lines) and the *hokku* (seventeen syllables in three lines) and made other attempts to write the kind of poetry Hulme demanded. Hulme himself produced five poems in the new manner which Pound published as "The Complete Poetical Works of T. E. Hulme" in pages appended to his *Ripostes* (1912).

As soon as Pound moved in on *Poetry* he had an ideal outlet for the work of his Imagist friends. In the fourth issue Miss Monroe printed three poems by H.D. "Imagiste." Subscribers were not long left in doubt about the meaning of the strange epithet. When the sixth number appeared they learned about "Imagisme" from an essay contributed by F. S. Flint, to which Pound added "A Few Don'ts by an Imagiste."

H.D.'s three poems were a revelation to Miss Lowell and she determined to reform her poetical style and become an Imagiste. (The "e" in the appellation was soon dropped.) She hastened to London, heard the gospel at first hand, and straightway began reorganizing the Imagist movement. Pound, she felt, was using it chiefly as a means of calling attention to the poems of his friends. Several of the poets whose work he printed in his anthology *Des Imagistes* (1914) had no right to the splendid title. In the contest which followed Miss Lowell won handily, possibly because Pound was now busy with Vorticism. She lined up Aldington, "H.D." (his wife), John Gould Fletcher, F. S. Flint, and D. H. Lawrence and proposed that the six true Imagists — now rid of the masqueraders — should issue an annual anthology of their poems written in accord with the true faith. When she returned to America she promptly found a publisher and the first of three Imagist anthologies was issued in 1915.

This collection carried a preface which set forth the correct doctrine in six explicit rubrics. (1) Imagists must use the language of common speech and employ the exact word. (2) They must create new rhythms. Free verse is

not the only poetical form but poets must be accorded
the right to use it. (3) There must be absolute freedom
in the choice of subject. (4) Poetry must "render particulars exactly and not deal in vague generalities" (hence
the term "Imagist"). Clauses five and six called for poetry
that is hard and clear and concentrated in its effect.

In the war of words which Miss Lowell's generalship
provoked the strictly Imagist articles in the manifesto were
not much debated. Actually there was little that was new
in them. Many poetical revolutionists have denounced in-
flated diction and have demanded a return to the language
of common speech. It was the second article which caused
most of the uproar — the call for the creation of new
rhythms, that is to say free verse, or "cadenced verse" as
Miss Lowell decided it should be renamed. Precedents
might have been invoked even here. The example of Whitman frequently was, but the "organic rhythms" of Emerson
and Arnold might also have been brought into court as
exhibits for the defense.

The trouble with Miss Lowell's campaign was that few
poets joined up and even fewer good poets. She had tried to
narrow their art to the use of "cadenced verse" and the
search for the pure image. They refused to be confined.
Three poets of real stature remained faithful to the Imagist
doctrines, D. H. Lawrence, H.D., and William Carlos
Williams. For a few others, Pound, T. S. Eliot, and Hart
Crane, for example, Imagism was a brief though useful
episode in their apprenticeship.

IV

It may seem ironic that the two poets of this remarkable
era whose achievement is of a high order, E. A. Robinson
(1869–1935) and Robert Frost (b. 1874) were not active
in the revolution of the word which the new movement
brought about. They belonged to no coterie and they

signed no manifestoes. Yet, through the asseverations of Miss Monroe and Miss Lowell, and of reviewers and anthologists, the public was made to think of them as "new" poets though each had been trying for twenty years to persuade magazines to print their verse. Actually they owed a great deal to their new-found champions. Robinson's *The Man Against the Sky* was abundantly praised when it appeared in 1916. On Frost's return in 1915 from his four years of self-imposed exile in England, where his first two volumes had been issued, he found readers waiting for him.

Great poets "represent" only themselves and Robinson and Frost are great poets. Yet in some particulars their poetical aims paralleled those of Masters, Sandburg, and the Imagists. Like Masters and Sandburg they were biographers of their region. Like the Imagists they returned to the language of common speech. But they were "new" poets chiefly because their subjects and their styles were unique.

In the recent revival of interest in Robinson's work one can see signs that he is coming to be rightly valued as one of the best of American poets. It was through an odd combination of circumstances that he failed to receive wide acclaim in his lifetime. His first volumes — *The Torrent and the Night Before* (1896) and *Children of the Night* (1897) — gave him the reputation of being "Browning-esque" (a bad word). The mingling of sententiousness, pathos, and Bohemian high spirits in his long poem about "the pauper" — *Captain Craig* (1902) — puzzled readers. Many thought it trivial and its length wearied. Robinson was making his way slowly when the new movement of the years 1912–1922 swept him along with the current for a time. But measured against the novelties of Lindsay and Amy Lowell his somber lyrics and short narratives in conventional meters looked old-fashioned. (He scorned

free verse.) This discrepancy between his style and contemporary fashions in verse became all the more marked
in the 1920's when Pound, Eliot, Hart Crane, Wallace
Stevens, and Allen Tate began to dominate the scene. In
the 1920's Robinson turned back to the long narrative
poem so loved by Victorian readers. By doing this he put
himself still further out of fashion, though his *Tristram*
(1927) was popular. After 1914, too, the increasing reputation of Robert Frost, accompanied by the growth of the
legend of Frost as the lovable poet-in-the-pulpit, overshadowed Robinson. Their names were usually coupled
(an annoyance to which poets are peculiarly subject) but
the notion prevailed that Frost was the superior poet.
Robinson has long been popular with anthologists but the
fact that "Richard Cory," "Miniver Cheevy," "The Dark
House" and "Flammonde," excellent poems though they
are, turned up so often must have convinced readers that
there was little else to put beside them.

It has often enough been said that Robinson's best
poems are psychological portraits of men and women whose
lives are failures. What has not been sufficiently noticed
is that his derelicts and defeated ones possess a fortitude
that is peculiarly Robinsonian. In his own life Robinson
experienced defeat many times but he met the successive
blows with the courage his characters evince. The family
business in Gardiner, Maine (the Tilbury Town of the
poems), went to smash in the hands of a brother who soon
died of tuberculosis. Another brother took to drink and
drugs to relieve the strain of his country medical practice.
Until his mid-forties Robinson was often on the verge of
destitution. The one job he was good at and really liked
was that of time-checker in the New York subway. Yet,
through the worst of times and even when he was drinking
heavily, Robinson kept at his task of learning to be a poet.
Fortunately there were friends who believed in his genius.

They helped him when they could, though they often had to be secret in their giving.

It would not be surprising if Robinson had vented his misery in the nihilism of a James Thomson or blamed Hardy's "purblind Doomsters" for the ills of humanity. He did neither. He comes nearest to despair in his long ode, "The Man Against the Sky," in which he explores relentlessly the ways men confront death. He spares neither the cowardly nor the indifferent, the cynic nor the materialist. It is the conclusion of the poem which has disconcerted many readers:

> If there be nothing after Now,
> And we be nothing anyhow,
> And we know that,— why live?

But these lines must be read in the light of Robinson's own life and the import of his other poems. He loved life too much to take his own, no matter how much misery he had to bear; and in his poems about human failure what he is bent on showing is how men and women endure. The speaker in "Mr. Flood's Party" is old, and strangers are in the doorways of Tilbury Town where once there were friends. But Mr. Flood can tilt his jug and drink to himself and for "auld lang syne." The mother in "The Gift of God" knows that her son is worthless and that the town knows it, too. Yet she

> arranging for his days
> What centuries could not fulfill,
> Transmutes him with her faith and praise,
> And has him shining where she will.

But life was worth living to Robinson not merely because endurance can be transmuted into triumph. Among his best poems are many which give thanks. His cryptic "The Dark House" celebrates his having conquered alcohol. "Hillcrest" is a moving tribute to Mrs. Edward MacDowell whose colony for writers at Peterborough, New Hampshire, sheltered him each summer for the last quarter-century of his life.

From the beginning Robinson was an accomplished prosodist. Working with traditional meters, stanzaic forms, and rhyme schemes, he enlarged the possibilities of poetics in English, an achievement that is rare. Yet there is seldom any bravura in his metric. All seems so easy that the precision and the elegance can easily be overlooked. In one particular skill — psychological portraiture — he improved greatly over the years. As Louis O. Coxe has noted (*Sewanee Review*, Spring 1954), such poems as "The Gift of God," "Eros Turannos," "Veteran Sirens," and "The Poor Relation" (all of these are in *The Man Against the Sky* volume of 1916) are not merely succinct little dramas touched with irony or pity. In them Robinson works "toward a condition of total communication by means of suggestion and statement." They are not didactic because there is no need for the poet to sum up after the totality of his "plot" is disclosed. Every recorded fact, every guess at motive, every symbol and allusion carries us deeper into a particular human mystery. When the last lines are spoken we feel that all has been told that anyone could tell. And the telling has required no more than a half-dozen stanzas.

While Robinson slowly came into his own, Robert Frost enjoyed a popularity in his lifetime unequaled by any American poet since Longfellow. He had to wait until he was forty for recognition, but after 1915 it came in abundance. Colleges showered him with honorary degrees. He was four times awarded the Pulitzer Prize. In 1950 the United States Senate, in an unprecedented gesture toward the arts, cited him (in Resolution No. 224) for having written poems which "have helped to guide American thought with humor and wisdom, setting forth to our minds a reliable representation of ourselves and of all men."

His unofficial laureateship did Frost no harm. A staunch farmer-poet, he continued to "build soil" past seventy. There are poems in his late volumes which are as good as his earlier best: "The Silken Tent," "The Most of It," "The Gift Outright," in A *Witness Tree* (1942); and, in *Steeple Bush* (1947), "Directive" and "An Importer."

Though Frost was born in San Francisco, it was inevitable that he should be New England's poet. He inherited a claim to the region from his parents and he began to pre-empt it in his poetry as soon as he began to write. After his father's death, when he was ten, his mother returned to Lawrence, Massachusetts, three miles from the New Hampshire border. From his twelfth year, to help out, he worked at all kinds of jobs, as a cobbler, farm hand, bobbin boy in a textile mill. After a few months at Dartmouth and two years at Harvard, he alternated school-teaching with farming. Farming won, though Frost has always been a teacher, sometimes in college classrooms, but always in the long sessions of talk after his public readings.

Unlike William Faulkner, another great regionalist writer, Frost has not mapped the land he claimed. There is no mythical Yoknapatawpha County in his New England. We do not know how far the Hill Wife lives from the Gum Gatherer or whether The Runaway colt belongs to the neighbor who is Mending Wall. Only in his topographical poem "New Hampshire" is there any roll call of the towns. Blueberries, "real sky-blue and heavy," are in "Patterson's pasture" and The Wood Pile warms "the" frozen swamp as best it can. This indefiniteness of place enhances the mood of loneliness and desolation in the poems. Most of Frost's New England lies outside the village. The landmarks are a solitary white house and its gray barn, a fenced-in family graveyard near by, cellar holes, and a wood road whose track grows fainter or disappears as you go deeper into the forest dark.

The special quality of Frost's nature poetry must account, in large part, for his popularity. As Americans have left the country for the city they have looked back with longing to their agrarian past and they still escape into nature on hasty week ends. Nature no longer has transcendental meaning for them but it does connote simplicity, peace, beauty, wonder. These qualities they find, separately or in happy combination in such favorite poems as "Birches," "The Oven Bird," "The Cow in Apple Time," "Stopping by Woods on a Snowy Evening," and "In Looking Up by Chance at the Constellations."

But Frost is no nature mystic. Nature is over there, beyond the wall. She takes no account of man, yet man is most himself when he measures his courage and faith against her pace and strength. "Come In" shows this separateness as well as any of his poems. The poet is listening, entranced, to thrush music deep in the woods. It sounds to him almost like a call to come in and lament.

> But no, I was out for stars:
> I would not come in.
> I meant not even if asked,
> And I hadn't been.

As a poet Frost always moved on. Each new volume was a new departure. The style of the lyrics in *A Boy's Will* (1913) is close to that of the English Georgians, though if there was influence flowing either way, it was Frost who did the influencing. In *North of Boston* (1914) one finds many of the well-known dramatic monologues and dialogues, such as "The Death of the Hired Man" and "The Code." Having mastered this form, Frost explored a new vein in *Mountain Interval* (1916). The result was a meditative lyric prompted by a person or an episode which compelled his attention. But there is no lack of drama in "The Road Not Taken" and "An Old Man's Winter

Night," brief as they are. A new self-consciousness about his art appears in *New Hampshire* (1923). Frost begins to argue with his reader (a habit he never abandoned) and the poems in his riddling manner — "The Lockless Door" and "I Will Sing You One-O" — appear for the first time. In *West Running Brook* (1928) man and nature move farther apart and one hears a ground bass of stoic fortitude which drops to a despairing minor in "Acquainted with the Night." Eight years later, in *A Further Range*, Frost teaches by parable (in the section entitled "Taken Singly") but who can object when his little sermons are such perfect works as "Design" and "On a Bird Singing in its Sleep"?

The depression, the second World War, and the incipient horrors of the atomic age diverted Frost increasingly to argument and satire. The poems induced by the diseases of his time are his poorest. He had no cures to offer and he took a perverse pleasure in jibing at planners who suggested any.

Though Frost likes to argue in verse, he is by temperament antirationalist and romantic. He believes in the validity of intuition and his aim in each poem has been to create "a particular mood that won't be satisfied with anything less than its own fulfillment." In "The Constant Symbol" (the introductory essay to the Modern Library edition of his poems) he offers a rule of thumb by which one may judge whether a poet has made a success of his poem. "Had he anything to be true to? Was he true to it? Did he use good words? You couldn't tell unless you made out what idea they were supposed to be good for. Every poem is an epitome of the great predicament; a figure of the will braving alien entanglements." In these words Frost provides the test by which his own poetry should be judged. His best poems begin with a "tantalizing vagueness." One cannot guess the road that will be taken. But the reader's awareness increases as the metaphor expands and his excitement mounts as he approaches the moment of disclosure. This is why one remembers so many of Frost's concluding lines: "He says again, 'Good fences make good neighbors' "; "With the slow smokeless burning of decay"; "The question that he frames in all but words / Is what to make of a diminished thing." If a Frost poem yields in its last line "the pleasure of ulteriority," it succeeds.

v

When Lloyd Morris in 1917 assembled his anthology of opinion "concerning the spirit and aims of contemporary American literature," many of the writers who responded to his queries believed that the new developments in poetry were far more promising than any improvements they could discern in fiction. Some of them neglected to comment on the novel at all. Present critical opinion would tend to sustain these contemporary judgments. There are, it is true, only a few memorable works of fiction surviving from the decade 1912 to 1922; possibly when one has named Joseph Hergesheimer's *The Three Black Pennys* (1917), Sherwood Anderson's *Winesburg, Ohio* (1919) and *Poor White* (1920), Sinclair Lewis' *Main Street* (1920) and *Babbitt* (1922), Edith Wharton's *The Custom of the Country* (1913) and *The Age of Innocence* (1920), and Willa Cather's *O Pioneers!* (1913) and *My Ántonia* (1918) one has named them all. But what the novelists accomplished in those years has been obscured by the fame of Fitzgerald and Dos Passos and by the sustained careers of Hemingway and Faulkner. There is another reason why the earlier generation of novelists has been pretty well forgotten. With the exception of Dreiser, Tarkington, Sinclair Lewis, Ellen Glasgow and Willa Cather, none of them seemed impressive even in the late twenties. Anderson's novel writing career was brief; it ended, in 1925, with *Dark*

Laughter. Carl Van Vechten's last success was *Nigger Heaven*, in 1926. The "Cabell era" was over by the mid-twenties. Joseph Hergesheimer's later novels (he ceased writing in 1934) were elegant costume pieces in which furniture and finery played more important parts than the characters.

And yet, if one will take the trouble to read or reread a dozen of the best and most representative novels of this neglected decade, he will be struck by the changes which took place in so short a time. The stereotyped plots and the black and white characters of the Age of Innocence have vanished. The new novelists had learned some profitable lessons from European masters, in particular Wells, Galsworthy, Anatole France, D. H. Lawrence, and even James Joyce and the Russians. The result was a greater probability in the action and a new psychological subtlety in the treatment of character.

Most notable is the changed attitude toward the American experience. In place of the earlier chauvinism and optimism there is a persistent questioning of the assumptions by which Americans lived. The novelist was in search of America and he was not apprehensive about what he might find in the darker places. It had become his duty to discover what America was like beyond the confines of Sunnybrook Farm and the Limberlost. Characteristically Anderson's *Poor White* opens in Mudcat Landing, Missouri, where the yellow, shallow, and stony soil is tilled by a race of "long gaunt men who seemed as exhausted and no-account as the land on which they lived." Hergesheimer, in his second novel, *Mountain Blood* (1915), took to the West Virginia hills and the village of Greenstream where two local skinflints hold the lesser folk of the valley in miserable bondage.

Not all these fictional excursions into unexplored America begin in dreary villages or the slums of big cities.

Many of the novelists were delighted with the new America they had found. Sinclair Lewis, for example, planned *Free Air* (1919) as a gay-hearted grand tour of the northwest. Country boy gets eastern girl after he has followed her and her father across the continent in his Teal "bug." As Claire sheds her eastern sophistication, she falls in love with Milt — and with his country.

> Often there were no fences; she was so intimately in among the grain that the fenders of the car brushed wheat stalks, and she became no stranger, but a part of all this vast-horizoned land. She forgot that she was driving, as she let the car creep on, while she was transported by Armadas of clouds, prairie clouds, wisps of vapor like a ribbed beach, or mounts of cumulus swelling to gold-washed snowy peaks. The friendliness of the bearing earth gave her a calm that took no heed of passing hours. . . .
>
> Claire had discovered America, and she felt stronger, and all her days were colored with the sun.

In some of these novels we follow the country boy to the great city and witness his excitement as he stands looking out over its teeming life. Typical of these enchanted youths is Felix Fay in Floyd Dell's *The Briary-Bush*. Newly arrived from Iowa, he gazes across Michigan Avenue to the lake, thrilled with the beauty of Chicago, yet half ashamed to be so deeply moved. Here life begins.

Other novelists moved back, with equal excitement, into the American past. They continued the tradition of the costume novel popular in the Age of Innocence, but they took more pains with sets and costumes than did Charles Major or Maurice Thompson. A great deal of research went into the writing of Ellen Glasgow's "Commonwealth" novels, and Hergesheimer's recreations of colonial life in Pennsylvania (*The Three Black Pennys*) and New England (*Java Head*, 1919) are as full of authenticated furniture as an antique shop.

A recurrent theme in many of the novels of this decade

is the degradation of American life caused by rapid industrialization. The movement from an agrarian to an industrial society had been accelerating, of course, for nearly half
a century, a fact well known to the novelists with the
muckrake. But most of them had been so much concerned
with the corruption in particular businesses and industries
that they had little to say about the profound changes
which industrialization was effecting in men's lives.

By temperament Sherwood Anderson (1876–1941) was
the writer best suited to describe the blight which factories
were spreading in the land. His first three novels, *Windy
McPherson's Son* (1916), *Marching Men* (1917), and *Poor
White* (1920), are studies of the problem. The son of a
ne'er-do-well father, Anderson understood the compulsion
to success in business which a family situation like his
own often produces. His still mysterious flight, in a state of
amnesia, from his "Roof Fix" company, a traumatic experience which turned him from business to writing, shows
how deeply he detested industry, though outwardly he had
made a success in it. Because he was so emotionally involved in the story he was trying to tell, he introduces into
these novels many of his personal frustrations. As a result,
only the first half of one of them, *Poor White*, dramatizes
objectively the consequences of industrialization.

Poor White is the story of Hugh McVey, an awkward,
lonely boy with a streak of inventive genius in him. He
comes to life in the Ohio village of Bidwell where he begins to experiment with models of farm machinery. In the
end Hugh is a wealthy man but he is still closed within
the walls of loneliness. What he has created is sterile and it
brings sterility and fear into the lives of those who admire
him and are grateful for his machines. The inhabitants of
Bidwell, like all men and women who live in industrial
cities, are "mice that have come out of the fields to live
in houses that do not belong to them."

One of the strongest indictments of the new industrial

society turns up, unexpectedly, in Booth Tarkington's *The Magnificent Ambersons* (1918). Tarkington loved the vanishing America of his Hoosier boyhood but his earlier chronicles of this region show little concern about the changes which were transforming it. In *The Magnificent Ambersons*, the story of the decay of a once proud and respected family, he indulges himself in a five-page diatribe against the effects of industrialization: the befouled and darkened sky, the raw new houses, the ghettos where immigrant labor lives.

In truth [he concludes], the city came to be like the body of a great dirty man, skinned, to show his busy works, yet wearing a few barbaric ornaments; and such a figure carved, coloured, and discoloured, and set up in the market-place, would have done well enough as the god of the new people. Such a god they had indeed made in their own image, as all peoples make the god they truly serve; though of course certain of the idealists went to church on Sunday, and there knelt to Another, considered to be impractical in business. But while the Growing went on, this god of their market-place was their true god, their familiar and spirit-control. They did not know that they were his helplessly obedient slaves, nor could they ever hope to realize their serfdom (as the first step toward becoming free men) until they should make the strange and hard discovery that matter should serve man's spirit.

Another of the assumptions of American life which the new novelists challenged was the myth of the friendly village. No matter if corruption were rampant in the smoke-blackened cities, life was supposed to have remained sweet at the crossroads. Meredith Nicholson said so in his *The Valley of Democracy* (1918): small town folks still possessed "a breadth of vision and a devotion to the common good at once beneficent and unique in the annals of mankind." A few earlier novelists had tried to destroy this persistent myth, but good novels though they are, E. W. Howe's *Story of a Country Town* (1883) and Harold

Frederic's *The Damnation of Theron Ware* (1896) produced no offspring.

It was Anderson's *Winesburg, Ohio* (1919), his most
powerful and influential book, which finally touched off
the novelists' revolt from the village. These stories of lives
twisted by toil and failure, of illicit affairs which the whole
village follows with lascivious interest, of secret lusts and
perversions, were not written by Anderson to "expose" the
village. But he reveals so starkly the spiritual deformities
of the inhabitants of Winesburg that he seems to be writing to the thesis that life in the American village is foul and
mean. And this was the impression he left with his readers.

The "village virus" was at last isolated and given a
name by Sinclair Lewis (1885–1951) when he published
*Main Street** in 1920. Americans must have been waiting
for this kind of attack on the shoddy architecture and the
hypocritical mores of all our Main Streets, for the novel
was a best-seller as well as a sensation. Readers at the
time sided with Carol Kennicott, the culture-hungry wife
of the town doctor who in bringing his bride to Gopher
Prairie exiles her among the Philistines. Few noticed that
the novel concludes with Lewis' usual compromise between
his love for the midwest and his revulsion from its drabness.
After living alone for a time in Washington, Carol consents to go back and try again. So Dr. Will wins in the
end and Lewis hints that his solid virtues are more admirable than Carol's yearning for beauty.

But the satire in *Main Street* (1920) has not lost its savor
after thirty years. And Lewis made sure that no one then
or later could say Gopher Prairie was the exception. Its
Main Street, he says in his preface, is the continuation of
Main Streets everywhere in America.

Main Street is the climax of civilization. That this Ford car
might stand in front of the Bon Ton Store, Hannibal invaded

* Lewis' first sketch of the novel was entitled "The Village Virus."

Rome and Erasmus wrote in Oxford cloisters. What Ole Jenson the grocer says to Ezra Stowbody the banker is the new law for London, Prague, and the unprofitable isles of the sea; whatsoever Ezra does not know and sanction, that thing is heresy, worthless for knowing and wicked to consider. . . .

Such is our comfortable tradition and sure faith. Would he not betray himself an alien cynic who should otherwise portray Main Street, or distress the citizens by speculating whether there may not be other faiths?

For more than ten years after *Spoon River, Winesburg,* and *Main Street* no novelist ventured to write about plain folks in friendly small towns. Significantly, a back-to-the-village movement can be observed in the early 1930's (Phil Stong's *State Fair*, 1932; Ruth Suckow's *The Folks*, 1934), at the moment when the darkened factories and empty store-fronts in the depression-wracked cities made Americans long once more for a garden patch and neighbors on the front porch across the street.

For a young writer in the years between 1912 and 1922 there were other ways of escaping the American village than "exposing" it as a *Winesburg, Ohio* or satirizing it in a *Main Street*. He could seek sanctuary in one of at least a half-dozen Bohemias in the larger cities, New York's Greenwich Village being the largest and the gaudiest. Here was a refuge from all that was boring and ugly in American life. Once you had hung the batik curtains in your attic in Macdougal Alley, there were all kinds of emancipated young Americans to argue the future with. At the famous salon of Mabel Dodge (23 Fifth Avenue) you could meet, in a single evening, Carl Van Vechten, the most sophisticated man in America, Bill Haywood, I.W.W. leader, Max Eastman, whose magazine, *Masses*, was Socialist in politics and *avant garde* in all the arts, John Reed, who later witnessed the Russian Revolution, and Robert Edmond Jones, who was helping to bring into being the new American theater. The passport to this charmed society was a determination never to go home again and an absolute belief in emancipation, intellectual, artistic, and sexual.

The novelist who best represents the liberated spirits of this time is James Branch Cabell (b. 1879), though it is doubtful if he ever left Virginia long enough to set foot in Greenwich Village. In the early 1920's his *Jurgen* (1919) was the breviary of all young men and women who were sworn enemies of Puritanism, political earnestness, realism in art, and middle-class morality. Many critics said many foolish things about Cabell (Carl Van Doren, V. L. Parrington, and H. L. Mencken among others), but none of them colored his praise with so deep a purple as Joseph Hergesheimer in his elucidation of the magic of *Jurgen:* "There is reach on reach above even the purity of the Trojan Helen . . . up, up to the port of Heaven which smelt of mignonette." .

The plot of *Jurgen* resembles the plots of most of the fifteen novels that make up what Cabell called "the Biography." The hero goes on a journey and incredible things happen to him. He is usually wandering about Cabell's imaginary Poictesme, sometime between 1234 and 1750, and he always deserves the fine adventures which befall him because he inherits the great Dom Manuel's chivalry and sexual prowess and gift of words.

The Jurgen vogue will be the more readily understood if one remembers that many young men in 1920 looked back on the age of Wilde and Beardsley much as young people thirty years later sighed for the golden age of F. Scott Fitzgerald. In Cabell's prose there is something of the preciousness of Pater, the slyness of Anatole France, the naughtiness of Beardsley, and the wit of Oscar Wilde. Furthermore there was literary snob appeal in Cabell's casual allusions in "the Biography" to myths and legends and historical episodes, classical and medieval, French and German. And how pleasant to meet Helen of Troy and

Shakespeare, Merlin and Alexander Pope, and hear them talk.

There was also sex. And if Cabell's language failed, at times, to be explicit about Jurgen's amours, Papé's illustrations supplied the details. Joyce's *Ulysses*, one should remember, was published three years after *Jurgen* and until 1934 could be owned by an American only if he smuggled it through customs. Henry Miller was still in swaddling clothes — if he ever wore them. The phallicism of *Jurgen* was in 1920 God's plenty. What could be more delightful than this jousting in the dark between "the plump brown-haired bright-eyed little creature, this Chloris" and King Jurgen?

"And how does a king come thus to be traveling without any retinue or even a sword about him?"

"Why, I travel with a staff, my dear, as you perceive: and it suffices me."

"Certainly it is large enough, in all conscience. Alas, young outlander, who call yourself a king! you carry the bludgeon of a highwayman, and I am afraid of it."

VI

The decade of the "new American literature" saw the rise of one novelist, Willa Cather (1873–1947), whose work is today as exciting as it seemed in those years when readers awaited with eagerness the appearance of her newest book. She achieved mastery through a happy combination of circumstances. A woman of great vigor of mind and body, she succeeded in transferring to her novels the strength of her own personality. (She also had the staying power to turn out twelve novels and several volumes of short stories.) Her response to life was open and eager and in time she came to love, with a deep passion, her native region, the great plains which lie between the Missouri and the Colorado mountains. The tradition of western civilization, its art, music, architecture, literature, religious rituals, and national traits, continuously affected her outlook on life and no modern American writer has made so much of the cultural continuity between the Old World and the New.

Willful as a girl and strong-minded as a young woman, she was none the less devoted to her family and to the friends of her years of growing up. She entered fully into their lives, and the joys and defeats of her characters were drawn from the life stories of people she had known. She was a born writer. The dramatic criticism she wrote for the *Nebraska State Journal,* when she was a student at the University, reminds one, in its wit and good sense, of Shaw's *Dramatic Opinions and Essays.* The travel-letters she sent back to the same paper during her first trip to Europe, in 1902, already evince the vividness and purity of style which characterize her best work.

Extraordinarily gifted as she was and destined to bring to life a whole region, Miss Cather was a long time, seventeen years to be exact, in finding her way back to the village of Red Cloud, Nebraska. Then, novel by novel, it was successively transformed into the Hanover of *O Pioneers!* (1913), the Moonstone of *The Song of the Lark* (1915), the Black Hawk of *My Ántonia* (1918), the Frankfort of *One of Ours* (1922), the Sweetwater of *A Lost Lady* (1923), and the Haverford of *Lucy Gayheart* (1935). Red Cloud ranks with Concord and Hannibal as one of the most famous villages in American literature.

After graduating from the University in 1895 and spending a discontented year at home, Miss Cather came east to Pittsburgh where she worked as a journalist and then taught high-school Latin and English. She continued to write, publishing the usual slender volume of verse, *April Twilights,* in 1903, and in 1905 a book of short stories, *The Troll Garden.* The plots of these first stories have so little to do with the people of "the Divide" that one might suppose she had never lived there. For the most part they are concerned with the life of the artist, his struggle for success in a Philistine world and the sacrifices he makes for his art. From one story in the group, "A Wagner Matinée," we learn that Miss Cather's memories of Red Cloud were at this time anything but tender. The narrator tells how his Aunt Georgianna comes on from Red Willow County in Nebraska for a brief vacation in Boston where she had once taught in the Conservatory. When he was a farm boy in that desolate country, she had awakened his interest in music, providing him with the link to all she had given up to go west and become a pioneer's wife. When the magnificent concert is over, she bursts into tears and sobs: "I don't want to go, Clark, I don't want to go."

I understood. For her, just outside the concert hall, lay the black pond with the cattle-tracked bluffs; the tall, unpainted house, with weather-curled boards, naked as a tower; the crook-backed ash seedlings where the dish-cloths hung to dry; the gaunt, moulting turkeys picking up refuse about the kitchen door.

From this dreariness Willa Cather had escaped and she had no desire to return to it, even in her stories.

Leaving Pittsburgh, she moved on to New York to become an editor for S. S. McClure, one of the most farsighted magazine publishers of his time. She served him well, from 1906 to 1912. Through her connections with *McClure's Magazine* she entered the larger world of art, music, and literature in New York and Boston. The momentous event of these years was her friendship with the greatest of American regionalists in fiction, Sarah Orne Jewett. Miss Jewett recognized that Willa Cather's genius was still unfulfilled and helped to set her on her true course. "You must find a quiet place," she admonished her in a persuasive letter written in 1908. "You must find your own quiet center of life and write from that."

Willa Cather was not quite ready to assent. The influence of Henry James on her style and themes was still strong and would be responsible for her first novel, *Alexander's Bridge,* published in 1912. But three events of that year accomplished the turning-back to Nebraska Miss Jewett had hoped for. Willa Cather resigned from *McClure's* and prepared to live by her fiction-writing alone. She published "The Bohemian Girl," the first story which shows, though faintly, her reconciliation with the life she had escaped from seventeen years before. And she went with her brother Douglas into the parts of Arizona and New Mexico which would figure importantly in many of her novels. She delighted in the Indians and Mexicans in whom she saw survivals of Aztec beauty, and her imagination was stimulated by the ruins of the Cliff Dwellers in Arizona's Walnut Canyon. In these new scenes she discovered an older America than that of her childhood. It would become a refuge for many of her later characters — for Thea Kronborg in *The Song of the Lark* and Tom Outland in *The Professor's House.* Death comes for her Archbishop in that enchanted land to which he had given his hope and his life.

In *O Pioneers!* (1913) Miss Cather turned at last and with success to her country and to old neighbors whom, as she later wrote, she had "almost forgotten in the hurry and excitement of growing up and finding out what the world was like and trying to get on with it." She did not expect that the novel would make much stir. Nebraska, she felt, was "distinctly déclassé as a literary background" and her farmers were not only Nebraskans, they were Swedes, traditionally comic characters in American writing.

O Pioneers! is somewhat faulty in construction. One is not sure whether the story belongs to Alexandra Bergson, the strong and enduring woman who saves the family's land and makes it prosper, or to her talented younger brother,

Emil, whose love for Marie Shabata incites the wronged husband to murder them both. But there is no denying the functional beauty of the descriptive passages and the power with which the scenes are evoked, especially the tragic killing under the white mulberry tree. For the first time Miss Cather makes use of her version of the theme of the true pioneer. Like Alexandra he can make the land blossom and bear fruit if he loves it: "the history of every country begins in the heart of a man or woman." He must have imagination and be able "to enjoy the idea of things more than the things themselves." This is the touchstone by which she will test many later characters who falter or give up in despair as well as those who are true to the "genius of the Divide."

In her next book, *The Song of the Lark* (1915), Miss Cather essayed, not very successfully, to follow the career of a great opera singer from her childhood in a western village to her triumphs in Europe and New York. The novel is overburdened with detail and in places scarcely moves at all. Fortunately *My Ántonia* (1918) took the road of *O Pioneers!* It is the most masterly of her novels and one of the classics of our literature. The story is told by Jim Burden who as a boy arrived in Black Hawk on the train which brought the Shimerdas, the first Bohemian family to come to that country. Though Jim is the narrator (and we follow him from the farm to the village, on to the University, and the world beyond), the story belongs to Ántonia, the affectionate little Shimerda girl who becomes in the end a strong, great-hearted woman, the most completely realized of Willa Cather's true pioneers. With a sure hand Miss Cather develops the contrast between the serene life in the house of Jim's grandparents, with its ways and furnishings carried thither from Virginia, and the squalor and suffering in the sod house of the Shimerdas. After Jim leaves Black Hawk, Ántonia, the brave, the gay of heart, is left pregnant by a man who had promised her marriage. She recovers from the hurt, marries, and when Jim sees her twenty years later she is the mother of a fine brood of young Cuzaks. She has become the kind of woman who lends herself "to immemorial human attitudes which we recognize by instinct as universal and true."

That Willa Cather hoped she could give significance to the lives of her pioneers in *My Ántonia* we know from a chapter describing Jim's Latin studies at the University. He has been reading Virgil's Georgics and one passage in particular lingers in his mind.

I turned back to the beginning of the third book, which we had read in class that morning. *"Primus ego in patriam mecum . . . deducam Musas"*; "for I shall be the first, if I live, to bring the Muse into my country." Cleric had explained to us that "patria" here meant, not a nation or even a province, but the little rural neighborhood on the Mincio where the poet was born. This was not a boast, but a hope, at once bold and devoutly humble, that he might bring the Muse (but lately come to Italy from her cloudy Grecian mountains), not to the capital, the *palatia Romana*, but to his own little "country"; to his father's fields, "sloping down to the river and to the old beech trees with broken tops."

The words are Jim's; the hope that was not a boast was Willa Cather's.

Though Miss Cather used the region of the Divide in later novels and short stories none of these works possesses the idyllic tone of *My Ántonia*. The reasons why this is so are plain enough. As she remarked in *Not Under Forty* (1936), for her "the world broke in two in 1922 or thereabout." The devastation caused by the War in France, to which she was devoted, affected her deeply. Her growing pessimism over the degradation of American life darkened her feeling about her region and showed increasingly in her work. At heart a true conservative, loving the heroic generation and disliking the new machine-made civilization, she turned the coin over to reveal what disgusted her in the postpioneer age. In *One of Ours* (1922) she showed how Claude Wheeler's life is made miserable by his marriage to a shallow, bigoted girl and by his unsympathetic brothers, symbols for Miss Cather of the generation which had inherited, without deserving, what the pioneers had created. Claude escapes into the War and knows some moments of contentment and beauty in France before he is killed.

In *A Lost Lady* (1923) she contrasts the two generations, "in one of those gray towns along the Burlington railroad," as seen through the eyes of Niel Herbert who grows up there. Mrs. Forrester, the lady who in the end is "lost," is married to a man twenty-five years older than herself, one of the builders of the region. She stands by him in his poverty and long illness but she has taken (and lost) a lover in the railroad aristocracy and at the end she has fallen so far that she submits to Ivy Peters, a local boy who has made good as a lawyer, though he is as shady in his profession as in his morals. *A Lost Lady* is a novella perfectly told. The stages of Mrs. Forrester's decline and fall are subtly stressed. Like young Niel who has seen it all we can not admire her but we can pity and understand. "This was the very end of the road-making West." The great age was gone and nothing could bring it back — "the taste and smell and song of it, the visions those men had seen in the air and followed." What Niel most held against Mrs. Forrester was that she was not willing to die with the pioneer period to which she belonged. "She preferred life on any terms."

A second turning point in Willa Cather's career is marked by *The Professor's House* (1925). In writing it she found her way out both in method and in theme, as Edith Wharton and Sherwood Anderson, in their time of despair about America, had failed to do. If she could no longer write with devotion about the land and people she knew, she could go back in time and find solace in the heroic past. At the center of the novel is Professor St. Peter's determination to cling to the shabby house where he had written his monumental study of the *Spanish Adventurers in North America*. The domestic struggle is symbolic of his resistance to the success-worshipping life of his wife and daughters. What strengthens him is his memory of his most brilliant student, Tom Outland, who died before his scientific genius could be exploited for profit. Before Tom arrived at the midwestern college where St. Peter teaches, he had discovered in a New Mexico canyon a Cliff Dweller village perfectly preserved against the erosions of time. (The account of the discovery — "Tom Outland's Story" — is the intercalated middle section of the book.) Here again, though now carried back into history, is Miss Cather's dominant theme of the true pioneer who with his hands and faith builds and leaves behind a civilization.

She was ready to cast the shell of modern life and write only about the past. Her next two novels, *Death Comes for the Archbishop* (1927) and *Shadows on the Rock* (1931), celebrate the builders of civilization in the New World. Into the first, the story of the first archbishop of the southwest who begins in 1851 his long struggle to revive the Catholic faith in his immense parish, she could pour all her love for the region she had first seen with her brother in 1912. In the second, through the heroic builders of Quebec, from Count de Frontenac and the indomitable Bishop Laval to the wise and gentle apothecary, Auclair, in whose shop most of the scenes are laid, she could express her admiration for French civilization, its love of order and the good life — above all its genius for creating a New France in the wilderness. Critics who have called these two historical novels wan have not noticed how perfect they are of their kind, that they are indeed unique. Willa Cather was not interested in battles and affairs of state, in costumes or folkways. She was writing about men of strong and simple faith and their adherence to God's will to plant in dry and stony soil.

There were to be two more novels — *Lucy Gayheart* (1935), another study of a musician who grows up in a small town on the Platte, and *Sapphira and the Slave Girl* (1940), in which Miss Cather turned to the Virginia of her early years. They are good novels — the portrait of the cold and imperious Sapphira is especially fine — but they do not rank with her best. At her death she left unfinished a novel about Avignon, the Papal city in southern France which had first engaged her imagination forty years earlier. The novel — it was to be called *Hard Punishments* — would have furnished a symbolic climax to her career. In one way or another Europe had entered all her novels: through the memories and stories which her immigrants bring to Nebraska, through Claude's brief but happy days in France, through Professor St. Peter's French garden, with its "glistening gravel and glistening shrubs and bright flowers." The opening scene of *Death Comes for the Archbishop* is in the garden of a villa in the Sabine hills where three cardinals are talking about Catholic missions in the New World. In *Shadows on the Rock* one is constantly reminded of the ties that bind Auclair and his Seigneur, de Frontenac, to the Quai des Célestins in Paris. Here at the end, in the Avignon novel, Europe was to have usurped America.

THREE

Dramatic Interlude, 1915-1940

I

COINCIDENT with the coming-of-age of American poetry and fiction in the years between 1914 and 1925 was an upsurge of serious interest in the drama. One cannot call this remarkable dramatic interlude, which lasted twenty-five years, a renaissance. There had never been an American drama of any literary distinction to undergo a rebirth. From the early days of the Republic down to the period under consideration not more than a half-dozen plays had been produced which are still read by any except historians of the theater. Suddenly playwrights whose work was distinguished for more than "good theater" turned up in surprising numbers. Many of their plays seem destined to survive as literature.

Looking back on this episode from the vantage point of the 1950's one is struck by the crusading enthusiasm for the new drama on the part of playwrights, actors, producers, and audiences and by the length of time this new spirit in the theater persisted. A little earlier there had been a similar burst of vitality in the theaters of Germany, France, Ireland, and England but in none of these countries was the ardor created by the movement so great or the impact on the national life so strong. Young Americans in the 1920's and 1930's got an education in the theater, for almost every subject of importance was discussed in the best plays of these years, from social and political philosophy to sexual

63

morality. The censors, official and unofficial, had not yet moved in.

It is difficult to convey to the young the quality of this enthusiasm for the new drama. What they were seeing on Broadway in the 1950's was a pale reflex of what their elders saw twenty or thirty years before. Except for an occasional revival in the college theaters or the off-Broadway playhouses, they have had no chance to learn why their parents still talk excitedly about first nights of plays by O'Neill, Sidney Howard, Maxwell Anderson, Robert Sherwood, and foreign importations by Shaw, Molnar, and Pirandello. So evanescent is the art of the theater that they cannot be expected to be thrilled by reminiscences of Louis Wolheim as Yank in *The Hairy Ape* and as Captain Flagg in that shocking war-play *What Price Glory?* No one can make them imagine how "young, beautiful, gracious, and obviously civilized" Jane Cowl was as Amytis, wife of Fabius, the Dictator, in Sherwood's *The Road to Rome*.

Beyond Broadway in those years, furnishing the audiences for the new plays and sending to New York a continuous stream of young actors, directors, and scene designers, were the little theaters. In communities all over the country everyone, so it seemed, wanted to save America by directing or performing in plays by Lord Dunsany and Shaw and the bright young playwrights trained at Harvard in Professor George Pierce Baker's 47 Workshop. They painted flats and struggled with switchboards. They talked knowingly of light-bridges, cycloramas, the duties of the *régisseur*, and the possibilities of the futurist drama. Their first gods were foreign — Adolphe Appia (the begetter of modern lighting in the theater), Gordon Craig, Jacques Copeau, Stanislavsky, Shaw, Strindberg — but as soon as Broadway was converted to the new drama and the new theater, they added to their pantheon Robert Edmond Jones, Lee Simonson, and O'Neill.

Almost every season was a banner season. It seemed as if there would never be an end to the procession of highly original plays, admirably cast and expertly produced. In 1924, before the hiatus of Christmas, theater-goers had seen Anderson and Stallings' *What Price Glory?*, O'Neill's *Desire under the Elms,* Sidney Howard's *They Knew What They Wanted,* and Philip Barry's second play, *The Youngest.* George Kelly's hilarious comedy *The Show-Off,* a hold-over from the season before, was still selling out. Ten years later the pace had not slackened. The best plays of the 1934–1935 season were Lillian Hellman's *The Children's Hour* (a first play which was not expected to do well), Sherwood's *The Petrified Forest,* starring Leslie Howard and Humphrey Bogart, Zoë Akins' *The Old Maid,* with Judith Anderson and Helen Mencken to help it on its way to a Pulitzer Prize, and Clifford Odets' *Awake and Sing!,* his first full-length play. Then came a slackening in the war years, a premonition of the rapid decline in the 1950's.

During these twenty-five years audiences looked on with delight as the dramatists took them into the byways of the nation and aquainted them with people they would not know in real life — gangsters, beachcombers, stevedores, Negro preachers and fish venders, Bohemian artists, and the ultra-rich. They received with pleasure just about anything the dramatist offered them, if it was novel, honest, and exciting. In the 1920's they were delighted, though puzzled, by experiments in Expressionism, such as Elmer Rice's *The Adding Machine* and O'Neill's *The Great God Brown.* When the Moscow Art Theater came to America in 1922–1923, audiences sat enraptured through *The Cherry Orchard* and *Tzar Fyodor* without understanding a word spoken by the actors. When O'Neill's nine-act *Strange Interlude* was playing in 1928 they thought it a great lark to come to the theater in the afternoon, take eighty minutes out for dinner, and return for another long session in the evening. They came faithfully three days in succession to follow to the end the cycle of plays which made up Shaw's *Back to Methuselah*. In the 1930's they cheered the social propaganda in the Federal Theater's plays whether they believed it or not.

II

One cannot point to any one season before or after the first World War and say in that year the new drama came into being. In the mid-twenties, when the Theatre Guild was doing its most experimental work and the new movement was in the ascendant, the vacuous and sentimental *Abie's Irish Rose* ran for five years (1922–1927) and piled up a record of 2,532 performances. Yet there is a very great difference between the theater of Minnie Maddern Fiske and that of Katharine Cornell and the difference is measurable. In the 1900's audiences attended the theater to be amused, much as people today go to the movies or watch television. They wanted bravura acting and happy endings. They did not expect to be exposed to ideas, especially if they were unpleasant ideas. There was no popular protest when the producer (Arnold Daly, a Shaw enthusiast) withdrew *Mrs. Warren's Profession* after its one New York performance on October 31, 1905. Most of those who had blundered into the theater that night probably agreed with the outraged reviewers, one of whom declared that the play could not be made fit for public view: "You cannot have a clean pig stye."

Conditions under which actors were hired and plays produced were inimical to good drama in the early years of the century. The Theatrical Syndicate, founded in 1895 by a group of theater owners, controlled most of the houses across the country and soon had all the better actors in its keep. So tight was the Syndicate's monopoly that when

George Tyler took Sarah Bernhardt on tour he frequently had to play her in a circus tent. The rivalry soon offered by the Shubert's chain of theaters worsened the situation. The individuality of the local houses was destroyed and the quality of plays and productions was lowered even further. Dramatists worked like hacks to keep up with the demands of competitive booking. Since the so-called "ten-twenty-thirty" houses played an attraction for only one week, a dramatist like Owen Davis who worked for the Stair and Havlin Circuit had to prepare each year a large number of the thirty-five plays needed to keep the Circuit's companies moving around the "Wheel."

Under the conditions which prevailed between 1895 and 1905 there was little chance that plays of any literary merit could emerge. There are probably no more than three written in this period that could be revived today: Langdon Mitchell's *The New York Idea* (1906),* a genuinely witty satire on "advanced" ideas about marriage and divorce; William Vaughn Moody's *The Great Divide* (1909), a "problem" play which, in the persons of the hero and heroine, brings into conflict the puritanical east and the lawless Arizona frontier; and Percy Mackaye's *The Scarecrow* (1910), a fantasy which anticipated the plays on folk themes, an important feature of the experimental drama of the 1920's.

There were, of course, many plays which dealt with contemporary ideas and problems, such as Augustus Thomas' *The Witching Hour* (mental telepathy); Eugene Walter's *The Easiest Way* (the woman who succumbs, but is abandoned at the end); and Edward Sheldon's *The Nigger* (a rising southern politician who has to face the fact of his Negro "blood"). What is wrong with these plays, and others like them, is, as Alan Downer

---

* In this chapter the dates given in parentheses are the years in which the plays were produced.

has pointed out, the meretricious theatricalism which inevitably vitiates their themes.[1] Frequently they get off to an excellent start. The settings are realistic, the problem is well stated, the characters show promise of development. But before long the values and devices of the older theater invade the action. The unexpected gun goes off, the long-lost heir knocks at the door in the nick of time, the incriminating document turns up. The playwrights who used these tricks were not looking at life. They were remembering scenes invented by Boucicault and Daly. Downer's observation about Sheldon's plays can be extended to the work of his contemporaries: "[They] are startling proof of the determination of the theater of the early twentieth century to live in a world of its own." Whatever reality is in them is "only a device; it is not organic, it is not in the theme."

Why was theatricalism so swiftly abandoned? The causes are many but not in the least obscure. First to be reckoned with is the fertilizing effect of a renewed contact with the artistic life of Europe. In the first decade of the century America had been singularly isolated from contemporary culture abroad. The situation changed rapidly just before the War. Symphony orchestras were inducing their audiences to listen to Debussy, Ravel, Mahler, and Stravinsky. The great exhibition of modern painting (chiefly the French Impressionists) gathered for the famous Armory Show in New York (1913) had a profound effect on the thousands who visited it. The performances of the Ballet Russe, under the direction of the mighty Diaghileff, opened up a new world of delight in the theater. Americans had never seen anything so dazzlingly beautiful as the choreography of Fokine, the dancing of Nijinsky, and the spectacular sets of Léon Bakst. By 1918 many stage-struck young people had made some contact with the "free theaters" and "art theaters" abroad. If they had not seen the work of the director André Antoine at the Theâtre Antoine or the Odéon in Paris or visited the Abbey Theatre in Dublin, they had read the plays produced there and had read about them in Ludwig Lewisohn's revelatory *The Modern Drama* (1915). The visit of the Abbey Players to America in 1911 and the two-year sojourn in New York (1917–1919) of Copeau's Vieux-Colombier company brought the best Europe had to offer into direct competition with Broadway.

Inspired by the achievements of Brahm and Reinhardt in Germany, Antoine and Copeau in France, Yeats and Lady Gregory in Dublin, what could the young enthusiasts bent on reforming the American drama do in the face of the theatrical monopoly? They could do, of course, what their European predecessors had done — found free theaters and art theaters in defiance of the "system." In a short time little theaters (the American term) broke out all over the country. In 1912 the Toy Theater was organized in Boston. In the same year Maurice Brown established the Chicago Little Theater where the fare he offered — Euripides, Ibsen, Strindberg — nourished his patrons but bankrupted his enterprise after five years. Soon the Cleveland Play House, the Vagabond Players of Baltimore, the Carolina Playmakers, the Dallas Little Theater, Le Petit Théâtre du Vieux Carré in New Orleans, and scores of other groups were spreading the gospel. By 1924, so Kenneth Macgowan estimated, five hundred such theaters had been founded and their actors were playing to an audience of half a million.[2] The professional producers on Broadway and the Road did not mount as many plays in a season as did these groups.

Though many of the little theaters were to have a long and prosperous life — the Pasadena Playhouse and the Cleveland Play House, for instance — none of them has had so great an effect on our dramatic history as the Washington

Square Players which opened their first season in 1915. The organizers were remarkable for the variety of their talents, good taste, and ability to survive the hazards of life in the theater. Lawrence Langner, a patent lawyer, furnished the business brains. Philip Moeller wrote plays and directed them. Helen Westley was their character actress. Lee Simonson, recently returned from art study in Paris, and Rollo Peters designed sets. Among the first to act in their productions were Katharine Cornell, Glenn Hunter, and Roland Young. The company played everything good that was obtainable — Chekhov, Maeterlinck, Andreyev, Ibsen, Shaw, and new plays by young Americans, including several in the Players' own circle. When their fourth season ended in 1918 they had presented, all told, sixty-two short pieces and six full-length plays. Their tenacity and their insistence on standards were known and admired by every other little theater group in the country.[3]

Late in 1918 some of the Washington Square veterans organized the Theatre Guild, the most influential theatrical organization this country has ever known. This was not a little theater, but was founded with the intent of taking Broadway by storm. The Introduction to *The Theatre Guild Anthology*, published in 1936, declares that when the Guild began to function it was "without a theatre, without a play, without an actor and without a scrap of scenery. Its sole artistic asset was an idea." This statement is a pleasant fiction. The Guild owned greater assets than material ones: the intelligence and experience of Langner, Moeller, Helen Westley, and Lee Simonson. They soon added to their group one of the shrewdest theatrical managers of the century, Theresa Helburn, a great compounder of differences in a traditionally quarrelsome profession, and the possessor of an uncanny ability to spot new acting and writing talent.

Though it had some failures along the way, the Guild

established itself as a tough competitor on Broadway. As events proved, there was an audience ready for the excellent plays it produced. Its success might not have been so complete if it had not made several astute moves. It avoided the problem of raising money, show by show, from "angels" by setting up a subscription plan which offered patrons six productions a year for a reduced price. In 1925 the Guild acquired an excellently equipped playhouse and thus solved the Broadway rental problem which was even then vexatious. Another wise move was its establishment of a play-reading department, the only professional theater to have one at the time. A group of eight experts searched the repertory of Europe and came up with plays by Benavente, St. John Ervine, Molnar, Tolstoy, and Strindberg. In 1919 when Shaw had trouble finding a producer on either side of the water for his *Heartbreak House* (it was considered too pacifistic), the Guild gave it a production which was a financial as well as an artistic success. Shaw subsequently entrusted fourteen of his plays, four of them in their world premières, to the Guild. In the early seasons it was rightly accused of producing only foreign plays, but as soon as the young American playwrights came along, Howard, Lawson, Behrman, Barry, Sherwood, Anderson, it was quick to take them in. O'Neill came over to the Guild in 1928 with *Marco Millions.*

While the Washington Square Players were evolving into the Theatre Guild, the Provincetown Players carried on through the War in their Macdougal Street barn in Greenwich Village. The group survived until the depression struck in 1929. Their first productions, in the summer of 1915, were presented in a fish house in Provincetown, Massachusetts, then a vacation retreat of Villagers. The guiding spirits of the Provincetown were George Cram Cook, Susan Glaspell, Robert Edmond Jones, and Eugene O'Neill. Eventually the directorate was O'Neill, Jones, and

Kenneth Macgowan, an ideal combination of playwright, designer, and director. Though many of the productions were memorable (in spite of the miniscule stage and a limited budget), the Provincetown was primarily a theater for young dramatists. Only a few of them — O'Neill, Susan Glaspell, Hatcher Hughes, and Paul Green — went on to make play-writing their profession, but the list of the others who later became well known as poets, novelists, and critics is impressive. Their brief connection with the venture was significant in the development of Edna St. Vincent Millay, Theodore Dreiser, Floyd Dell, Edmund Wilson, and Stark Young. But the Provincetown Players' greatest service to American drama was the fostering of O'Neill's talent. It was a decisive night in our dramatic history when in midsummer, 1916, O'Neill's *Bound East for Cardiff* was presented in a bill of four one-acters in the now famous fish house on a Provincetown wharf.

In reckoning up the transformations effected by the art theaters one must not overlook some balances in favor of Broadway. As John Gassner has reminded us,[4] several hard-headed producers were willing to be shown. They were particularly ready to adopt the innovations in stage lighting and décor in which Joseph Urban, Robert Edmond Jones, and Lee Simonson pioneered. When Arthur Hopkins ventured to produce Tolstoy's *Redemption* and Benelli's *The Jest* and starred Barrymore in *Hamlet* and *Richard III*, Jones was his designer. In the 1920's Urban, who had come from Vienna to design sets for the Boston opera, was called in to mount the lavishly produced Ziegfeld *Follies*. Hopkins gave O'Neill his first phenomenal success by his production of *Anna Christie*. It was the conservative Brock Pemberton who introduced Pirandello to American audiences. Even William A. Brady, one of the last representatives of the old romantic theater, producer of scores of melodramas (including *Way Down East* and *The Two*

Orphans), once gave his all for art. The play was Elmer Rice's *Street Scene*, the Pulitzer prize-winner in 1929. It had been refused by the insurgent theaters, but as usual Brady made money for himself and his playwright.

III

When a young writer today sends his first play to an agent or producer he is likely to have had some training in his craft in a university department of drama. At last the academic recognition accorded music and the visual arts has been won, in most colleges, by the arts of the theater. In some colleges and universities, notably Yale, Iowa, Indiana, Amherst, and Williams, they are magnificently provided for. Things were very different in 1920. Some of the writers of the new drama left vaudeville for which they had been writing one-acters. Some oldtimers simply got tired of the crude stuff they had been turning out and, moved by the time spirit, reformed their ways.[5] Others turned from reporting and column-writing to the drama, with the encouragement of some art theater group.

A few young dramatists could find in university courses the training they needed. Pittsburgh's Carnegie Institute of Technology has had an important department of drama since 1914. Frederick H. Koch, founder of the Dakota Playmakers in 1910, moved to the University of North Carolina in 1918 to teach play writing. Most influential of the university professors of drama as a living art was the austere George Pierce Baker of Harvard. His famous 47 Workshop, which got its name from the catalogue number of his course in play writing, was organized to produce the prentice work of his students at Radcliffe and Harvard. Baker's efforts to teach the elements of dramatic art was looked down on by his scholarly colleagues, but he did the best he could with his meager equipment in old Massachusetts Hall. What mattered was his skill as a teacher and the quality of the dozen or so students he admitted each year to his course. When Eugene O'Neill, the most famous alumnus of English 47, said of Professor Baker in 1939, "He helped us to hope," he undoubtedly spoke for Thomas Wolfe, Sidney Howard, John Dos Passos, George Abbott, Philip Barry, Theresa Helburn, and all the other students who had at some time been members of "Baker's dozen."

By the mid-twenties audiences had been persuaded to enjoy many plays which were experimental, but the change which was taking place in the theater is most clearly seen in the honest realism of such characteristic plays as *Miss Lulu Bett* (1920), *Dulcy* (1921), and *What Price Glory?* (1924). The heavy villains and angelic heroines, the soubrettes and ingenues have vanished. The plot-solutions follow from the clash of characters whose motives are understandable. The action in these plays lies close to life. Everyone has encountered at least one Miss Lulu Bett, the sister-in-law, soon to become an old maid, who is so imposed upon by her family that she has become a drudge. In every circle there is a Dulcy, the wife who talks in clichés, who does her best to help her husband, but makes a mess of things. It was not merely the uninhibited Marine language of *What Price Glory?* and the competition to get into Charmaine's bed which made that play a success. Here was the War as A.E.F. veterans in the audience had known it. It was also the War these men had forgotten to tell their wives about or had not been able to make them understand.

Of the ten Pulitzer Prize awards between 1917 and 1927, eight went to realistic plays, a fact of some significance when one remembers that under the terms of the Pulitzer will the play receiving the award must raise the "standards of good morals, good taste and good manners" in the theater. On through the 1920's and 1930's plays of

this genre continued to be the mainstay of the theater —
Street Scene in 1929, *The Children's Hour in* 1934, *Awake
and Sing!* and *Dead End* in 1935 — to mention only
four of the best. Like the novelists contemporary with them
— Willa Cather, Sinclair Lewis, Booth Tarkington — the
playwrights were rediscovering middle class America.

Two early plays in this genre, Owen Davis' *Icebound*
(1923) and George Kelly's *The Show-Off* (1924), are the
more remarkable because they were written by men who
had no connection with the insurgent theater. Davis had
written hundreds of melodramas, of the order of *Convict
999* and *Nellie, the Beautiful Cloak Model,* for the popular-
price circuits. Kelly had spent five years writing one-acters
for the two-a-day. (How little use he had for art-struck
amateurs of the theater he made plain in 1922 with his
satire on the little theater movement, *The Torchbearers.*)
Davis, Portland-born, knew the people and the place he
wrote about in *Icebound.*

Scene: The parlor of the Jordan Homestead at Veazie,
Maine.

Here, in the room that for a hundred years has been the
rallying-point of the Jordan family, a group of relatives are
gathered to await the death of the old woman who is the head
of their clan. The room in which they wait is as dull and as
drab as the lives of those who have lived within its walls.

Each Jordan, jealous of the others, hopes for the inheritance. A few moments after the mother's death the blow
falls. The lawyer tells them that the money is to go to their
second cousin, Jane Crosby, who has loved the old woman.
Shortly before this, Ben, the scapegrace of the family, has
arrived, prompted partly by love for his mother, partly
by greed. Early in the play one guesses that Jane will reform
Ben, that the charge of arson which stands against him
will be withdrawn, and that they will marry.

One can imagine how Davis might have handled this not unusual dramatic situation in his unregenerate days. But *Icebound* is true in nearly every line. The dialogue is Down East without a trace of folksiness. Davis stays by his theme, the icebound lives of his characters. At the end the only ones whose hearts have been thawed are Jane and Ben, because only they could escape, through love, the chill of that parlor.

Kelly's *The Show-Off* gave a memorable character to American drama. Aubrey Piper is the little man with the big ego, the bluffer and back-slapper who is always telling people what a whiz of a fellow he is. To the disgust of the Fishers their romantic daughter Amy insists on marrying him. The family conversation is so excruciatingly real that one would think Kelly had been listening for years at the keyholes of lower middle class Philadelphia suburbia. Here, for example, is Mrs. Fisher questioning her husband about an item he has just found in the paper: a fellow has been left a million dollars but won't claim it.

MRS. FISHER. Well now, what becomes of money like that, Neil, that people won't take?

MR. FISHER (*squinting at her over his glasses*). What'd you say?

MRS. FISHER. I say, what becomes of money that people won't take that way?

MR. FISHER (*resuming his paper*). Why, nothing at all becomes of it; — they just come and get it. (*She looks at him steadily.*)

MRS. FISHER. Who does?

MR. FISHER. The people that won't take it. (MRS. FISHER *is puzzled for a second.*)

MRS. FISHER (*resuming her knitting*). Well, I'll bet if they left it to *me* they wouldn't have to come and take it.

MR. FISHER (*looking at her again with a shade of irritation*). *Who* wouldn't have to come and take it?

MRS. FISHER (*losing her temper*). Why, the people that won't take it!

MR. FISHER. What are you talkin' about, Josie, do you know?

MRS. FISHER. Yes, I do know very well what I'm talkin' about! — but I don't think *you* do.

MR. FISHER. Let me read this paper, will you?

Sidney Howard, whose realistic *They Knew What They Wanted*, introduced by the Theatre Guild, also won the Pulitzer Prize (1924), was a man of more varied experience than Davis or Kelly. A graduate of the University of California, he had lived abroad, studied under Baker at Harvard, served in the War as an ambulance driver, and had proved himself an able reporter on such matters as narcotic rings, coal strikes, and company spies in labor unions. In consequence his plays are more sophisticated than theirs and do not suffer from the touches of theatricalism which linger in *Icebound* and *The Show-Off*. In *They Knew What They Wanted* the Paolo and Francesca theme is translated to the vineyards of Napa Valley, California, whose people Howard knew well. Tony, an aging Italian winegrower, has made money and seeks a wife to share it with. In his wooing by correspondence he sends, as his, a photograph of Joe, his handsome hired man. When Amy, the San Francisco waitress who agrees to marry Tony, discovers the fraud, she is outraged but carries out her bargain. On the wedding day Tony's legs are broken in an accident and Joe (who is a rover and has wanted to pull out) sleeps in Amy's bed that night. Here is a situation which the older theater would have resolved by heroics — probably by a revenge-murder or a double suicide. True to the new creed of honesty, Howard resorts to no such formula. These three tortured human beings knew what they wanted and they get it. For Amy and Joe it is not the passion of young love (one night was enough). For Tony it is not just a faithful wife. Amy does not win forgiveness nor does Tony take the child as his merely to make a happy ending. As

Howard wrote to his friend Barrett H. Clark: "After all, the play is a little (and unimportant) treatise on the obsessions which make the world go round. The woman's obsession for security — the man's for a dynasty, on the one hand (Tony), and for rebellion on the other (Joe's)." Howard also knew what he wanted.

IV

But it was not merely to further the cause of realism, no matter how important this might be, that the insurgent theaters in America had come into existence. Like the European theaters on which they modeled themselves, they were in close touch with the new movements in art and literature which were searching beyond realism and its close relative, naturalism. These successive revolutions — expressionism, futurism, surrealism — sought to show more than mere external reality and by penetrating deep into human consciousness to reveal man in his essence. The disturbing new concepts of man which Freud and Marx had introduced required a new kind of drama. As techniques, realism and naturalism were too elementary to present man at war with his buried life and Collective Man at war with the bourgeois state.

For two special reasons the theater had responded quickly to these new ways of presenting experience. Directors and dramatists were finding the traditional stage a great handicap. Under the gilded proscenium arch was an invisible fourth wall through which audiences for two hundred years had spied on the actors moving about in their secret world beyond. But the spectator could see no more through his large peephole than a camera might. He could not look inside the minds and emotions of the characters. The invisible wall also sealed him off from the action in another way. It deprived him of the rapport between spectator and actor which had existed in the theater of Aeschylus and Shakespeare. The new dramaturgy which the little theaters were quick to seize on — and the commercial theaters to adopt spasmodically — ought, therefore, to accomplish two things: to present the inner lives of the characters and to bring audience and actors so close that the spectator would have the sense of participating in the action.

Of the new literary modes available to the dramatist expressionism proved to be the most useful. Expressionism seeks to show how experience looks to the man who is having the experience. What goes on in his dream-life, in his reveries of childhood, and his fantasies about the future must be realized in the action. His fears and hates must not be talked about, merely, but symbolized audibly and visibly. Experience, even to the normal person, does not come in measured quantities. A small span of time may seem like eternity or eternity may fill a moment. Such distortions of experience expressionism seeks to present.

The inventor of expressionism was the Swedish dramatist August Strindberg (1849-1912), but the movement made theatrical history in Germany about the time of the first World War. There the leading exponents were Georg Kaiser and Ernst Toller. By 1924 any little theater in America which knew its business had produced Kaiser's *From Morn to Midnight* or Toller's *Man and the Masses*. The commercial theater had also begun to take notice, especially after the success of O'Neill's *The Emperor Jones* (1920) and *The Hairy Ape* (1922), both of which employed expressionistic techniques.

When the Theatre Guild produced *The Adding Machine* in 1923 Broadway audiences had no difficulty in understanding what Elmer Rice was trying to say by means of expressionistic methods. The play is about Mr. Zero, an accountant, who is fired when the firm buys an adding machine to do his work. Here — developed in the expressionistic manner — is the way Mr. Zero gets the news:

ZERO. Wait a minute boss. Let me get this right. You mean I'm canned?

BOSS (*barely making himself heard above the increasing volume of sound.*) I'm sorry — no other alternative — greatly regret — old employee — efficiency — economy — business — business — BUSINESS — (*His voice is drowned by the music. The platform is revolving rapidly now. ZERO and the BOSS face each other. They are entirely motionless save for the BOSS'S jaws, which open and close incessantly. But the words are inaudible. The music swells and swells. To it is added every off-stage effect of the theatre: the wind, the waves, the galloping horses, the locomotive whistle, the sleigh bells, the automobile siren, the glass-crash. New Year's Eve, Election Night, Armistice Day, and the Mardi-Gras. The noise is deafening, maddening, unendurable. Suddenly it culminates in a terrific peal of thunder. For an instant there is a flash of red and then everything is plunged into blackness.*)

Mr. Zero has shot his boss.

Rice's *The Adding Machine* is not pure expressionism. It opens with a long soliloquy by Mrs. Zero which is reminiscent of Molly Bloom's famous self-communion in Joyce's *Ulysses*. There is a wistfully realistic passage when Zero meets Daisy, his office-mate, in the Elysian Fields and the satire in Scene VII, when Zero is told that he is doomed to be a wage-slave in perpetuity, is presented directly.

Though many dramatists made use of expressionism — O'Neill did so in a half-dozen plays* — the movement produced no American "school." Our only completely expressionistic play is Sophie Treadwell's *Machinal* (1928) which tells the story of a loveless marriage, the wife's adultery, her murder of her husband and her trial and execution. The plot is banal but the expressionistic technique conveys poignantly the woman's bewilderment, sexual frustration, fear, sense of guilt, and final hopelessness.

---

* O'Neill's work is discussed in the last section of this chapter.

American dramatists and directors experimented with many devices which would eliminate the invisible fourth wall and bring back into the theater a sense of participating in the mystery and the wonder. The stage was extended over the footlights or was built up on different levels. Actors spoke from the boxes and in the aisles. Masks, dancing, music (especially jazz) were used to re-enforce the symbolism of the action.

One of the most effective of the new devices was the dream sequence. To American dramatists it opened up great possibilities for farce, satire, and extravaganza, though it had been used for far different purposes in Strindberg's somber *A Dream Play* (1902). George S. Kaufman and Marc Connelly made the most of it in their hilarious *Beggar on Horseback* (1924), based on Paul Apel's *Hans Sonnenstössers Höllenfahrt*. After it is established, realistically, that Neil McRae, a struggling composer, loves his apartment-house neighbor but is being maneuvered into a marriage with the daughter of the vulgar-rich Cadys, the play takes off on a wild rampage (Neil's dream) which moves at a faster and faster pace. Everyone talks at once, rooms dissolve into larger and larger rooms, butlers multiply, characters are metamorphosed, dancing masters and business men appear from nowhere and take over the stage. In the whirling climax of the first part Neil murders the entire Cady family. In the second part he is tried in a comic opera court in which the clerk is a ticket-taker and the jurors are the audience assembled to judge Neil's pantomime, *A Kiss in Xanadu*. But all of this has been a dream.

Even more in the American vein is John Howard Lawson's *Processional* (1925), the most original of the experimental plays of the 1920's. The setting is a town in the West Virginia coalfields during a strike. This is the only declarative statement that can be made about the play. Lawson maintained that American life in the Harding-Coolidge era was one vast vaudeville show and only the vulgar slapstick of vaudeville could mirror its madness. He modeled his characters on the comedians of the two-a-day. The heroine's father, Isaac Cohen, performs all the antics of the traditional Jewish comedian. The brash "newspaper feller" is a George M. Cohan song-and-dance man. Vaudeville tricks explode in every scene. While the Sheriff is reading the charge against Dynamite Jim, "his chair falls to pieces and he goes heavily to the ground." The Klan meeting is a burlesque litany, with responsive chants sung and danced to jazz rhythms. Lawson succeeded in his avowed purpose of reflecting "the color and movement of the American processional as it streams about us." Beneath the flavor of the fun was a strong physic of satire on prohibition, professional veterans, labor-baiters, the venalities of the law, tabloid journalism, the Klan, and mother love.

In the 1930's only a few attempts were made to try anything as boldly experimental as *The Adding Machine* and *Processional*. Eugene O'Neill, great technician that he was, continued to seek new functional means for projecting his ideas. There are traces of expressionism in Philip Barry's *Hotel Universe* (1930) and Robert Sherwood's *Idiot's Delight* (1936). In *Our Town* (1938) and especially in *The Skin of Our Teeth* (1942) Thornton Wilder made skillful use of non-representational methods. Maxwell Anderson attempted successfully to go beyond realism by casting his dialogue in free verse. The best of his verse plays was *Winterset* (1935), suggested by the Sacco-Vanzetti case.

The art theaters, at a slower pace than before, continued their search for new dramatic techniques. Most significant was the work of the Vassar Experimental Theatre, organized in 1925 by the indefatigable Hallie

Flanagan. In 1927-1928 its audiences saw Chekhov's *Marriage Proposal* produced in one evening in three different manners: realism, expressionism, and constructivism. The futuristic manner in painting was translated to the stage in one bill of the season of 1930-1931. Plays from the classical repertory, *Antony and Cleopatra*, *The Knight of the Burning Pestle*, *The Barber of Seville*, were overhauled and presented in various modern styles. Any form or technique which required new ways of writing and directing was given a try — the Japanese No Play, the Hawaiian ritual, commedia dell'arte, the Greek mime, ballet in the Mayan mode. Hallie Flanagan's experiments at Vassar would soon have consequences at the national level. When Harry Hopkins telephoned her in February, 1934, and said, "We've got a lot of actors on our hands. Suppose you come in to New York and talk it over," her work as Director of the Federal Theatre Project of the Works Progress Administration had begun. She brought to her task the fund of ideas she had developed at Vassar.*

During the general excitement over the achievements of the new theater there was talk about the possibility of an American folk drama. The Abbey Theatre Players had made a deep impression during their tours in this country. Could not our dramatists, drawing on the lives of people in remote sections of America, where the blight of standardization had not yet penetrated, do for us what Yeats and Synge had done for Ireland? Several directors working in provincial theaters believed that a genuine national drama could come to life only at the grassroots. At the University of North Carolina "Proff" Koch preached this doctrine, and the tours of his Carolina Playmakers, whose repertory included folk plays by Thomas Wolfe and Paul Green, stirred up an excitement comparable to that produced by the Abbey Theatre performances. In 1919 Pro-

* The work of the Federal Theatre is discussed on p. 98.

fessor A. M. Drummond of Cornell established a country theater at the New York state fair and began presenting rural life plays at various towns in the state. There was a similar movement at the University of Wisconsin.

A number of excellent plays on folk themes did well on Broadway and thus seemed to justify the hope for a folk drama. Hatcher Hughes's *Hell-Bent fer Heaven*, which dramatized the machinations of a half-crazy evangelist in the Carolina mountains, won the Pulitzer Prize in 1924. So, in 1926, did Paul Green's *In Abraham's Bosom*, a play about the tragic struggle of a young Negro in the turpentine woods of eastern North Carolina. In 1927 the Theatre Guild presented Du Bose Heyward's *Porgy*, which also received the Pulitzer award. (Gershwin's operatic version, *Porgy and Bess*, was started on its road to worldwide fame in 1935.) Marc Connelly's *The Green Pastures*, based on Roark Bradford's stories in *Ol' Man Adam an' His Chillun*, was another Pulitzer winner in 1930. Lynn Riggs's *Roadside*, a comedy about a latterday Davy Crockett who wrecks a courtroom in Indian Territory and lights out for Texas with Hannie and her Pap, was withdrawn after two weeks. But in writing the foreword to the play when it was published, Arthur Hopkins, who produced it, called it "the first American dramatic classic." When the Theatre Guild offered Riggs's *Green Grow the Lilacs* in 1931 it had a modest run of eight weeks, but the musical based on it, *Oklahoma!* (1943), piled up the phenomenal record of 2,248 performances. It was also an immense success on the road and in England.

Despite this brilliant beginning, few folk plays reached Broadway after the 1920's. How is one to account for this fading enthusiasm? It is true that the writers of folk drama lost interest in the cause and, in the case of Hughes and Connelly, turned to other forms. Paul Green, the most gifted of the group, occupied himself with "symphonic dramas," historical pageants presented out of doors before audiences which come by the thousands, summer after summer, to see *The Lost Colony* at Manteo, North Carolina, and *The Common Glory* at Williamsburg, Virginia. But the defection of the dramatists is not the only answer. In the nature of things American folk drama was destined to die aborning. New York audiences do not care very much about feuds in the Cumberland mountains or the woes of Cajuns or Georgia crackers. With the help of memorable tunes and eye-catching dances the musical versions of *Porgy* and *Green Grow the Lilacs* filled the theaters for years, but the two-hours' traffic of the stage does not give the writer of folk drama time enough to accustom his audience to unfamiliar dialects and strange folkways. Furthermore, can it be said that there is any "folk" in mid-century America? Was not the attempt to find it made too late? In his cabin in Beersheba, Tennessee, the mountaineer drinks, not white mule, but boughten bourbon. His dulcimoor lies unstrung in the loft and the hillbilly songs he listens to come over the air waves from Nashville.

Aside from the lasting merit of the plays themselves, the folk drama movement made one important contribution to the American theater. It gave Negro actors their first chance to perform in something better than vaudeville, an occasional all-Negro revue, and plays requiring a pert Negro maid or comic butler. Charles Gilpin achieved stardom in the title role of O'Neill's *The Emperor Jones*. Rose McClendon got her start in Paul Green's *In Abraham's Bosom* and went on to further successes as Serena in *Porgy* and as Cora Lewis in *Mulatto* (1935), written by a Negro, Langston Hughes. The Negro actor and playwright came into their own during the Federal Theatre days (*The Swing Mikado* and *Haiti* were fabulous successes) but it was the writer of the earlier folk plays who

had released them from bondage to the old Jim Crow stereotypes.

v

As the American theater matured rapidly in the 1920's,
four exceptional writers of high comedy emerged — S. N.
Behrman, Philip Barry, Sidney Howard, and Robert E.
Sherwood. They would have many deserved successes in
the next twenty years. Like Eugene O'Neill they were prolific and the body of their work, with O'Neill's added, makes
up the bulk of the playwriting of real distinction in the
1920's and 1930's. These four have much in common.
Their plays are sophisticated and witty and are constructed
with a sure sense of craft. (Behrman, Barry, and Howard
learned it under Baker at Harvard.) The exposition is
effortless and is never disjoined from the action. Entrances
and exits are natural.

As a group they admired tolerance and personal integrity.
They were interested in man as an individual, not man in
the mass. They disliked stuffy people, mean people, hypo-
crites, phonies, zealots, and messiahs. The characters who
come off best in their plays are artists, refugees from European dictators, and strong-minded but beautiful women
(played by Jane Cowl, Lynn Fontanne, Ina Claire, and
Katherine Cornell). They were very definite in their tastes
— their stage directions are precise about the picture over
the mantel, furniture, dress, and background music. Their
presiding gods were Anatole France, Shaw, Freud, Molnar,
and Richard Strauss. When their characters take a breather
in Europe, which is often, they head for Vienna or Paris.

Though S. N. Behrman (b. 1893) was reared in a middle class Jewish environment in Worcester, Massachusetts,
his setting is usually the country house or the apartment of
the rich or an artist's studio. The people who inhabit these
scenes are talented painters, writers, actresses and their

foils — the idle rich, radicals, businessmen, politicians. These oppositions of temperament produce the clash of ideas from which the action develops. A typical Behrman play — and he seldom departed from the pattern he evolved — is really an exciting two-hour argument, with many decisions and revisions before the resolution is achieved. The arguments are always urbane and the point at issue is decided by the character (usually a woman) who is Behrman's spokesman. The decision is made rationally, not emotionally, and from a determination to preserve personal integrity.

In his first play, *The Second Man* (1927), Clark Storey, a writer of no very pronounced talent, must choose between a life of comfort offered him by a rich woman and the infatuation for him of a young woman, Monica Grey. In order to capture him Monica tries to appeal to his idealism but Storey knows there is a "second man" within, who does not want to be made over in the image the romantic Monica has of him. Common sense wins and Monica is turned back to an adorer who has been patiently standing by. In *Biography* (1932) a woman portrait-painter with a past is besieged by a radical journalist and a politician (her first lover) who try to tell her how to live her life and what she is to do with the autobiography she is writing. In the end she rejects the arguments of both men, throws the manuscript into the fire, and walks out, a free spirit. In *Rain from Heaven* (1934) Lady Wyngate has to choose between a famous but simple-minded explorer, with Fascist sympathies, and a refugee from a concentration camp. She rejects the explorer and the refugee goes back to carry on the struggle in Germany.

Though Behrman's plays deal with ideas, they are not thesis plays. What gives them their special quality is the way in which the comic spirit quietly mocks the arguments. As Joseph Wood Krutch says: "They are comedies of illumination. They turn to the uses of the moment the most valuable of comedy's gifts — the gift of disinterested insight." [6]

As the world grew darker in the 1930's Behrman found it difficult to keep the arguments free from passion and bitterness. In *No Time for Comedy* (1939) he questioned whether the comic spirit should not retire from the scene in the age of the dictators. Gay Esterbrook, a successful writer of light comedies, is about to desert his wife for whom he has written his plays and marry a woman who is encouraging him to write drama with a serious import. In the following exchange between Gay and his wife Behrman seems to be arguing with himself.

LINDA. One should keep in one's own mind a little clearing in the jungle of life. One must laugh.
GAY. It is easy for us here in America to laugh. We have the illusion of safety.
LINDA. This putting of dead people in plays does them a disservice really, strips them of the dignity of their silence. Aesthetic body-snatching! We know nothing of death and can know nothing. When we describe it even, we are describing life. . . . I beg of you, Gay, don't throw away your charming gift, don't despise it. . . . Is it more profound to write of death of which we know nothing than of life of which we may learn something, which we can illuminate, if only briefly, with gaiety, with understanding? Gay, I beg of you, don't turn your back on the gift you have, the instinct you have, the power you have. . . .

Gay returns to Linda. He has a new play all formed in his mind. It will be a witty treatment of a serious theme (the crisis they have just been through) and he will call it *No Time for Comedy*.

What Behrman did for Gay he could not do for himself. He tried two — unsuccessful — plays on serious themes. Then, for some reason, probably his hesitation about the direction he should take, he ran out of ideas and turned to adapting for the stage the work of other men.

There are many paradoxes in the career of Philip Barry. He wrote with great facility: from 1923 until his death in 1949 there was a Barry play nearly every season, and sometimes two. Though he usually judged nicely what his audience wanted, he had several failures. He was the darling of the sophisticated and his most successful plays deal lighthandedly with the marital troubles of the rich. Yet he made several excursions into psychological and political drama, satire, and extravaganza. There is even one biblical play, *John* (1927), which closed after eleven performances. Sometimes he could make his audiences accept these aberrations. (Reviewers and spectators hated to see a Barry play fail.) After three failures in a row (1934–1936) he came back with *Here Come the Clowns* (1938), a baffling allegory about a stagehand who tries to get some cosmic answers from God but is kept from the truth, for a time, by the tricks of the show's illusionist who is, of course, Satan. The reviewers were puzzled but respectful and returned to have a second look, on their own.

Barry was a man of divided allegiance, and this fact may account for his ups and downs in the theater and his rebellious attempts to shake off the destiny he shaped for himself by such comedies as *Paris Bound* (1927), *Holiday* (1928), and *The Philadelphia Story* (1939). There are unexpected religious themes in his plays which indicate that memories of the Roman Catholic instruction of his youth had survived. He consorted with the rich and, like Fitzgerald, he anatomized their behavior, though with less mordacity. But the freedoms of Bohemia also appealed to him and his tormented characters often escape into it. Barry's extraordinary fluency induced him to write too much and too precisely on the event. In consequence few of his plays measure up to the best work of Behrman, Howard, and Sherwood.

In *Hotel Universe* (1930) Barry successfully brought together the several worlds in which he lived. The characters who are gathered on Ann Field's Mediterranean terrace, which is angled toward sea and sky like a wedge into space, have come from the haunts of the rich and from Bohemia and their conversation, after the curtain rises, suggests this will be another Barry comedy involving nothing more serious than a rearrangement of lovers. But the mood soon deepens. The strangeness of the place and the recent suicide of a young man several of them have known bring on a series of self-revelations. Each of these is presented ingeniously by means of a kind of trancelike charade which permits the character to relive the moment which set him on the course that led to his present desperation. Under the spell of the words of Ann's father, a half-mad physicist who talks mystically of time and space, and illumined recurrently by a lighthouse beacon (the "Finger of God," Ann's father has named it), they are healed of their sicknesses. They have learned, at last, to live in Stephen Field's three estates — the everyday life, the life "in which one wishes, dreams, remembers," and "the life past death, which in itself contains all the others." In spite of its rather obvious symbolism, *Hotel Universe* is a moving play. Barry never created a group of characters with whom one can feel more sympathy.

Though quite as sure in his craftsmanship as Behrman and as prolific as Barry, Sidney Howard (1891–1939) was less devoted to the illusionism of the theater than they. He frequently wondered if the steady turning out of plays, season by season, was really the life he wanted and whether he should not strike out into some other activity. But he was always lured back. He once explained his restlessness to Barrett H. Clark, the dramatic historian.

I wrote plays in college when I went to California and was rather talked into going to the 47 Workshop course. I didn't like that, in which I was wrong and I have since eaten my words against it. I came very much under the influence of Sam Hume and his first new stagecraft show. But I chucked any idea of the theatre to go over to drive an ambulance in France. Later, much later, when I was working, after the war, for *Life* and *Collier's Weekly* and doing labor investigating in the period when I first knew you well, I translated D'Annunzio's *Fedra* for Nazimova and Hume again. That got me interested again and *The Rivet* [7] came along. In time Vildrac's [*S.S.*] *Tenacity* started me into an alley where I could function somehow for the theatre, and there I've been since. Always about to tumble out into a world I like better than the theatre and always picked up and put back. Clare held me hard to the theatre, of course.

Aside from the influence of Clare Eames, his actress wife, what probably kept Howard writing plays was his realization that the drama was for him the most natural means for projecting exciting new ideas, and he throve on ideas. Experiences of all sorts, immediate and vicarious, were grist to his mill. When he read Paul de Kruif's *Microbe Hunters*, he set to work transforming one chapter of it into *Yellow Jack* (1934). Sinclair Lewis' *Dodsworth* struck his imagination and was forthwith made into a play. Because he was the busiest — and most reliable — adapter on Broadway, he spoke of himself as a journeyman of the theater and was a little contemptuous of dramatists who were solemn about their high calling. One of the most successful script writers in Hollywood, he took its money without wincing.

Howard was not an adapter of the work of others because of any lack of ideas of his own. His correspondence shows that two or three plots were often buzzing in his head at the same time. In one typical letter from Hollywood, in which he expresses his weariness of the world of the theater and his intention of abandoning it, he remarks in passing that he is about to take a little time off to "finish my Yellow Fever play and a comedy about marriage and a tragedy about the conflict between the artist and the amateur"!

What is typical of Howard's plays is no recurrent situation but their novelty and humanity. He wrote equally well about many different kinds of people. The raffish characters in *Ned McCobb's Daughter* (1926) — the setting is a spa in Maine — are as believable as the Italian wine-growers of *They Knew What They Wanted* (1924). He understood the devious alliances formed in the shadowy speak-easy life of prohibition days (*Lucky Sam McCarver*, 1925) as well as he did the ruthlessness of the true professional who invariably sacrifices friendship and love to art (*Alien Corn*, 1933).

After seeing a Howard play one left the theater with the feeling that the dramatic situation had been thoroughly and satisfactorily explored. In *The Silver Cord* (1926), his best play, he did up the mother complex so completely that no dramatist has touched it since. Mrs. Phelps ("great woman," "your own marvellous self, mother") has drawn the umbilical cord so tightly around the neck of her sons, now grown men, that one of them, Robert, cannot disentangle himself and marry the girl to whom he is engaged. David, the older, slips the soft knot only with the help of his wife who fights Mummy with the weapons of love and a devastating knowledge of the mother-fixation in the male. But *The Silver Cord* is no clinical case history and Howard was right in objecting violently when the Theatre Guild's directorate insisted on discussing it as if he had found his plot in Freud. These sons and lovers are people — David and Robert, the young wife, the bewildered and hysterical fiancée. Even Mrs. Phelps is not an ogress and she is given some moments of pathetic loneliness.

Robert E. Sherwood (1896–1955) marked out the stages of his career in the theater in the Preface to his play about

Finland's resistance to the Russian invasion, *There Shall Be No Night* (1940). (He was attempting to answer the accusation that he had identified himself again and again as a pacifist and now had suddenly turned warmonger.) Sherwood's development as a dramatist may not have been quite so evenly consistent as, in retrospect, he believed it to have been, but, of these four dramatists, he was the one most concerned with the issues of his time. Like other liberal writers of his generation he tried to think his way through the problems thrust on America by the international crises of the years between the two wars. It was logical that he should become a friend and adviser of President Roosevelt and should write one of the most substantial accounts of his years in office, *Roosevelt and Hopkins* (1948). What was consistent in Sherwood's career was his unrelenting search for answers. Fortunately he had great gifts as a playwright and made exciting drama of his changing convictions.

Sherwood served in the Canadian army during the first World War. He was wounded in action and was not expected to recover from a heart condition brought on by his injuries. Naturally enough he joined the ranks of the disillusioned veterans who cursed the warbreeding consequences of nationalism. In his first play, the enormously successful *The Road to Rome* (1927), he inserted a pacifist message which mirrored the mood of the liberals in the mid-twenties: war is utterly irrational and should be laughed out of existence. His Roman senators and generals, looking very like Americans in fancy dress, are narrow-minded, hypocritical, materialistic. Even the mighty Hannibal has no idea why he must go on with his monotonous conquests. As he confesses to Amytis, wife of the Roman dictator, who has ventured forth to a parley with him:

For ten years I've followed the road that leads to Rome — and it's a hard road to travel, Amytis. It's littered with the bones of dead men. Perhaps they know why they died. I don't.

Sherwood's answer is to have Amytis sleep with Hannibal so that he will forget about conquering Rome. Not that she is sacrificing herself to save the city. She wants a son whom the impotent Fabius cannot give her.

After four failures in a row, Sherwood was again successful with *Reunion in Vienna* (1931). By this time he had lost hope in rational solutions. Hypertrophied rationalism was now the enemy. To be true to his principles, Dr. Anton Krug, a famous psychoanalyst, must stand by without protest while his wife visits a secret reunion of the Hapsburg court and — we suppose — spends the night with her former lover, His Serene Highness Rudolph Maximillian. The mummeries of Rudolph's shabby court during its night of escape into the past represent one way in which modern man confronts the black doubt before him.

The title of Sherwood's next play, *The Petrified Forest* (1935), symbolizes its theme: life in America has become a waste land — the setting is the Black Mesa Bar-B-Q in the Arizona desert — in which decent human impulses have become hardened into stone. The man who should be the play's hero is a defeated intellectual, one of T. S. Eliot's hollow men. The only useful thing he can do is to make a graceful exit into death. At his request the killing is performed by the gangster, the new American, who is also "the last great apostle of rugged individualism." Sherwood was partial to *The Petrified Forest* because it had given him, à *rebours*, a sense of direction. He wanted to get out of the intellectual wasteland as rapidly as he could.

His next play, *Idiot's Delight* (1936), may not have seemed very optimistic to the thoughtful in the audience, but it was a merciless exposure of the way mankind would behave when the next war came — made hilarious, as Sherwood intended, by the acting of the Lunts. When the bombs start falling on the Hotel Monte Gabriele, in the

Austrian Alps, the guests are true to form. The munitions manufacturer is calm because his cartels are secure and he will win no matter how many others lose. The German scientist deserts his cancer research to work for the Nazis. The American vaudeville manager is just trying to get his troupe of blonde cuties across the border into Switzerland. While the play was having successful runs in London and New York, the Germans occupied the Rhineland and invaded Austria. The newest and most monstrous idiot's delight had arrived.

One other play helped Sherwood along the road to his conviction that the Fascist and Communist threats must be met before it was too late. In *Abe Lincoln in Illinois* (1938) he viewed Lincoln as the man who has brooded much on death and human fallibility, the sensitive intellectual who is reluctant to lead men in a time of crisis. In his younger years the importuning of his friends and the ambition of his wife forced him into action. But as he leaves Illinois for Washington, his convictions are his own. Sherwood makes him say to the citizens of Springfield, when the train is about to pull out of the station:

We gained democracy, and now there is the question whether it is fit to survive. Perhaps we have come to the dreadful day of awakening, and the dream is ended. If so, I am afraid it must be ended forever. I cannot believe that ever again will men have the opportunity we have had. Perhaps we should admit that, and concede that our ideals of liberty and equality are decadent and doomed. . . . And yet — (*Suddenly he speaks with quiet but urgent authority.*) . . . Let us live to prove that we can cultivate the natural world that is about us, and the intellectual and moral world that is within us, so that we may secure an individual, social, and political prosperity, whose course shall be forward, and which, while the earth endures, shall not pass away. . . . I commend you to the care of the Almighty, as I hope that in your prayers you will remember me. . . . Good-bye, my friends and neighbors.

VI

If Sidney Howard and Robert Sherwood had not induced American audiences to enjoy themselves while watching ideas in action Lillian Hellman (b. 1905) might have had a harder time of it when she came on the scene in the mid-thirties. Her plays are always serious and sometimes even grim. They have none of the modishness of a *Hotel Universe* or the hilarious madness of an *Idiot's Delight*. Yet nearly all of them were successes. Miss Hellman seems to have come by her art naturally, though some years of experience as publicity director for a stock company and as a Broadway playreader must have helped. Her plots are carefully constructed but they are not "well made" in the manner of Scribe and Sardou. She delights in strong situations which in other hands might have been shaped into melodrama rather than tragedy. She made them believable because the conflicts which arise from the clashing temperaments of her characters are significant. She is a specialist in the evil in men's lives, and as the titles of her plays suggest, she is also an ironist.

In her first play, *The Children's Hour* (1934), she shows how two young women are ruined by malicious accusations of Lesbianism made against them by one of the girls they teach. In *The Little Foxes* (1939) and *Another Part of the Forest* (1946), its sequel in reverse (the characters are carried back twenty years), she exposes the naked evil in the lives of two rapacious southern brothers and a sister who are consumed by hatred for one another. These plays were evidently intended as parables about the opposition between the decadence of the southern aristocracy and the money-hunger of the New South generation. Audiences were more impressed with the bitchery of Regina (superbly played by Tallulah Bankhead) and the criminal maneuvers of Ben and Oscar in their effort to outsmart each other. In *The Watch on the Rhine* (1941) and *The Search-*

ing Wind (1944) Miss Hellman turned to the immediate
issues of the years leading up to the second World War.
In the first she brought the struggle between the Nazis
and their underground opponents violently into the drawing room of a liberal American family. In the second she
was in search of an answer to the question why American
journalism and diplomacy had done nothing to head off
the Nazi and Fascist conquests.

In the 1930's when Americans were recovering from the
effects of the depression (and asking questions about its
causes) and while the warclouds enveloping Europe threw
darkening shadows over this country, there was a second
resurgence in the theater comparable to that of the 1920's.
This revival was nourished by the playwrights' serious concern for the fortunes of the Republic. But there were other
forces at work in the new theater groups whose achievements at this later time rivaled those of the Washington
Square Players, the Provincetown Theatre, and the Theatre
Guild. The Playwrights' Company was founded in 1937
by Elmer Rice, Maxwell Anderson, Behrman, Howard,
and Sherwood to support American dramatists in their effort to secure better contractual arrangements with producers, to present plays of their own choice, and to lower
the costs of admission. At the Mercury Theatre Orson
Welles and John Houseman were seeking to reassert the
stage's "power over words, music, and light" and to create
a people's theater that could compete with the movies in
the price range of seats. Their modern-dress *Julius Caesar*,
with its anti-Fascist implications, was a sensation of the
1937-1938 season. In New York the efforts of various left-
wing groups to bring into existence a proletarian drama
culminated in the successes of the Theatre Union. In the
Civic Repertory Theatre in Fourteenth Street (one of the
oldest theater buildings in New York) audiences in the
mid-thirties applauded the plaster off the walls at perform-

ances of *Peace on Earth, Sailors of Cattaro,* and *Stevedore.*

Most far-reaching in its influence throughout the country was the work of the Federal Theatre which came into existence in 1935 and was killed by Congress four years later. Organized to give work to unemployed actors and theater technicians, the Federal Theatre employed 10,000 people at its peak and operated theaters in forty states. It presented all kinds of theatrical entertainment — classical and modern plays, musicals, plays for children, dance dramas, religious dramas. These were performed in theaters which the depression had closed down, in public parks, community houses, church and school auditoriums. Many of its best productions — notably *Triple A Plowed Under, One-Third of a Nation, Chalk Dust, Haiti,* and the dramatization of Sinclair Lewis' *It Can't Happen Here* — were original work. No theater group in America has ever had such a fine repertory or has reached so many people. As an article in *Federal Theatre Magazine* said of it:

We're the Caravan theatre in the parks, Shakespeare on a hillside, Gilbert and Sullivan on a lagoon, the circus under canvas, Toller on a truck. We're the theatre for the children of the steel mills in Gary; we're the theatre for the blind in Oklahoma. We're dramatic companies and vaudeville companies and marionette companies touring the C.C.C. camps, touring the flood areas, playing in schools, playgrounds, prisons, reformatories, hospitals. [8]

But a group of suspicious Senators persuaded themselves and their colleagues that the Federal Theatre was presenting indecent plays (*Love 'em and Leave 'em* and *Up in Mabel's Room* were viewed with alarm), harboring Communists, and handing out Red propaganda — at the taxpayers' expense. The end came on July 1, 1939.

Of the new developments along Broadway in the 1930's none gave greater promise than the work of the Group Theatre. Formed under the aegis of the Theatre Guild, this was a close-knit organization of actors, directors, and dramatists who adopted the methods of the Moscow Art Theatre, rehearsing until every nuance of speech, gesture, and movement had been realized and coordinated. Its first independent success was Paul Green's *The House of Connelly* (1931), a play ideally suited to this style of acting. During the years of its existence the organization had notable successes with such plays as Sidney Kingsley's *Men in White*, Maxwell Anderson's *Night over Taos*, Irwin Shaw's *Bury the Dead*, and William Saroyan's *My Heart's in the Highlands*. Among the gifted actors who came up with the Group Theatre were Luther and Stella Adler, Morris Carnovsky, Jules Garfield (new-baptized John by Hollywood), and Elia Kazan who was later one of the most sought-after directors for both stage and screen. Clifford Odets (b. 1906), whose plays soon became as closely identified with the Group Theatre as O'Neill's had been with the Provincetown Players and the Theatre Guild, was acting minor roles when its production of his strike-play, *Waiting for Lefty* (1935), gave him sudden fame.

American Leftists of all shades of opinion could point with pride to the eight Odets plays written between 1935 and 1941. At last the leftist movement had produced a dramatist of distinction. But the Communists were not entirely satisfied and they frequently had to scold him. Though nearly every Odets play makes some use of "proletarian" formulas, his spokesman for the great day coming generally delivers his one revolutionary speech in the last few minutes of the play. Odets did not always know what was going to happen to his characters beyond the last act and a burst of Marxist rhetoric was an expedient way of bringing down the curtain.

No American dramatist has known so intimately the people who cling to the precipices of lower middle class life in the city and for whom, in the 1930's, the idea of revolution was a persuasive dream. Though his small tradesmen, factory workers, and taxi drivers come to the brink of disaster, few of them descend to the lowest depths. Someone helps out — a neighbor or a relative or a friend with a little horde of money — and the sons and daughters, a few of them, at least, escape to freedom. Yet there is tragedy along the way and the substance of an Odets play is the incommunicable loneliness of his characters. Critics on the extreme left believed, hopefully, that in concerning himself with the particular sorrows of the lower middle class Odets was writing allegories about the sickness of the American capitalist society. He does, it is true, sometimes blame "the system," just as he usually remembered to write a peroration in praise of the revolution to come. But his chief concern is to show us what frustration and insecurity make his characters say and do — their impulsive acts of violence and of love, their sharp words which are used to wound, their shifting moods of bitterness, despair, hope, forgiveness, guilt, and tenderness. What Odets says of his characters in *Awake and Sing!* may be said of the characters in all his plays: "They share a fundamental activity, a struggle for life amidst petty conditions."

Awake and Sing! (1935) was Odets' first full-length play. Its success — it made an excellent run of 209 performances — proved that he could create an interesting family microcosm (his typical form), make appealing the "petty conditions" under which parents and children struggle towards the light, and suggest that what happens in the Bronx flat of the Bergers was happening along the mean streets of a thousand American cities. His next play, *Paradise Lost* (1935), is more doctrinaire, and its leftist doctrine is applied to a plot which does not substantiate it.

Odets' most popular play, *Golden Boy* (1937), is the story of a gifted young violinist who wants what money can buy in America and tries to get it quickly by using his second talent, prize-fighting. Once Joe Bonaparte (the setting has shifted from a Jewish to an Italian-American family) has sold himself to the fight-promoters and the petty racketeers who prey on them he becomes their commodity. No part of him belongs to himself, not even his hands which are broken in a fight. He cannot return to music. His defection has brought sorrow to his father. In desperation he and his girl burn up the night in the car his fight money has bought and they crash. In spite of the unlikelihood that any young man could double in violin-playing and prize-fighting, *Golden Boy* was an appealing play. As Harold Clurman, the Group Theatre's brilliant director, has noted, much of its power derived from its subjectivity. Odets was himself a kind of golden boy, eager for dazzling success in the theater yet too conscientious to prostitute his gifts.

None of the three plays which Odets went on to write before Hollywood claimed him — *Rocket to the Moon* (1938), *Night Music* (1940), *Clash by Night* (1941) — measures up to *Awake and Sing!* Never resourceful in construction he loosened his plot line until it became little more than improvisation. He depended almost exclusively on his ability to create distinctive and appealing characters and to give them poetic speech.

Odets was the last dramatist of great talent to make a name for himself before the second World War. During the War itself the second resurgence of the theater of this century slowed down and there was no marked upswing in the 1950's. Few producers ventured plays with any ideological content, understandably in the years when legislators were out hunting for un-Americans. Largely because of mounting production costs there were only sporadic attempts to experiment in dramatic technique and scene design. Postwar Broadway fare consisted of expensively mounted musicals, sure-fire adaptations of best-selling novels, and static little domestic dramas tailored by television script writers. The older dramatists had ceased to write and there were few new ones to take their places. George Kelly offered no play after 1946 and Behrman none after 1945.* Sidney Howard was killed in an accident in 1939; Philip Barry died, at forty-three, in 1949. Robert Sherwood who had been drawn into work for the Roosevelt administration died in 1955. O'Neill, though ill, continued to work as he could, but little came from his workshop. After *Days without End* (1934) only two plays reached the stage before his death in 1953: *The Iceman Cometh* (1946) and *A Moon for the Misbegotten* (1947). He had finished two others which have been produced with success, the autobiographical *Long Day's Journey into Night* (1956) and *A Touch of the Poet* (1958).†

Only three playwrights of distinction emerged after the second World War and continued, from play to play, to reach and hold their audiences. William Inge (b. 1913), Tennessee Williams (b. 1914), and Arthur Miller (b. 1915). Inge was slow to develop but the popular success of *Come Back, Little Sheba* (1950), *Picnic* (1953), and *Bus Stop* (1955), and the favorable critical reception of *The Dark at the Top of the Stairs* (1957) established him as a shrewd and sympathetic reporter of the little tragedies of middle class life. The realism of his plots and dialogue suggest the kind of dramas with which the playwrights of the early 1920's broke the earlier tradition of sentimentality and melodrama in the theater.

Williams is one of the most expert dramatists of this

* As this volume was about to go to press (December 1958), Behrman's *The Cold Wind and the Warm* was having a successful run on Broadway. It is a dramatization of *The Worcester Account*, a book of essays about his youth.

† From about 1934 to 1943 O'Neill worked on two immense cycles of plays which were to be called *A Tale of Possessors Self-Dispossessed* and *By Way of Obit. A Touch of the Poet* was planned as the fifth play in the first cycle. Three other plays for this cycle were completed. The drafts of two of these O'Neill destroyed. A typescript of the third, *More Stately Mansions*, survives. Of the second cycle only a one-act play, *Hughie*, is extant.

century and his plays keep an audience enthralled because of their skillful construction and the liberal amounts of sex, bawdry, and violence they contain.* In such phenomenal successes as A *Streetcar Named Desire* (1947) and *Cat on a Hot Tin Roof* (1955) he seems to be saying something about the South, in which he was born. What really interests him are his neurotic women and his lusty (or perverted) men. As the English dramatist John Osborne says: "Williams's women — Blanche, Maggie the Cat, Alma in 'Summer and Smoke', Baby Doll — they all cry out for defilement, and most of them get it."

If Inge suggests the realists of the 1920's, Arthur Miller calls to mind the class-conscious dramatists of the 1930's. Yet Miller does not attack particular social ills or propose specific cures for them. His aim is more general. He believes his *Death of a Salesman* (1949) made such a strong impression in the theater because it fulfilled his intention of picturing a man "who was not even especially 'good' but whose situation made clear that at bottom we are alone, valueless, without even the elements of a human person, when once we fail to fit the patterns of efficiency." Miller would like to do something through his plays to cure this deep moral uneasiness among us. As he says, in a perceptive essay, "On Social Plays" (printed with A *View from the Bridge*, 1955): "There is a world to make, a civilization to create that will move toward the only goal the humanistic, democratic mind can ever accept with honor." The dramatist can help men move toward this goal by showing them that the peace we may get "may leave us without the fruits of civilized life."

VII

From the early twenties until his death in 1953 Eugene

---

* This generalization does not hold for *The Glass Menagerie* (1945), Williams' quietest and most tenderly human play. It makes no attempt to compel attention by means of shock.

O'Neill was recognized as the most gifted of the many playwrights who were helping to create the new American drama. His first full-length play, the idealistic *Beyond the Horizon,* was an immediate success in 1920 and won the Pulitzer Prize. For eight years O'Neill continued to entrust the production of most of his work to the Provincetown Players but several of his plays were so popular — *The Emperor Jones* (1920) and *Desire under the Elms* (1924), for instance — that they were moved to large theaters uptown. By the mid-twenties critics were saying that at last America had a dramatist worthy to join the company of Chekhov, Pirandello, and Shaw. In 1936 O'Neill's European reputation was certified by the award of the Nobel Prize.

Though O'Neill read widely, he drew only occasionally on the ideas and techniques of other writers. What he wrote came straight from his observation of life. His father, James O'Neill, was a famous actor who had been diverted from Shakespearean roles to the profitable performance, year after year, of *The Count of Monte Cristo.* Eugene's convent-trained mother disliked the theater but accompanied her husband on tour. As a result the boy was literally brought up in the theater and thus gained an uncanny knowledge of what audiences can be made to like.

The serious tensions in his family are reflected in several O'Neill plays in which a stern father and a suffering mother appear. They were at last fully objectified in *Long Day's Journey into Night* (1956), a play which, painful as the subject was to him, O'Neill felt he had to write. The young O'Neill's flight from his father led to months of seafaring life. On his voyages to the Argentine, South Africa, and England he met the sailors who appear in his early one-act plays and acquired the sense of the sea's mystery and cruelty which pervades his first work. At this time, too, his favorite hangout in New York was the waterfront saloon of Jimmy the Priest which he used as the setting of *Anna Christie* (1921) and *The Iceman Cometh* (1946). The turning point in O'Neill's life came in 1913 when he spent six months in a tuberculosis sanatorium, an experience later recorded in *The Straw* (1921). It was then that he decided to become a playwright.

Two other influences must be mentioned. O'Neill's pride in his Irish ancestry is evident from the number of Irish characters he created, notably Driscoll in *Bound East for Cardiff* (1916), Mat Burke in *Anna Christie*, and Larry Slade in *The Iceman Cometh*. Though his family had only a slight connection with New England, through their home in New London, he was fascinated by the Puritan temperament and dissected it again and again, from *Ile* (1917) and *The Rope* (1918), through *Desire under the Elms*, to the climactic *Mourning Becomes Electra* of 1931.

In the twenties O'Neill wrote several plays that make use of themes with which the other dramatists of the time were concerned. *Diff'rent* (1920) is a study in the then much discussed subject of sexual repression. Yank, in *The Hairy Ape* (1922), is outraged when he is called a "filthy beast" by a society girl who goes slumming in the stokehole, but the play's "social consciousness" does not require him to join the Communist party. *All God's Chillun Got Wings* (1924) explores the tragic consequences which follow from the marriage of a white girl to a Negro. *Marco Millions* (1928) satirizes the commercialism of the twenties in the person of the young Venetian supersalesman, Marco Polo. In *Dynamo* (1929) O'Neill attempted, not very successfully, to say something about those who desert the faith of their fathers and, going to the other extreme, worship fanatically the gods of technology. But these contemporary themes are so unconventionally stated and the resolutions which O'Neill worked out are so unexpected that it is pointless to force comparisons between his work and that of other dramatists who made drama out of the social and ethical problems of their time.

Yet in one important respect O'Neill resembles the serious dramatists contemporary with him. Like them he was not content with surface realism but attempted to express unusual ideas in as striking a way as possible. He differed from them in the greater range of his ideas and the more imaginative methods he invented to present them. He was, indeed, the most persistent experimenter in technique the modern theater has known. Any sequence of O'Neill productions bears out the truth of this statement. Take, for example, the six plays he offered between 1924 and 1928. *Desire under the Elms* (1924) is a grim tragedy involving incest and infanticide, set in the New England of 1850. His next play, *The Fountain,* romantic in form and elevated in tone, follows Ponce de Léon's search for the fountain of youth which becomes, in O'Neill's version of the story, a search for religious certainty through mystical vision. In *The Great God Brown* (1926), by an intricate use of masks, O'Neill went deep into the divided soul of Dion Anthony who is at war with himself and suffers under the domination of his friend William Brown, "a visionless demigod of our new materialistic myth." For *Marco Millions* (1928) O'Neill required a huge cast and the scenes of his vast pageant range over most of the countries of the East. In the nine-act *Strange Interlude* (1928) the characters speak their private thoughts in long soliloquies while the action stands still. *Lazarus Laughed* (1928) is a religious play in which Lazarus, come back from the dead, opposes his ecstatic faith to the hopelessness of those who "fear life in fearing death." These six plays made unprecedented demands on producers and actors and compelled the strictest attention from audiences. Yet all of them, except *The Fountain,* were remarkably successful. Even *The Great God Brown,* O'Neill's most baffling play, ran for nearly a year.

Though O'Neill continued to try out new themes and techniques through his entire career, one can mark off certain stages in this experimentation. In the early years, roughly through the time of *Desire under the Elms,* he was preoccupied with primitive characters, homeless, rootless men who suffer but cannot articulate their suffering beyond the reiterated "Dat ole davil, sea" of Chris Christopherson in *Anna Christie.* O'Neill was attracted to these wanderers because he had known such men in his own wanderings and also because he was trying deliberately, and in defiance of the kind of drama his father admired, "to evolve original rhythms of beauty where beauty apparently isn't — *Jones, Ape, God's Chillun, Desire,* etc." (as he himself said). But he soon deserted his primitives and substituted for them the sensitive men and women of *The First Man* (1922), *The Great God Brown,* and *Strange Interlude,* intellectuals whose lives reveal, so he believed, the sickness of modern life — the doomed struggle to love and to believe and the failure and exhaustion (at best the quietism) with which the struggle invariably ends. As if in expiation for the nihilism of these plays, he was writing at the same time his "dramas of conversion" — *The Fountain* and *Lazarus Laughed* — which conclude with an affirmation which is grounded in a not very explicit mysticism. In one play, *Days without End* (1934), he turned back to the rejected Catholicism of his youth.

From the beginning O'Neill thought of himself as a tragic dramatist. (He wrote only one comedy, *Ah, Wilderness!,* 1933, based on an episode in his adolescence.) He was convinced that the only subject worth writing about was the eternal tragedy of Man in his glorious, self-destructive struggle to make the "Force behind" express him "instead of being, as an animal is, an infinitesimal incident in its expression." [9]

Because of the magnitude of the questions posed in

Desire under the Elms, The Great God Brown, Strange Interlude, Mourning Becomes Electra, and *The Iceman Cometh* O'Neill challenged comparison not only with Chekhov and Strindberg but with Shakespeare and the Greek tragedians as well. The critics debated — and are still debating — whether these plays are true tragedies and whether even so expert and gifted a dramatist as O'Neill could write tragedy in an age in which a pervasive naturalism has weakened man's faith in a moral order in the universe. For in the past, writers of tragedy have been able to rely on this faith to mitigate the calamities which befall their heroes.

At moments in his life O'Neill, who called himself a mystic, was persuaded of the eternal rightness of things, but the plays which end in affirmation are among his poorest. There is no escaping the fact that he was fundamentally a naturalist, but neither can it be denied that he was moved by pity and terror (and could move his audiences) at the spectacle of man illuded and erring; struggling to understand the human predicament and suffering for his failure to live by the best light he has.

O'Neill's two most ambitious and imaginative tragedies, *Mourning Becomes Electra* and *The Iceman Cometh,* passed the pragmatic test. They continued to impress and move audiences for months, yet in them O'Neill made no effort to go beyond naturalism. He was content to search for the springs of suffering and to bring his characters to the tribunal of their own consciences. But what scene in modern drama is more harrowing than the last act of *Mourning Becomes Electra?* Lavinia, the Electra of this retelling of the Aeschylean trilogy, has brought about the downfall of the Mannon dynasty. Consumed by jealousy, she has persuaded her brother Orin to murder her mother's lover. Driven by remorse for this deed and by guilt for his incestuous love for his sister, Orin shoots himself. How

can the modern writer of tragedy resolve this woe? Hardly
by imitating Aeschylus and appealing for a solution to the
equivalents (if they could be found) of the Areopagus and
patron-goddess Athena. The play ends as it rightly should.
Lavinia turns away her panic-stricken lover with the words:
"Love isn't permitted to me. The dead are too strong."
Then she goes alone into the empty house to shut herself
up with her dead, to keep their terrible secrets, and let
them hound her until the curse is paid out.

I know they will see to it I live a long time! It takes the
Mannons to punish themselves for being born!

The ending of *The Iceman Cometh* is likewise true and
right. The human derelicts who enjoy the bounty of Harry
Hope's bar live in an alcoholic dream which permits them
to retrieve their lost careers and wasted talents. Then comes
Hickey with his gospel of reform. Let them get off the
booze and abandon their pipedreams. They struggle briefly
to come back to reality and to take up life where they
abandoned it. But Larry Slade, the one of their company
who all along has stared straight at the truth, knows that
Hickey is the Iceman who is bringing them death. They
cannot live without their dreams and at the play's end
they have lapsed joyously into them again. All except Larry,
who says, as they are just a few drinks before the passing-
out stage:

Life is too much for me! I'll be a weak fool looking with
pity at the two sides of everything till the day I die! May that
day come soon! Be God, I'm the only real convert to death
Hickey made here.

The voice is Larry Slade's but he speaks, one guesses,
for Eugene O'Neill.

FOUR

Caste and Class in the Novel, 1920-1950

IN THE YEAR 1903 Frank Norris, a very popular novelist in his too-brief day (he died at thirty-two), wrote these prophetic words:

> Today is the day of the novel. In no other day and by no other vehicle is contemporaneous life so adequately expressed; and the critics of the twenty-second century, reviewing our times, striving to reconstruct our civilization, will look not to the painters, not to the architects, nor dramatists, but to the novelists to find our idiosyncrasy. [*The Responsibilities of the Novelist.*]

Norris exaggerated the adequacy with which the novel in 1900 expressed the issues and values of American life, but what he envisioned has come to pass. There is no doubt that the novel has been the dominant literary form in this country since 1920. In twentieth century America the long narrative poem, so much liked by our grandfathers' generation, *The Idylls of the King, Evangeline, Hiawatha,* has pined away and died. Only Robinson's *Tristram* (1927), Stephen Vincent Benét's *John Brown's Body* (1928), and Archibald MacLeish's *Conquistador* (1932) sold in figures which reached into the thousands. And though the drama came to vigorous life between the two World Wars and, as a result, the successful plays of each season were printed, editions were not large and reprintings were few.

The age of the enormously successful best-selling novel (required to place: a sale of more than a million copies) is the depression decade. Having little else to do for inexpensive pleasure people stayed home and read novels that were written to give the buyer a lot of pages for his money. Publishers still sigh for the quantities of gold dug out of the rich lodes hidden in Pearl Buck's *The Good Earth* (1931), Hervey Allen's *Anthony Adverse* (1933), Margaret Mitchell's *Gone with the Wind* (1936), John Steinbeck's *The Grapes of Wrath* (1939), and the six Erle Stanley Gardner mystery stories published between 1933 and 1938.

How insatiable the reading public's demand for fiction is today can be judged at a glance by anyone who will pause to inspect the paperbacks displayed in drug stores, supermarkets, railway stations, and bus terminals. He will find some popular psychiatry, several how-to-do books, religious best sellers (which demand nothing more of the sick soul than positive thoughts), two or three volumes of poetry (Frost, Ogden Nash), a stray movie-script, and — though this is rare — a play or two. The rest is fiction: hard-cover novels leased to the soft-cover trade when they went into a third printing, and "originals" written to order on subjects which the editors know will be sure-fire. To realize the impressiveness of this phenomenon of cheap books for the millions, and in essence this means cheap novels for the millions, one has only to look at the figures for a single year. In 1953, for example, the publishers of paperbacks issued 1,061 titles in a print order of 259 million copies.

Most of these novels are negligible, but the surprising fact is that a fair proportion of them are by our best writers. By browsing from rack to rack, from Bantam to Dell to Avon, the shrewd purchaser can acquire, at the cost of two steak dinners, a whole library of Farrell,

Steinbeck, Dos Passos, Hemingway, Fitzgerald, Bellow, and O'Hara. A few years back, at a time when several of Faulkner's eighteen books were out of print in hardcover editions, fourteen were procurable in paperback series. This is all the more surprising (and gratifying) in view of the fact that as late as 1950 Faulkner was considered a difficult novelist and was known to the public chiefly as the author of one sensational novel, full of sex and violence, *Sanctuary.*

Since it will not be possible to examine in this chapter the diverse themes to which the novelists of the twenties and thirties were drawn, we might try to find — if it is to be found — one theme to which many of them returned again and again, and then explore the variations made on it. A convenient place to start the hunt is the year 1936. It happened to be both an exceptional and a representative year. Such exceptional works appeared as Faulkner's *Absalom, Absalom!,* Farrell's *A World I Never Made,* Mrs. Rawlings' *The Yearling,* Steinbeck's *In Dubious Battle,* Dos Passos' *The Big Money,* and Erskine Caldwell's *God's Little Acre.* But most of the tried and true plots, some of which were popular in the early 1900's, were still around. Since in 1936 it was still true, as William Dean Howells observed, that women are the chief readers of novels in America, we should expect to find — and we do find — a large number of novels written for women: exotic love stories, novels in praise of noble women who "come through" by saving their marriages or even (since this is 1936) the family business. Since we are only three years beyond the phenomenal success of *Anthony Adverse,* many fiction writers are in pursuit of high romance — in the California of pioneering days, in France just after the burning of Joan of Arc, even unlikely Siberia. Historical novels were still in request, the best of them being Kenneth Roberts' *Northwest Passage.* A few of these costume novels show some influence of the times; for example, Edmonds'

Drums along the Mohawk, which is concerned with the proletariat (if you will) in New York State at the time of the American Revolution. There are regional novels in abundance, so many, indeed, that you may almost choose your state. The novel of the generations still persists, under the influence of Galsworthy's *Forsyte Saga.* Novels about the first World War are surprisingly abundant and vary in content from heroics to bitter disillusionment. Some of these were evidently written under the impending shadow of another war which was only three years off. The influence of Freud is still to be seen, though it is slight in comparison with the revival of themes and techniques based on Freudian concepts in the fiction written since the second World War.

But what stands out as one examines the novels, good and bad, published in 1936 is the persistence of some variation of the social theme — an interest in status, class, and social mobility and, often, the effect which the depression had on these phenomena. Strangely enough, in this particular year no proletarian novels with a marked revolutionary bias were published. In 1935 there had been several which presented what Communist theorists designated "the revolutionary situation" (a strike or some other form of civil violence) that pointed the way toward the "great day coming" in America; for example Tom Kromer's *Waiting for Nothing,* William Cunningham's *The Green Corn Rebellion,* and Clara Weatherwax's *Marching! Marching!* which won a *New Masses* prize for the best novel on a proletarian theme. In 1936 not even John Steinbeck's *In Dubious Battle* quite fills the bill since it is rather a study in the pathology of Communism than a defense of it. Coleman and Raushenbush's *Red Neck,* an account of the tortuous training of a labor leader, is certainly leftist in its sympathies, but is a New Deal rather than a Communist novel.

But this is not all. What is most significant is that two

social themes, directly related to the depression, turn up again and again, sometimes in unlikely places. In the first group of novels of this kind the setting is proletarian, though the author shows no leftist bias and is not writing with the coming revolution in mind. Thus we can move in one novel among the old brick tenements of Williamsburg (Brooklyn), in another among Negro sharecroppers in the south, or in another among migratory fruit workers. So common had the proletarian setting become by this time that in one detective story the murder takes place in the midst of a fruit-pickers' strike in California! The work of these novelists who were making use of a proletarian setting should be remembered because their concern with the lives of Americans who balance on the edge of failure had a lasting effect. They had inverted the success novel of the 1900's and were persuading readers to interest themselves not in the country boy who makes good in the big city (possibly his kind had vanished) but in the city boy who cannot resist the downward pull of joblessness, racketeering, and interracial violence. The proletarian novel in this sense, without any ideological bias, that is, had come to stay. Much of the subliterary paperback fiction produced in the 1950's is of this kind.

The other type of novel, so frequently encountered as to be representative, deals with the impact of the depression on the middle class. Typically, we see an urban family sink lower and lower in the economic scale until there is nothing left to do except to abandon the struggle and try to start again in a new environment. Escape is generally to a farm or a small village; at any rate, to a distant and idyllic place where the old American virtues of thrift, honesty, and willingness to work count for something. These novels are a curious mixture of conventional patterns. They begin realistically enough with pictures of the distress and anxiety which the depression caused. But the theme of escape relates them to the "I-can-go-home-again" novels of the decade. And the return-to-the-village theme carries the reader back many years to the local color novels of the nineteenth century. A few of these depression novels bring their characters face to face with new social realities. Hamilton Basso's *Courthouse Square* is the most striking. His hero returns to his boyhood home in the south, thinking to leave behind in New York the mess of his private life and the inanities of Greenwich Village arguments over sex and art and Communism. But he is soon in the midst of a violent upsurge of race hatred. He is forced to take sides and does so with a quiet heroism.

In arguing, as this chapter will do, that social themes in the novel persisted through the twenties and thirties and on into the period after the second World War, it may be objected that the choice of 1936 as a representative year loads the dice. The country was slowly climbing out of the depression, and what would be more natural than that the novelists should concern themselves with urgent social and economic problems? But, as we shall see, the novelists had been interested for many years in the manifold implications of caste and class in American society. In the mid-thirties they fixed their attention on two particular effects of the depression on the class structure — the emergence for the first time in America of a self-conscious proletarian class and the effort of the middle classes to maintain their status by holding on to all the things which guaranteed it to them — job security, the ownership of property (other than the tools of one's trade), access to higher education, and the chance to rise in the world.

II

One can make out a good case for the novelists as the discoverers of class-consciousness in America. Frank Norris, Theodore Dreiser, Sinclair Lewis, and even Willa Cather were aware of class differences and were making use of them in fiction several years before the sociologists began investigating "cleavage" in the American city, "caste and class" in southern towns, "the status system" in modern communities, "prestige classes" and "occupational mobility." Much of what teams of interviewers and graph-makers discovered about social classes in "Middletown," "Plainville, U.S.A.," "Elmtown" and "Yankee City" in the thirties and forties the novelists had already dowsed with their divining rods.

It is possible to find American novelists who anchored their plots to the concept of class structure and class conflict as far back as the time of T. B. Aldrich's *The Stillwater Tragedy* (1880), John Hay's *The Bread-Winners* (1883), and Henry Francis Keenan's *The Money-Makers* (1884). (In the first two of these the authors side with the owners; Keenan's crusading editor-hero is a partisan of the workers.) The struggle between the California wheat-farmers and the Pacific and Southwestern Railroad dominates two-thirds of Frank Norris' *The Octopus* (1901). Jack London preached revolution in tract-novels which sometimes also advanced his contradictory belief in the superman and in Nordic supremacy.

During the first twenty years of this century the Presidential voting strength of the Socialist Party increased from 96,000 to 900,000 (the high point). In the same two decades forty-nine Socialist novels were published which were directed at this rapidly growing audience. Few of them possess any literary merit though I. K. Friedman's *By Bread Alone* (1901), based on the Homestead (Pennsylvania) steel strike, and Leroy Scott's *The Walking Delegate* (1905), which deals with the struggle for power in the New York locals of the Iron Workers Union, are exceptional in vigor and realism. Ironically, the best-known of these novels, Upton Sinclair's *The Jungle* (1906), which ends in the conversion of the hero to Socialism, was widely read only because it exposed the filthy horrors of the meat-packing industry.

Why is it that so few novelists in these two decades — forty-nine novels is a mere handful — thought in terms of economic class and of the class-struggle, in spite of the fact that there was a growing working-class audience which might have read novels on this theme? I can find three answers. Certain novelists — Edith Wharton is the best example — continued to explore the acquisition of status and the loss of status as determined by moral behavior, business ethics, education, attitudes toward religion, and other causes. William Dean Howells had made this kind of novel popular and had exploited its theme in a great variety of middle-class settings. Mrs. Wharton's characters moved on a higher social level than his but in story after story she writes of the struggle to maintain status (*The House of Mirth*) or to acquire it (*The Custom of the Country*). The persistence of this theme is a significant commentary on the American myth of the egalitarian society. The novelists believed the myth to be untrue.

The second reason why so few novelists dealt directly with economic causation was that many of them — Dreiser, for instance — who were beginning to write about the lower castes in American society were under the influence of naturalism. The evolutionism in their novels brings into play autochthonous forces which move mysteriously within society and individual lives, are beyond human control, and block human efforts toward cooperation. In *Sister Carrie* (1900) Dreiser conceived and judged his two main characters in ways which are opposed. Sister Carrie's naturalistic tropism would, it seems, have drawn her upward toward her dreams of affluence and ease no matter in what class she was born. Hurstwood, on the other hand, is a much more credible character because he was not created to illustrate a naturalistic dogma and because Dreiser weighs the economic causes of his destruction, as well as the physical and psychological.

In the third place, the muckraking novelists of the 1900's, though they dealt with all kinds of abuses in business and industry and found their villains among the oligarchic rich, were not radicals but reformers. The cures for the social ills they observed were to be the exposure of wrong-doing and legislation to prevent its recurrence. Moreover the muckraking movement in fiction was short lived. The novelists who belonged to it soon ran out of exposable evils as legislation rapidly deprived the malefactors of their power to defraud on a grand scale.

At first glance it would seem that the American novelists of the twenties were little concerned with social issues. The important names — Elinor Wylie, Carl Van Vechten, James Branch Cabell, Willa Cather, Conrad Aiken, F. Scott Fitzgerald, Sinclair Lewis, and Ernest Hemingway — suggest retreat to Europe or flaming youth or Freud; nostalgia for the American past or light-hearted satire of the present. According to the legend, the answer of the novelists to the materialism of the decade was a demand for more gin and more sex. Yet, when we reread their novels now, we can see that many of them viewed the Harding-Coolidge era with disgust. There was a prophetic urgency in what they wrote and often an effective anger. And most of them were concerned with caste and class.

Sometimes their intentions were misunderstood, as those of F. Scott Fitzgerald (1896–1940) certainly were. To call him "the historian of the jazz age" is to belittle the novelist who comprehended the American rich better than any writer ever has. This was his speciality, and his training for practicing it brought, finally, the collapse of his personal life. Fitzgerald understood, because he wanted, as a young man, what the rich had: all that money can buy —

things, parties, and irresponsibility. It is this glittering but phantasmic world which Jay Gatsby tries to enter. He has the money to pay the entrance fee; why should he be refused? It is the world that Gloria and Anthony (of *The Beautiful and Damned*, 1922) hold out for until they are damned in the end just when it is in their hands. The theme is more profoundly analyzed in *Tender is the Night* (1934), which is essentially a study of the vampirism of the rich. All the talent and vitality and nobility of Dick Diver is sucked out of him by the woman whom he, as a psychiatrist, married in order that he might cure. When she is well, she is well enough to leave him for another man.

No wonder Fitzgerald was annoyed with his friend Hemingway for introducing into one of his stories this uncomprehending judgment: "He remembered poor old Scott Fitzgerald and his romantic awe of [the rich] and how he had started a story once that began, 'The rich are different from you and me'; and how someone had said to Scott, 'Yes they have more money.' But that was not humorous to Scott." Most of Fitzgerald's best writing centers on this theme of what makes the rich "different from you and me." And he knew the answer because he had known the American rich in all the places they spent their money during those years, New York's Hotel Plaza, Paris, the Riviera. In large part Fitzgerald's present reputation is due to the realization that he was an accurate historian of their motives and actions.

Meanwhile Sinclair Lewis was doing an equally thorough job on the middle class. He was, of course, from *Main Street* on, a thesis novelist, but in developing each new thesis he worked up and down the scale of middle class life, from the Dodsworths in the upper bracket to Shad Ledue, the provincial fuehrer of *It Can't Happen Here*. In *Main Street* (1920) his target is the mediocrity which had invaded the American village. He uses *Arrowsmith* (1925) to expose the degrading effects of materialism in the quest for truth in medical research. All of the obscene activities of the lunatic religious sects and cults are spotlighted in *Elmer Gantry* (1927). In *It Can't Happen Here* (1935) he showed how far native Fascism had crept into American society. Even in his later novels, in which he reversed his field and praised the solid virtues of middle-class, middle-western Americans, he was still attacking something, still picketing some imbecility of American life. In *Gideon Planish* (1943), for instance, it is the world of "organizators and philanthrobbers and propheteers," inhabited by do-gooders of all kinds, from simple-minded humanitarians to prophets of revolution.

But in all Lewis' novels the frame of the picture is the daily routine of the middle class man.* He was a specialist in the ways of the business and professional men who determine the norms of their class. Few American novelists, perhaps none except Dos Passos, have equaled him in bringing into the picture all the symbols of achievement which are necessary for middle class morale, everything from gadgets to booster clubs. Few, if any, excel him in defining precisely how his characters lived in a particular year or even a single month. If our memories were sharp enough we could say of a chapter in a Lewis novel: "This must be the summer of 1925." He will have the car model right, the brand of cigarettes, the cocktail of the day. When, on page 9, Babbitt empties his pockets, the contents are a kitchen midden revealing the culture of middle-class America in 1922.

Because *Babbitt* was influential enough to give the lan-

* At one time Lewis considered writing a novel about labor but abandoned the idea. As a remark in one of his letters indicates, he could not think himself out of the class he knew best: "I come from the middle class and know only middle class speech. The labor people I have met . . . have no special speech which I can *hear*." (Grace Hegger Lewis, *With Love from Gracie, Sinclair Lewis: 1912–1925*, 1955, p. 215.)

guage a name for the group its hero represents, it is important to note what Lewis thought he had discovered about George F. Babbitt and his friends. In the first place, they maneuver almost invariably with the cash nexus in mind. While Sir Gerald Doak is being lionized by the McKelveys (who can look down on the Babbitts), George F. discovers that the Englishman is over here to buy coal. In one evening they become firm friends over a bottle of bootleg Scotch and business. When Babbitt is asked to reorganize the Sunday School he sizes up the situation as a merchandizing problem. Money talks all through the novel. Status is also terribly important and the Babbitts have to work constantly at maintaining it. This is hard labor and the struggle kills the potential pleasure. In the midst of an important dinner party at the Babbitt house the host ruminates:

> The others, from their fitful unconvincing talk, their expressions of being slowly and painfully smothered, seemed to be suffering from the toil of social life and the horror of good food as much as himself.

Lewis is also a master at showing how closely interconnected are all the institutions which a Babbitt has to belong to and support — family, church, one's college class, clubs, realtors' organizations. No defection is possible, as Babbitt learns in his one season of revolt when he tries to avoid joining the Good Citizens League. His intransigence nearly causes him to be driven from the tribe. Gradually, as the novel draws to its conclusion, Lewis shows how Babbitt has become a prisoner of every group he has joined. There is no escape, no other life, both because he cannot escape and because he cannot imagine, though he tries fitfully, what another life might be.

Very early in a Lewis novel the leading character is assigned to his subgroup of the middle class. The reader comes to expect a paragraph of definition just as he expects the slambang Lewis idiom and the minutiae of going to bed and getting up, of eating and travelling and luncheon-club joshing. In *Dodsworth* (1929) it arrives on page 10:

> Samuel Dodsworth was, perfectly, the American Captain of Industry, believing in the Republican Party, high tariff and, so long as they did not annoy him personally, in prohibition and the Episcopal Church. He was president of the Revelation Motor Company; he was a millionaire, though decidedly not a multimillionaire; his large house was on Ridge Crest, the most fashionable street in Zenith; he had some taste in etchings; he did not split many infinitives; and he sometimes enjoyed Beethoven. He would certainly (so the observer assumed) produce excellent motor cars; he would make impressive speeches to the salesmen; but he would never love passionately, lose tragically, nor sit in contented idleness upon tropic shores.

But this paragraph is, of course, only a direction-finder. In following Dodsworth from Zenith to Europe, where he is on his second honeymoon, we pick up hundreds of details which expand and refine the definition. Though he and his wife have drifted apart, he has had no time for quarreling. (Too busy at the office and on the golf course.) He is endlessly fascinated by figures, from population statistics to grade-percentages. His investments are so sound and diversified that there would be no point or pleasure in changing them. When he goes to his class reunion at Yale, he notices that his friends (now fathers and grandfathers) "looked as though they overworked and overdrank." When he gets to Europe he is sure that the English condescend to him. Having given Europe a quick once-over, he wants to return home and make something, "even if it's only a hen-coop."

There is some truth in Maxwell Geismar's observation (in *The Last of the Provincials,* 1947) that the middle class which Lewis depicted is "essentially without a home life, without children, without religion . . . and, hardly established in power, has every appearance of dissolving — including the escape into a dream world of the middle class." Yet it cannot be denied that Lewis caught the middle-class man and his family on his black and white film before the scene changed or faded.

Towards the end of the twenties and in the first years of the next decade there were several novelists who took their readers down the scale to the lowest classes, to the group that Americans would soon, though self-consciously, call the proletariat. Erskine Caldwell's *Tobacco Road* (1932) defined "poor white." Nelson Algren's *Somebody in Boots* (1935) was the first of his studies of the lumpen-proletariat. The years covered by this novel are roughly 1927–1930, and the record is a terrifying one — boys on the road, the railroad jungles, police beatings, filthy, vice-ridden jails.

The novelist who specialized most successfully in the lower classes, as Fitzgerald and Lewis specialized in the classes above them, is James T. Farrell (b. 1904). Because the novels which followed his Studs Lonigan trilogy (1932–1935) and the Danny O'Neill tetralogy (1936–1943) are a devitalized repetition of his earlier work we forget with what exactness Farrell marked off his chosen segment of American society. Like Fitzgerald and Lewis, he stays within certain degrees of his scale. His characters do not move higher than the self-respecting, hard-working Irish-born father of Studs Lonigan. They do not sink lower than the O'Neill family who struggle with poverty and the birthrate. The street the O'Neills live on is not in Nelson Algren's skid-row Chicago though some of Studs Lonigan's companions are on the way down to it.

Farrell's second novel, *Gas-House McGinty* (1933), early showed the segments of the social scale he would continue to mark out for himself. Around the central figure, Ambrose J. McGinty, proud of his job as Chief Dispatcher in the Wagon Department of the Continental Express Company, swirl the others in the outfit, from the Old Man down through Wolfe, the much-feared inspector, to the Old Man's nephew who is hated by even those who dare to talk back to him, to the young punks whose minds are on nothing but the women they have had and how they had them and in what numbers. "Gas-House" worries about his health and his troubles in bed (Mame holds out on him). He envies the inspectors ("you got pensions"), hates Jews, Bohunks, Wops, and Polacks, has twinges of fright when he sees a bum (could it happen to him?). Most of all he worries about his job. Just when he thinks he has made the grade and the white-collar promised land is in sight (he has thought up the speech he will make to the Happy Expressmen's Club), he is given the boot, and only because when his piles were acting up he made a scene and got the Old Man sore at him.

This is not a great novel but it comes near to being a classic account of the two-fisted American working man who almost lifts himself into the pension-holding class, only to be denied at the moment of his elevation. The moral is in the epigraph.

"One place that's always busy is the Call Department. They threw away the key to the office when they opened it, and it's one sure house of grief," Mac said.

"Don't let the kid stay in this game. There's too many kids who started in it, and are rottin' away in it now, gettin' nowhere."

In the Studs Lonigan trilogy (*Young Lonigan*, 1932; *The Young Manhood of Studs Lonigan*, 1934; *Judgment Day*, 1935) Farrell was after another theme. He defined it in "How *Studs Lonigan* was Written":

Studs Lonigan was conceived as a normal American boy of Irish-Catholic extraction. The social milieu in which he lived and was educated was one of spiritual poverty. It was not, contrary to some misconceptions, a slum neighborhood. Had I written *Studs Lonigan* as a story of the slums, it would then have been easy for the reader falsely to place the motivation and causation of the story directly in immediate economic roots. Such a placing of motivation would have obscured one of the most important meanings I wanted to inculcate into my story: my desire to reveal the concrete effects of spiritual poverty. It is readily known that poverty and slums cause spiritual poverty in many lives. One of the important meanings I perceived in this story was that here was a neighborhood several steps removed from the slums and dire economic want, and here, too, was manifested a pervasive spiritual poverty.

This spiritual poverty arises from a number of causes. One is the inability of Studs's family to impress on him the immigrant generation's respect for hard work and decent behavior. Another is the unrealistic Puritanism of the Catholic Church. Studs and his friends come to despise the priests almost as soon as they learn how to play tricks on the nuns who teach them. Set against these ineffectual forces, and winning over them in the end, are the degenerative influences of the Prohibition era and its tawdry myth of success, repeated in a thousand movies.

In all the early novels by Farrell the characters are on the edge of economic failure. For one young man, like Danny O'Neill, who climbs upward there are a score who are defeated, who are hired one day and fired the next and are pushed down into the proletariat. Farrell created a pattern which would persist. There are many more novelists who use his stencil today than there are who show any influence of Fitzgerald or Sinclair Lewis. He has imitators by the score among those who turn out paperbacks to order. And his own novels, banned in city after city, are out on the stands again as soon as the phone calls to the police stop coming. Studs Lonigan — the "guy who didn't have mushy feelings . . . the hard-boiled egg they had left in the pot a couple of hours too long" — seems as certain of immortality as Tom Sawyer and Penrod, though for very different reasons.

III

In the early thirties the depression novel, usually with a leftist bias, was quickly created to fit the mood of the time. A whole school of fiction writers had been trained by the *New Masses*, founded in 1926 on the ruins of the old *Masses* and its successor *The Liberator*. For avowed Communists and fellow travelers alike this magazine had become by the early 1930's a rallying point. Those of its contributors who believed in the Marxian gospel detected the signs of final social disintegration as one Congressional investigation after another explored the venality of American capitalism in the postwar years. They were ready to believe that what had happened in Russia might happen here, for in 1935 there was more talk of revolution than at any time since 1776.

By the mid-thirties American writers in sufficient numbers were debating social causes and attempting to embody them in their work so that a considerable group felt the urge to unite and assess their position. America was climbing out of the deepest depression it had ever known, but at the moment the chances for capitalism's full recovery still seemed slender to many writers on the left. Possibly this was indeed the "revolutionary moment," and, if so, did they not have a responsibility to help the workers seize it? As one now looks back on the first Congress of American Writers, held in 1935, the revolutionary zeal and the bright words of hope expressed by many of the speakers are almost incredible. Some of those present have long since recanted and made public confession of their error. Some are now as bitterly antiradical as an investigating Congressman.

Some have won peace by turning to pure art. Some have disappeared from the literary scene, leaving no trace.

The tone of this first Congress is unmistakably revolutionary. In his introduction to the volume which records the speeches and discussions, Henry Hart declared that from 1930 on American writers had begun to take sides against a barbarism "deliberately cultivated by a handful of property owners." They were now depicting the struggle of the mass of Americans. They must join forces with the International Union of Revolutionary Writers in fighting Fascism, defending the Soviet Union, and strengthening the revolutionary labor movement all over the world. The sixty-nine writers who issued the call for the meeting included such well-known authors as Erskine Caldwell, Theodore Dreiser, James Farrell, Robert Herrick, John Dos Passos, and Richard Wright. Present at the Congress were 216 writers from twenty-six states, as well as 150 guests from other countries. The Congress was blessed with good wishes from Aragon, Barbusse, Gide, Malraux, Rolland, Gorky, and Shòlokhov.

In the various sessions the theme of revolutionary writing was developed by Waldo Frank, Jack Conroy, Granville Hicks, Edwin Seaver, and a half-dozen others. Some of the writers present, Malcolm Cowley and John Dos Passos for instance, were less interested in "the revolution" than in the discussion of questions of technique. But they were made to feel at home by Earl Browder who hospitably remarked that "the great majority of this Congress, being unaffiliated to the Communist Party, are interested in what it has to say because all recognize the necessity of establishing cooperative working relations . . . [with] all enemies of reaction in the cultural field." The Party wanted to help literature to be broad, for "we are all soldiers, each in our own place, in a common cause."

Harmony prevailed in most of the sessions, except on

such legitimate issues for debate among radicals as whether the only possible literature in a revolutionary society is proletarian literature. The League of American Writers was duly organized and staffed with officers. Before adjournment, James Farrell called for the singing of the *International*.

This brief period in the mid-thirties was the most propitious for the writing of fiction with a revolutionary bias. But within two years' time the newly formed League of American Writers began to lose its revolutionary zeal. New issues pressed for discussion. World events disturbed the comparative harmony which had prevailed in the 1935 Congress. Criticism, dissent, and defection began to draw off the less doctrinaire. But for the moment the record stood.

In the years from 1936 to the War novels based on social themes persisted but their numbers diminished. Such convinced Leftists as Michael Gold (*Change in the World,* 1937), Edwin Seaver (*Between the Hammer and the Anvil,* 1937), and Albert Malz (*The Underground Stream,* 1940) continued to turn out party-line novels in which the coming struggle for power between the workers and the owners is the central theme. A few writers with proletarian sympathies turned to new themes, the Loyalist cause in the Spanish Civil War being the most popular. Novels about racial intolerance continued to appear; so did fiction which dealt historically with the tragedy of the waste of human and natural resources in America.

It would be difficult to prove whether there is any close connection between this rapidly changing picture and the concurrent history of the League of American Writers. But it is an interesting fact that the League dropped its radical aims almost as soon as it proclaimed them. Its second Congress, held in 1937, ignored or played down the theme of revolution and demanded of the writers nothing more violent than a promise to "defend the political and social institutions that make for peace and encourage a healthy culture." The Communist Party, in its zeal for Loyalist Spain, was calling for a united front against Fascism, and the second Congress was dominated by this cause. The big public meeting held in Carnegie Hall was largely concerned with the plight of the Spanish Loyalists. At this session Hemingway made one of his few public addresses, on "The Writer and the War."

When the third Writers' Congress convened at the New School early in June 1939, there were signs that the disintegration of the United Front was imminent. Many members of the League had become aware of the fact that the Communists had infiltrated the organization and were in control. Before the report of the sessions of this Congress was in print (*Fighting Words*, 1940), the Russo-German pact had impelled many writers to resign from the League and from the Party as well. Others who had been known as fellow travelers abandoned the League with the flourish of a letter of resignation or by the simple process of not paying their dues. This was the end of the literary United Front.[1]

IV

It would be difficult to estimate to what extent all the talk among writers about Fascism, imperialist war, "agit-prop," formalism, and proletarian fiction, the calling of congresses and the making of speeches before them, influenced the writing of fiction during the decade. But one fact is inescapable. Something new had come into the American novel — a recognition of the failures of the American economic system and what these failures meant to men and women whose only resources, their work skills and their muscles, could not be put to use. It may be true, and this has often been said, that the proletarian novels of the thirties, of whatever variety, do not rank very high as works of art. But they have some value as historical documents. Even the most doctrinaire of them — for example, Grace Lumpkin's *To Make My Bread* (1933) and Ruth McKenney's *Jake Home* (1943) — are based on fact and tell us the inner history of actual strikes and of radical party politics.

Nor should we forget that at least three leftist novels of this decade surpass the novels in any other genre produced in these years — Dos Passos' *The Big Money* (1936), Steinbeck's *The Grapes of Wrath* (1939), and Hemingway's *For Whom the Bell Tolls* (1940). We should pause for a moment to examine these three, particularly since they were spectacular popular successes and influenced the beliefs of many readers.

The Big Money is Dos Passos' finest novel. His generalized hatred of the waste of war, the theme of *Three Soldiers* (1921) and *1919* (1932), is here transformed into a particular hatred of what American society does to the men who fight its wars. Charlie Anderson comes home a hero and expects a hero's reward — stocks and bonds, a mink-coated wife, a place at the directors' table. What he gets is options and a broker's account, a cold bitch for his marriage bed, and, in the end, a drunken race with death who beats him to the railroad-crossing. This is the story, several times retold by Dos Passos, of the cheaters and the cheated. Those who should inherit this land have been cheated. How could they have overcome the cheaters? Dos Passos cannot say. Socialism? Communism? The New Deal? These are not the answers. So far as one can interpret him, the only valid answers are what the Wobblies knew, the insights of Veblen, and the wisdom of Frank Lloyd Wright, one of the nine "representative men" whose careers are signposts in the novel.

glass
concrete;
and needs. (Tell us, doctors of philosophy, what are the needs of a man. At least a man needs to be notjailed notafraid nothungry notcold not without love, not a worker for a power he has never seen
that cares nothing for the uses and needs of a man or a woman or a child.)

Steinbeck's *The Grapes of Wrath*, published three years after *The Big Money*, in many ways complements it. Dos Passos' characters move in the old, ill-planned, rusting cities or those that are new and glittering. The Joads of Steinbeck's novel are from the land and move from the once fruitful acres that are now a dust bowl to the California paradise whose fruit they pick but may not enjoy.

Both novelists hate the exploiters and the wreckers who have made a waste land of America and have deprived the people of their heritage. For Dos Passos the wreckers are the efficiency experts who treat men as if they were machines, the speculators, and the rich who live only to consume. For Steinbeck the wreckers are the impersonal banks which deal in mortgages and human lives, the Farmers' Association, and the canneries. The unholy alliance that binds them together keeps wages down and forces prices up. The end might be serfdom.

But the American people will not become serfs. They know too well, even the ignorant Joads, that it is man's nature to

build a wall, to build a house, a dam, and in the wall and house and dam to put something of Manself, and to Manself take back something of the wall, the house, the dam; to take hard muscles from the lifting, to take the clean lines and form from conceiving, . . . Man reaches, stumbles forward, painfully, mistakenly sometimes. Having stepped forward, he may slip back, but only half a step, never the full step back.

The great owners have cause to fear this going forward of a people who have gone forward in the past. Such people, the American people, will endure only so much. When they are "hungry and cold they will take by force what they need." Hunger and brutality will test them and unite them and make them strong to resist.

The theme of *The Grapes of Wrath* was not new in American literature. In earlier times and in other settings it had been touched by Freneau and Whitman and, momentarily, by Frank Norris. Some of Steinbeck's contemporaries also touched it. In 1936 Sandburg wrote, in *The People, Yes:*

> The people will live on.
> The learning and blundering people will live on.
> They will be tricked and sold and again sold
> And go back to the nourishing earth for footholds,
> The people so peculiar in renewal and comeback,
> You can't laugh off their capacity to take it.
> The mammoth rests between his cyclonic dreams.

And in the year of *The Grapes of Wrath* Archibald MacLeish was asking, "Who are the born brothers in truth?"; and answering his question:

> Hunger and hurt are the great begetters of brotherhood:
> Humiliation has gotten much love:
> Danger I say is the nobler father and mother:
>
> These are as brothers whose bodies have shared fear
> Or shared harm or shared hurt and indignity. . . .

Those who have labored together carry the common look like a card, "and they pass touching" ("Speech to those who say Comrade").

In the year 1940 many people who had never heard of John Donne were reading *For Whom the Bell Tolls* and quoting its epigraph about brotherhood from the seventeenth of John Donne's *Devotions upon Emergent Occasions* which gave Hemingway his title. There was much rejoicing on the left because Hemingway seemed at last to have been gathered into the fold. But Robert Jordan's story is no leftist novel cut to a pattern. Its theme is Hemingway's usual theme: how does a man prove he is a man? Jake Barnes, in *The Sun Also Rises* (1926), had to learn how to be a man even though a war-wound had deprived him of his potency. Lieutenant Henry, in *A Farewell to Arms* (1929), had to put his life together again through love after his world fell apart at Caporetto. And now Robert Jordan is in Spain, fighting for the Loyalist cause. He admires those Communists who are honestly in the fight and sees through the lies of others who are using the war for their own ends. He is fighting because he loves Spain and because he is the grandson of his Civil War grandfather, and because his father was a *cobarde* who committed suicide. He does not wish to be a coward and he knows he is not because he has found out that he is as good at this war business as his grandfather was.

Robert Jordan has much time in which to think why he is in a strange country, fighting with strange comrades, in a cause which will be lost. When he comes to die, alone, in the place where he should be, ready for the end, there are only two regrets. He wishes he could tell his grandfather what has happened to him; and he wishes he could pass on to the real fighters what he has learned. It might help, and next time, perhaps, the cause can be won.

This linking of the heroic American past with the future of free men everywhere gives *For Whom the Bell Tolls* a scope which is lacking in the other two novels. But the three taken together condense within the four-year span of their publication nearly twenty years of American belief. All three concentrate on the struggle between the social forces that are destructive and those which make life good and fruitful, but there is a progression from the negative wasteland atmosphere of *The Big Money* to the ardent Americanism of *The Grapes of Wrath* to Robert Jordan, dying and saying:

"I have fought for what I believed in for a year now. If we win here we will win everywhere. The world is a fine place and worth the fighting for and I hate very much to leave it. . . . You've had just as good a life as grandfather's though not as long. . . . I wish there were some way to pass on what I've learned, though. Christ, I was learning fast there at the end."

The fiction written during the second World War reflects little social interest. Americans had turned from domestic problems to a struggle for survival. What most readers wanted was escape-writing. There were novels which attempted to deal with the impact of the war on men so recently civilians, but this fiction is largely autobiographical. It lacks scope and is seldom reflective.

Although it is true that social themes have largely disappeared from American fiction since 1940, there are a fair number of novelists who discovered new areas of social disorganization which they utilized for their settings. The most interesting novels of this kind have been written by Negroes. At last, in this generation, the Negro novelist has found a public. Not many years ago publishing houses carefully rationed in their lists the novels by and about Negroes and would take such fiction only if it conformed to certain acceptable patterns — for example, exotic black and white relationships in Harlem. This situation changed rapidly after the second World War. Some of the pocketbook publishers discovered that the literate Negro public was eager to read books written by members of their own race. The fact that Chester Himes or Ann Petry or Richard Wright or James Baldwin or Ralph Ellison is a Negro is plainly advertised on the cover.

These novels give a picture of Negro life, north and

south, which has never before been attempted. Some of the more usual themes are the struggle for an education and for an existence in which it can be used, the bewilderment of the southern Negro who has escaped to what he thinks will be a better chance in a northern city, the pressures which drive decent Negroes toward crime and vice, and the vicissitudes of the Negro worker.*

In the great flood of novels about the second World War there were several which were built around themes that are a carry-over from the social-crusading, proletarian thirties. Irwin Shaw, for example, takes for one of his three leading characters in *The Young Lions* (1948) a Jewish boy who has experienced to the full the harshness of anti-Semitism. The scenes in which Noah fights, one after another, the ten men in his company who have baited him are among the most terrifying in recent American fiction. James Jones's *From Here to Eternity* (1951) exhibits the enlisted man's hatred of rank and the petty privilege which goes with it, but Jones is careful to motivate the refusal of Prewitt to take his appointed place in the military hierarchy. Young Prew, the bugler who will not become a jockstrap for the glory of Captain Holmes, is the son of a striking Harlan miner who was in jail with two stab wounds and a fractured skull on the day Prew's mother died. Prew endures the torture of the stockade and eventually meets death because he comes of proud mountain stock which could never take an insult or an unjust order. The only person to whose advice he listens, in the novel's 860 pages, is Malloy who had been in and out of every radical movement of his youth and in the end had respect only for the Wobblies: "Nobody ever really understood them. They had the courage, and what's more important, they had the soft heart to go with it."

* Some of the difficulties faced by Negro novelists are discussed in Chapter VII, pp. 260–261.

Another war novel, Norman Mailer's *The Naked and the Dead* (1948), is the most class-conscious work of fiction written since the thirties. Between the enlisted men and non-coms at the bottom of the scale, all of whom have proletarian backgrounds, and General Cummings, an American Fascist who plans for the bigger war yet to come, is Lieutenant Hearn, the liberal who has never known how to put his vague liberalism to work. In the midst of war all the hatreds and destructive ambitions of these men are naked and on the loose. As the flashbacks of their early lives reveal, Mailer sees their actions almost entirely in terms of the class which formed, or more exactly, warped and frustrated each — general, lieutenant, or private.

v

The one novelist of the years between 1920 and 1950 who touched in some fashion most of the important social issues of the time was John Dos Passos (b. 1896). Only two of his novels — *1919* (1932) and *The Big Money* (1936) — seem undated now, but almost all of the others, from *Three Soldiers* (1921) to *Chosen Country* (1951), are interesting to one who wishes to review the fortunes of the Republic during the past half century. As *The 42nd Parallel* (1930) opens, orators and editors are noisily greeting the new century ("American progress will give it color and direction. American deeds will make it illustrious"); at the novel's close Charlie Anderson, garage mechanic who will become a war ace, is on his way to fight for France. The effect of the War itself on a group of enlisted men and their buddies is the theme of *Three Soldiers*. What happened to Americans turned loose in Europe just after the Armistice is the substance of *1919*. In *Manhattan Transfer*[2] (1925) Dos Passos brings his characters from the 1890's down to present time — the mid-twenties. The Harding-Coolidge boom years and the stock-market crash are covered by *The Big Money*. The first section of *Adventures of a Young Man* (1939) is concerned with Glenn Spotswood's boyhood but when Dos Passos gets him to college we are in the depression years and we watch him join the Communists, become disillusioned with the intrigues and betrayals inside the Party, and in the end die fighting for the Loyalist cause in Spain. The one remaining gap was filled by *The Grand Design* (1949) which opens on the day of Roosevelt's first inauguration and closes with America at war. In *Chosen Country* Dos Passos took a long running start (the first of the six family biographies which frame the story begins in 1848) and leapt over eighty years of American life into the years when the threat of Fascism was first felt in this country.

Possibly Dos Passos would have been a greater writer if he had followed the bent of his earliest novels, *One Man's Initiation* (1920), *Three Soldiers*, and *Streets of Night* (1923). In the tradition of the *Bildungsroman* each shows the awakening of a young man to the beauty and terror of life and his revolt against authority and conformity. But Dos Passos' brooding on the folly of the first World War, in which he served in the medical corps, and his involvement in the cause of the striking miners of Harlan County, Kentucky, and the Sacco-Vanzetti case turned him away from his aesthetical young heroes to the ills and injustices of American life. Temperamentally he was not equipped to deal with them objectively, because he was too much a perfectionist to accept the realities of politics. He missed the tragedy in Wilson's career, for example, because he saw him only as the hypocritical politician who got us into war. Later, his view of Franklin D. Roosevelt was similarly myopic. Roosevelt, he believed, betrayed his New Deal because he was a power-hungry

Caesar who made the people dance to his seductive tune so that he could stay in office term after term.

Dos Passos was never a good loser, as honest politicians and sincere liberals have to be, retreating when they must in order that they may fight again. In his later novels (particularly *The Grand Design* and *Most Likely to Succeed*) his bitterness over the defeat of causes he once championed is directed at liberals as well as Communists. America is still his "chosen country" but because it has been betrayed again and again by the politicians, the money makers, the Communists and the gullible liberals, the only comfort an honest man can find is to go back to the roots, to find "the ground we stand on." The "theme is freedom," still, as Dos Passos maintained in an anthology of his political writings (1950) to which he gave this title. But how are Americans to win freedom? How are they to achieve the skill in self-government which will guarantee freedom to every man? Dos Passos has never ventured an answer, except in his praise of the philosophical anarchists of Italy and Spain and their American heirs. The nausea of his later writing suggests a sense of guilt for having never found a social philosophy in which he could believe very long.

In considering Dos Passos' defects as a social novelist — as well as his achievements, which we shall come to in a moment — it is important to note that the novel which uses socio-political themes is something of an anomaly. There are, actually, few superior examples of the genre. (Henry James's *The Princess Cassamassima*, oddly enough, considering its author's remoteness from social and political affairs, is one; Robert Penn Warren's *All the King's Men* is another.) If the author stays close to actual events, which Dos Passos always does, his scenes and characters may soon become dated, as the fire goes out of the issues of a particular moment in history. If, on the other hand, he abstracts and generalizes, his novel takes on the character of a Ruritanian romance. If he is too passionate about the issues he is concerned with, his novel may become more a tract for the times than a work of fiction.

Given the difficulties of the genre, it is all the more remarkable that Dos Passos should have surmounted his problems as often as he did. He showed early that his imagination could grasp the collective life of a group or class and by 1930 he had mastered the techniques he needed for presenting the collective life of the nation. In combination these assets made it possible for him to construct the vast panoramas which constitute his two trilogies — U.S.A. (The 42nd Parallel, 1919, The Big Money) and District of Columbia (Adventures of a Young Man, Number One, The Grand Design). Another resource was his ability to project himself into the lives of his characters, no matter from what region or class they came. He knew the look of the towns in which they grew up, what games they played as children, what the pressures at home would be, the requirements of the jobs they would have held, their ambitions, secret fears, frustrations, and defeats. Whenever one Dos Passos character meets another we are sure to get two life stories, told in a bar, at a Greenwich Village party, or in a boxcar banging across the western plains. There are hundreds of such encounters in his novels and their frequency gives the reader the impression that Americans are always on the move, touching other lives, in the hospital ward, on the picket line, in a chance love affair, then drifting off, some moving up the social scale, many moving down into defeat.

It has often been said that in his effort to represent the rootlessness and mobility of American life Dos Passos fails to give his characters any depth. At least they have extension, rather as if they could be known only by their relations with the other characters whom they touch, the coordinates, so to speak, which determine their position for us. Dos Passos seems to be saying that in our complex world individuality is almost null. A man, an individual, exists only in his relationships to others and these relationships are constantly changing.

In developing his main characters, such as the five protagonists in *The 42nd Parallel* (the first novel in which he successfully juxtaposed several parallel lives), Dos Passos defines their status as carefully as a sociologist or a social caseworker. We are told at once, in direct narration, about their parents' place in the social framework and the process by which they break from the pattern of life prepared for them at home. Gradually they acquire the status which will be theirs for the remainder of the novel; sometimes seeking it deliberately, as the Horatio Alger boy from Wilmington, J. Ward Morehouse does, sometimes drifting towards it, as does Eleanor Stoddard whose hyper-romanticism makes it inevitable that she shall be one of the many women who keep J. Ward's ego from collapsing.

It might be supposed that once the status of any of Dos Passos' characters is established the portrait would turn into caricature or stereotype. One can, it is true, sum them up in a few typifying words — J. Ward, the successful public relations expert who counsels tycoons and statesmen; Dick Savage, the college esthete, whose sensibilities are too refined to permit him to step into J. Ward's place which is being warmed for him. But Dos Passos prevents many of his characters from becoming stereotypes by strokes of the brush which make them human and believable. In the brief portrait of Ben Compton in *1919* (one of his few sympathetic characters) there are many of these touches. Ben is a Brooklyn Jew who becomes a radical. But he is no mere stereotype of the revolutionary, American style. (In the later novels there would be many Party members and fellow travelers stenciled into the plot.) Ben is an ambitious and intelligent boy, a fine school debater, and a hero-worshipper. He is also very bitter about the way Jews are treated in America. If things had gone differently he might have become a successful lawyer, but his friendships with Nick Gigli, an anarchist, and Bram Hicks, a Wobbly, both of whom he worships because they know about life and are kind to him, set him on the course leading to a ten-year jail sentence in Atlanta which he begins to serve on his twenty-third birthday. It is like Ben, the bright schoolboy orator, to address the court so eloquently before being sentenced that even the judge sits up when he recites his peroration, the last words of the Communist Manifesto.

For the novels of the *U.S.A.* trilogy Dos Passos invented an ingenious structural plan which served his purpose excellently and had a considerable influence on the fiction written in the next generation. He brings along the story of one of his characters in two or three chapters, then drops him for fifty pages in order to pick up a second character, then a third, and so on until five or six life histories which cross and recross have been told. To place the characters in time and to give the reader a sense of what it felt like to be living at the given moment, Dos Passos used three devices which serve as partitioning introductions to each new turn of the plot: the "newsreel," the "camera eye," and brief profiles of actual persons who influenced or epitomized the age. (In 1919 these are John Reed, Randolph Bourne, T. R., Paxton Hibben, Meester Veelson, J.P. Morgan, Joe Hill, and Wesley Everest, a Wobbly hero.) The "newsreel" is a montage of lines from popular songs, advertising slogans, headlines, and snatches of editorials and news stories. In the "camera eye" sections the author himself speaks — in poetic prose that doesn't come off very well. His intention was to suggest through one man's remembered sense impressions how the particular moment in time registered on the human consciousness. To conclude *1919* and *The Big Money* Dos Passos hit on still another device which enabled him to end each novel with a bang. The final section is the last of the profiles but in this instance the subject is collective man: in *1919*, The Body of an American (that is, The Unknown Soldier); in *The Big Money*, Vag, who carries down the endless road in his rubbed suitcase of imitation leather all the defeats of all the men made homeless by the depression.

> went to school, books said opportunity, ads promised speed, own your home, shine bigger than your neighbor, the radio-crooner whispered girls, ghosts of platinum girls coaxed from the screen, millions in winnings were chalked up on the boards in the offices, pay-checks were for hands willing to work, the cleared desk of an executive with three telephones on it;
> waits with swimming head, needs knot the belly, idle hands numb, beside the speeding traffic.
> A hundred miles down the road.

In the speculations of the leftist critics of the 1930's there was much talk about the "collective novel." It was, they decreed, the kind of fiction which socially conscious writers should produce, showing how men are determined by the society in which they live. In such a novel society was to be pictured as all important: the hero, if the revolution had taken place; in the case of a decadent bourgeois society, the villain.

Dos Passos never theorized much about his work, but whether he intended to or not, he produced, in *1919* and *The Big Money*, two impressive collective novels, not made to order for the Party theorists but of his own devising.

FIVE

The Persistence of Naturalism in the Novel

UNLIKE the French, Americans are not much interested in critical wars. But we have endured one critical war which went on for years and was fought with the violence characteristic of civil strife. This was the war over literary naturalism. From the 1890's until the mid-twenties naturalism was for its partisans a battle cry; for its opponents a term of abuse. Both sides fought with deep conviction. At stake was the acceptance of a particular technique of presenting human life in fiction. The literary naturalists were also fighting for the right to tell the truth about American society, as they envisioned it. Their opponents believed that if the naturalistic novels came to be accepted as truthful accounts of American life, all aspiration for whatsoever things are pure, lovely, and of good report would disappear from the national consciousness.

This drawn-out war is supposed to have ended in the 1920's. When Paul Elmer More, the staunchest opponent of the literary naturalists, read Dreiser's *An American Tragedy* in 1925, he wrote with regret of the novelist's wasted talent. If only Dreiser had known the finer things of life as he did its shabby underside; if he had known the larger tradition of literature instead of relying for his standards on police court records and the dregs of science;

143

if he had had a chance, in short, he might have produced "that fabulous thing, the great American novel." By implication, at least, More accepted the sad fact that Dreiser could no longer be fought off.

By this time, when the partisans of the two sides had effected their uneasy truce, the newer critics who were fixing their attention on the younger novelists — Fitzgerald, Dos Passos, and Hemingway in particular — found many more interesting things to discuss than such worn-out concepts as heredity, environment, chance, determinism, and the slice-of-life theory of the novel. It was evident that these newer novelists were superior as craftsmen to the literary naturalists. Consequently the naturalistic elements in their writing were disregarded in order that their contributions to form and style might be sufficiently noted and praised.

From this time on literary naturalism was supposed to be a dead issue. Writers like Farrell and Steinbeck who were obviously in the tradition established by Norris and Dreiser had to be accepted, of course, because they were novelists of some stature. But the analytical critics rejoiced as they watched Farrell repeat himself in novel after novel, never attaining again the excellence of his Studs Lonigan trilogy, and as Steinbeck lapsed too often into patriotism and sentimentality. During the 1940's the gods of the critics were Henry James, Dostoevsky, and Kafka. Small wonder, therefore, that scant attention was paid to novelists who carried on in the naturalistic vein.

Though critics have grown weary of the term and have become petulant towards those who use it, a review of American fiction written since the second World War shows that the naturalistic tradition still persists. Literary naturalism is of course not now what it was in 1900; Norman Mailer's *The Naked and the Dead* differs as much from Norris' *McTeague* as the philosophical naturalism of

John Dewey and his disciples differs from that of Herbert Spencer. But for more than fifty years there has been a persistent bias towards naturalism in American thought as well as in the novel. This bias has become deeply ingrained in the American mind. Events and ideas decade by decade have combined to strengthen it.

It is the purpose of this chapter to follow the changes in the modes of naturalistic fiction which two wars, an economic depression, and the stimulus of Freudianism and Marxism have effected. But first it will be necessary to establish, by a review of at least one novel written since the second World War, the fact that literary naturalism is still very much with us. The novel I have selected is Mailer's *The Naked and the Dead* (1948). It may be objected that the case has been too neatly set up in advance, for in this particular novel, if anywhere in modern American fiction, one might expect to find remnants of naturalism. Still, the literary historian, searching for trends, has a right to submit it as evidence. It has been very widely read and discussed and even those critics who found fault with it granted Mailer a measure of craftsmanship and psychological penetration.*

Mailer learned from many masters. From Hemingway he learned how to convey compassion without stating it explicitly. Much of his symbolistic technique is derived from Thomas Mann's *The Magic Mountain*. Dos Passos taught him how to keep the actions of his grouped characters moving in parallel lines and how, at the same time, to penetrate a little way into their consciousness. The scope of the novel is as large as its length and though the devices used to keep the internal and external action moving

* Other post-War naturalistic novels which would serve quite as well to prove my point are Nelson Algren's *The Man with the Golden Arm* (1949), James Jones's *From Here to Eternity* (1951), Saul Bellow's *The Adventures of Augie March* (1953), John O'Hara's *Ten North Frederick* (1955), and Vance Bourjaily's *The Violated* (1958).

ahead on many levels are sometimes mechanical, the novel's form helps, most of the time, to impart its meaning.

The naturalistic derivations of *The Naked and the Dead* are clear enough. To be noted first is the milieu — war, and war at its worst, the kind of war which reduces man to his lowest terms. The title is significant. Mailer's soldiers have been stripped naked of their humanity. They have died out of the world of the decent human relations which some of them, at least, have known, and they look back to it from hell. Mailer's depiction of war, the fear, the horror, the brutality, the charnel-house atmosphere, would have delighted the Zola of *La Débâcle* who tried in that novel to tell the French people what the Franco-Prussian war of 1870 had meant to the soldiers who fought it. But Mailer carefully provides us also with the earlier, shaping environment of each of his chief characters in order that we may the more clearly see what war does to them.

Mailer's work is in the tradition of the older literary naturalism because he makes use of a milieu in which man becomes a hunted and tortured animal and because for the most part his characters are determined by the pressures of their past and present. But in several respects he goes beyond anything Dreiser or Crane could have attempted. The most self-conscious of his characters, Lieutenant Hearn and General Cummings, engage in a battle of wills which carries the central meaning of the book. This power of conscious, willed action was seldom permitted earlier protagonists in the tradition. Hearn is pictured at first as a drifter, a half-hearted liberal who would like to believe in something, most of all in himself. Slowly he begins to realize how deeply corrupted by the lust for power the General is. Cummings intends to possess Hearn's mind and, possibly, his body. Horrifying as this is, Hearn soon penetrates to a greater horror, Cummings' long-nurtured

plan to use his prowess in war for illimitable Fascist maneuvers when the war is over. Mailer suggests here that unless
men like Hearn awake in time to what Cummings and his
kind intend to do, more than a war will be lost.

In his depiction of the struggle between these two wills,
Mailer covertly uses the concepts of Freud and Adler to
give authority to his characterization of the two men. It
should also be noted that Hearn and Cummings are well
read in the modern psychology, as their conversations reveal.
They are thoroughly onto themselves and onto each other.
It is of interest technically that though Mailer uses Freudian concepts in constructing his less complex characters, he
permits them only the vaguest understanding of their
traumas and sex drives and they do not know the words for
them as do Hearn and Cummings.

II

With at least one recent manifestation of literary naturalism in the record, it is time to turn back and look into
the origins of this extraordinarily long-lived movement.
How did it come about that great numbers of Americans
became so convinced of the rightness of a view which
permits no belief in supernaturalism, which may even, at
times, deny man those rights which democratic idealists
once asserted were inalienable? The question is all the
more in need of an answer when one looks across the
Atlantic and sees what has happened to the English novel
during these past fifty years. English fiction had its naturalistic exponents — one numbers Hardy, Gissing, and
George Moore among them — but the episode was of short
duration. The same is true of France. Why is the story so
different in America?

In the first place we must remember that Americans
were ready and waiting for the influx of post-Darwinian
concepts which poured in upon them. By 1880 the ad-

herents of Jeffersonian democracy and of Transcendental idealism were having a rough time of it. Post–Civil War America was not the country the founders had dreamed of. Cyclic depressions, bloody strikes, the growing slums in the cities, social dislocations of many kinds made it impossible for thoughtful Americans to hold to older views of man's nature which were once dominant. What was needed, by those who were sensitive to these ills of the new age, was a philosophy which would account for them. As it turned out, the concepts of Social Darwinism, which flowed in to fill this intellectual vacuum, did more than explain. For those who embraced them, they supplied a justification, as well, for the ruthlessness of powerful leaders in business and politics who had transformed American society into a jungle. Paradoxically, the new ideas could be warped in opposite directions. Dreiser could meditate at the end of *Sister Carrie* on the pitiful "blind strivings of the human heart." But Andrew Carnegie, who like Dreiser had been illuminated by Spencer, could affirm that "man was not created with an instinct for his own degradation, but from the lower he had risen to the higher forms." Pessimism came in view at one end of the telescope; if the telescope were reversed, vistas of a boundless optimism opened out.

It was Herbert Spencer, of course, who was chiefly responsible for bringing the new views to America.[1] It is recorded that the American sales of his various books, from their first publication in the sixties through 1903, amounted to 368,755 volumes. It may well be that no work save the Bible has had so much influence in America as Spencer's Synthetic Philosophy, which in its several parts carried his system upward from *First Principles* (1862) and *Principles of Biology* (1864–1867) to the capstone, the *Principles of Ethics*, in 1892–1893. The fact that he was a shoddy thinker, vulnerable in several of his doctrines, had no effect on his popularity. There was nothing he could not explain — from the origin of species (he was a Lamarckian) to the nature of evil. (It results simply and naturally from "the non-adaptation of constitution to conditions.") Evil tends to disappear — comforting thought to Americans then sadly perplexed by social evil — because the process of adaptation is rooted in the nature of the organism. It is true that man still has to cope with the vestiges of his animal heritage. That is why he is still predatory and brutal. But he will in time adapt himself to the needs of civilized life. Spencer's leading idea was the notion of the "survival of the fittest," a phrase which he invented. But the whole argument turned on the one word "fittest." In what sense "fittest"? Strict constructionists of Spencerian law doomed not only the stupid and the vicious but as well the idle and the poor. But no one need be poor if he were strong enough to compete.

If one were a thorough Spencerian, therefore, one must go the whole way with the master, ignoring the evil and suffering incidental to the ultimate working out of the great plan. Progress was not to be considered an accident, but a necessity. Civilization is a part of nature, "all of a piece with the development of the embryo or the unfolding of a flower." The human faculties will eventually be moulded into complete fitness for the social state. "So surely must evil and immorality disappear; so surely must man become perfect." Spencer fixed no date for this millennium. It would come to pass only in nature's good time.*

If the Spencerian dogmas made glad the hearts of the Carnegies and Rockefellers, they had a very different effect

---

* How radically the contemporary naturalistic view of the development of civilization has displaced Spencer's can be judged from Dr. Karl A. Menninger's dictum in *The Human Mind* (1949, p. 131): "Civilization and culture owe their existence to the thwarting of primitive tendencies, particularly the sexual and aggressive instincts, and in this sense *civilization itself is a neurotic product.*" Dr. Menninger cites Freud's *Civilization and Its Discontents.*

on those who were too impatient to wait for nature to reach — how many thousands of years hence? — her grand conclusion. The social reformers, and certain critics of Spencer on whom they relied, wanted to help nature speed up the process, chiefly by calling in the state as the accelerator. Though the literary naturalists responded in diverse ways, they were most often humanitarians. Some were fascinated by the species which nature was discarding in her upward movement towards human perfection, the grotesque and malformed, who could not adapt themselves and so could not survive. These writers seized on the idea of evolutionary regression or devolution. Their fascination with its possibilities sometimes amounted to a delight which their detractors called morbid. Others, while subscribing to the conclusion that evolution is moving upward and that man will not forever balance between good and evil, chose to survey the human striving and suffering that still persisted in this time of transition. Essentially this is the theme of Dreiser's *Sister Carrie*. He pauses to tell us so directly in the eighth chapter of that novel. As an animal, man is still chiefly ruled by his instincts and desires. As a man he has not learned to align himself with nature. He is a wisp in the wind, "moved by every breath of passion, acting now by his will, and now by his instincts, erring with one, only to retrieve by the other, falling by one, only to rise by the other — a creature of incalculable variability." The spectacle fascinated Dreiser, but he could never hold fast for any length of time to a conviction of what it portended.

The early literary naturalists left abundant testimony, direct and indirect, of Spencer's fecundating influence in their work. Hamlin Garland states in *A Son of the Middle Border* that he grappled with the mighty masters of evolution — Darwin, Spencer, Fiske, Helmholtz, Haeckel — but for him Spencer was philosopher and master. "With eager haste I sought to compass the 'Synthetic Philosophy.' The universe took on order and harmony. . . . My mental diaphragm creaked with the pressure of inrushing ideas." Frank Norris concludes *The Octopus* with words which echo Spencer's optimism: "The individual suffers, but the race goes on. . . . The larger view always and through all shams, all wickednesses, discovers the Truth that will, in the end, prevail, and all things, surely, inevitably, resistlessly work together for good." Two years after his first reading of Spencer, Dreiser recommended him in an editorial because he could summon up the "whole universe in review . . . showing you how certain beautiful laws exist, and how, by these laws, all animate and inanimate things have developed and arranged themselves."

Spencer was the fountainhead but he was by no means the only source from which the new generation of novelists carried away ideas useful to them. As the battle of the books went on they could pick up the notion of "race suicide" from E. A. Ross, a pioneer in American sociology, who invented the term. They could follow Theodore Roosevelt's call for the "strenuous life." From the Reverend Josiah Strong's *Our Country: Its Possible Future and Its Present Crisis* (1885) they might come to believe in the nobility and unconquerable strength of Anglo-Saxon civilization. About the time Norris was imbibing academic evolutionism from Joseph Le Conte, a popular professor of geology and zoology at the University of California, Jack London was acquiring a more dubious Darwinism from Benjamin Kidd's *Social Evolution* (1894). This work by a British government clerk was so much in demand that it was translated into at least nine languages. One of Kidd's chief arguments, which accounts, incidentally, for his great popularity, was that religion performs a useful service by impelling man to be socially responsible. London conveniently ignored this notion, but was so much taken with Kidd's belief in Anglo-Saxon superiority that, on the basis of it, he could justify the ruthlessness of English and American imperialism. Beginning about 1905 the Nietzschean idea of the superman was added to this growing assortment of useful naturalistic concepts. Few writers took the doctrine straight. It was easily accessible in Shaw's *Man and Superman* (1903) and Huneker's *Egoists: A Book of Supermen* (1909).

From whatever widely scattered "authorities" the novelists selected the evolutionary ideas they needed, they agreed in calling Émile Zola the master of their craft. There are several reasons for this, the chief being the example he set them. In novel after novel he worked for twenty years at the vast canvas he was painting of the natural and social history of one family under the Second Empire. Through the twelve-hundred characters of the Rougon-Macquart novels he graphed a whole society. Zola's powerful example is responsible for the trilogies and tetralogies which American novelists, who sought his scope and massiveness, later produced: Norris' three-novel epic of wheat, of which only two parts were completed; Dreiser's trilogy on the career of the business titan Frank Cowperwood; Dos Passos' *U.S.A.* trilogy, and Farrell's compound novels grouped around Studs Lonigan and Danny O'Neill.

In spite of his declarations of scientific objectivity as a novelist, Zola was by nature a humanitarian for he had known "bread and oil" poverty himself. Zola the aesthetician might say "we are experimentalists without being practitioners; we ought to content ourselves with searching out the determinism of social phenomena," but it was Zola the hater of human injustice who defended Dreyfus and who cried out against his critics when they attacked *L'Assommoir*: "Educate the worker, take him out of the misery in which he lives, combat the crowding and the promiscuity of the workers' quarters where the air thickens and stinks; above all prevent drunkenness which decimates the people and kills mind and body." Zola's American disciples would attempt to follow his doctrine of the novelist's obligatory objectivity, but they were equally faithful to his humanity. They proposed to deny themselves the luxury of pity, but it often breaks through: Norris' frustrated sympathy for the wheat farmers in the toils of the railroad octopus; Dreiser's pity for Hurstwood as he sinks lower and lower till there is no exit except by the gas jet; Farrell's sympathy for Studs Lonigan who might have been the hero he longed to be if nature had given him a few more inches in his biceps and in his conscience.

Zola also taught his followers to amass in their files every document bearing on their subject. Because Zola knew all there was to know about peasant life and the city markets and the *ménage* of the courtesan, Dreiser was justified in pouring all he knew — and it was a great deal — about the methods and maneuvers of the American captain of industry into his Cowperwood trilogy. It was in the true Zolaesque spirit that Sinclair Lewis documented, down to the newest centrifuge and biological theory, the career of Dr. Martin Arrowsmith.

By 1880 Zola was prepared to set down his theory of the naturalistic novel. His *Le Roman Expérimental* became the textbook of his school. However outmoded it may seem to us now, it is surely one of the most important treatises in the not very extensive "poetic" of the novel form. And its influence has been immense.

Zola's premise is derived from science. He had been greatly impressed by *L'Introduction à l'Étude de la Medicine Expérimental*, written by a physiologist at the Collège de France, Claude Bernard. He insists, throughout his essay, that one may educe the theory of the experimental novel by substituting the word "novelist" wherever Bernard uses the word "doctor" in his treatise. Carrying

Bernard's arguments over into the province of the naturalistic novelist, Zola arrived at this satisfying method of procedure.

The problem is to know what such a passion [love], acting in a given surrounding and under given conditions, will produce, from the point of view of an individual and of society. An experimental novel, Balzac's *Cousine Bette*, for example, is simply the report of the experiment that the novelist conducts before the eyes of the public. . . . In the end you will have knowledge of man, scientific knowledge, in both his individual and social relations.

In the course of his essay Zola set forth his ideas about the form and style appropriate to his new kind of novel. These ideas were to have considerable influence on his American followers. He declared that in the literature of his time form had been given an exaggerated emphasis. Form should depend on method alone. "We are actually rotten with lyricism; we are very much mistaken when we think that the characteristic of a good style is a sublime confusion with just a dash of madness." Zola's quarrel with the idealists in art was that they were content with verbal elaborations of the unknown and the unverifiable.

Partly in answer to his detractors, one supposes, Zola contends that novelists of his kind are really experimental moralists. The dream of the physiologist — to master maladies in order to cure without fail — is also the objective of the naturalistic novelist: "We also desire to master certain phenomena of an intellectual and personal order, to be able to direct them." To be thus the master of good and evil, to regulate life, to regulate society, to give justice a solid foundation by solving through experiment the questions of criminology — is a grand and noble work.

III

We are now in a position to ask how one may recognize the influence of naturalistic concepts in the work of the novelists who were writing at the turn of the century. What, in general, for the deviations were many, were the presuppositions about the nature of man which shaped the novels of Hamlin Garland, Stephen Crane, Frank Norris, Jack London, and Theodore Dreiser?

Almost without exception these American naturalistic novelists denied man's relation to any supernatural order. Even Herbert Spencer's "unknowable," which is manifested to man through the process of evolution, did not seem a very useful concept. Moreover, they agreed that the Idealists in literature had pictured man as far more capable of nobility and self-sacrifice and of the use of reason than the facts warranted. They proposed to turn their light on hitherto neglected aspects of human nature — on man frustrated, deprived, limited by atavistic regressions; man the victim of his own lusts and inadequacies as well as the brutal aggressions of his fellows. Here a vast area to be conquered by their art opened before them. Even if they followed Spencer in believing that human evolution was upward, they wished to study the stage on the evolutionary scale at which their characters had arrived. To do so required the scrutiny of what Zola named the "determining causes of phenomena." These causes were, of course, heredity and environment and the moment in history in which the characters lived. The proximate causes, the data of psychology and sociology being limited, were the only ones which could be ascertained with any degree of scientific certainty. This suggests the reason why the literary naturalists did not write historical novels. It was not possible to bring a Pericles or a Cotton Mather into the laboratory of the experimental novelist.

Fate was a word which they used in a special sense or avoided altogether. It could not mean any kind of theological predestination or any force operating on man which intervened in the natural order. The extent to which man possessed any freedom of will was arguable in the early years; he was generally permitted only a modicum of it. This issue was soon to be fought out by philosophers like William James and John Dewey in whose thought evolution played a large part. The decisions they arrived at helped to change the subsequent course of literary as well as philosophical naturalism.

Strangely enough there was less agreement on the nature of Nature than on any other problem that had to be faced. Nature could be viewed variously as hostile to man, or indifferent, or beneficent. These contradictions were possible because the hypothesis of natural evolution was the central argument. Nature could be seen as sublime and awe-inspiring in its universal dynamism if one were willing to take the waste of species and individuals as incidental to the grand upward movement. But as soon as one counted the cost in human terms, Nature must be viewed as Tennyson sees it: "careless of the single life" and of the thousand types now gone. Yet Nature was resorted to or appealed to inevitably by every literary naturalist. If it is not alluded to specifically, it appears in symbol and imagery.

Hamlin Garland (1860–1940) was the first novelist to domesticate literary naturalism in America, but he went only a short distance towards the naturalism of Norris and Dreiser. Having known as a boy the soul-destroying struggle of farm life in Wisconsin and Iowa, he produced his best work on this theme, in the stories collected in *Main-Travelled Roads* (1891) and *Prairie Folks* (1893), and his short novel, *Rose of Dutcher's Coolly* (1895). Herbert Spencer, he said, had given him a "measure of scientific peace," yet he did not read his master through to the end. His sympathies were too close to the farmers whose existence was unceasingly threatened by storms and droughts. He was not comforted by the idea that in some far-off time man and nature will be allies. He felt, rather, the force of Nature's forgetfulness of man.

Garland was one of the "discoverers" of Stephen Crane (1871–1900). Both Garland and Howells were quick to perceive the great talent evident in Crane's *Maggie: A Girl of the Streets* (1893) and were his champions in the difficult days before his *Red Badge of Courage* (1895) suddenly made him welcome in the publishing houses. In his honest depiction of the depths to which man can sink Crane was far more bold and searching than the two older novelists who were his champions, just as he excelled them greatly as an artist.

It is difficult to estimate just how much Crane owed to the increasing vogue of literary naturalism. He was frequently referred to as a follower of Zola, but he refused to acknowledge any discipleship. When he was living in England, he complained to Huneker that people at parties asked him how much money he made and from which French realist he planned to steal his next book. Yet Ford Madox Ford observed that Crane's explosive denials that he had read the French naturalists were not to be believed. When the conversation got around to Flaubert or Maupassant his comments displayed a considerable acquaintance with their work.

Some scholars maintain that Crane pilfered scenes from *L'Assommoir* and *La Débâcle* for use in *Maggie* and *The Red Badge of Courage*. The evidence is too slight to justify the charge. The supposed resemblances to Zola in Crane's fiction would seem to be fortuitous. He was by nature a rebel, a hater of sham and gentility. He knew life in the Bowery at firsthand and he had befriended more than one Maggie. As for war and what it does to men, he thought and dreamed about it as a boy and listened avidly to what Civil War veterans could remember of their experiences. Nevertheless, in two respects Crane's work has close affinities with Zola's, although one does not have to predicate any direct influence in order to account for them. It might be said that he followed the ideal of the experimental novel in making "clinical" studies of particular passions — usually the passion of fear, as in *The Red Badge of Courage*, "The Open Boat," and "The Blue Hotel." Secondly he left nothing out when he was describing a "milieu" which was filthy and sordid. There are enough horrors of this kind in "An Experiment in Misery" (a night in a New York flophouse) to satisfy any literary naturalist.

But these affinities are not strong enough to give a story by Crane any of the tone or texture of a novel by Zola. The distance between aspiration and outcome, between appearance and reality so fascinated Crane that in most of his work irony plays constantly over the surface and gives his fiction its characteristic tone. To the men in the open boat the safe shore is in sight, but the deadly surf lies between. The windmill tower (probably deserted) is in plain view on the beach, standing like a giant with its back to the plight of the ants. It represents ironically "the serenity of nature amid the struggles of the individual — nature in the mind, and nature in the vision of men." Here, explicitly, Crane connects the irony which is central to his vision with the indifference of nature, but this is one of the few places in which he attempts to explain it at all. It simply exists in human life as something to be encountered and recognized.

In contrast to Crane whose debt to literary naturalism is small, Frank Norris (1870–1902) was its avowed champion. His brother once remarked that "he was never without a yellow-covered novel of [Zola] in his hand." This corroborative evidence is hardly needed. Norris not only tried to follow the method and capture the spirit of Zola. Many of his scenes are borrowed and Americanized. Norris had to get up his naturalism. The son of a wealthy San

Franciscan, he had the advantages of a Harvard education and of art study in London and Paris. His early enthusiasm for Froissart and the *Chanson de Roland* made him for the time a devoted romantic and accounts for the romantic lapses in his fiction. Indeed Norris, during his brief writing career — from *Moran of the Lady Letty* (1898) through *The Pit* (1903) — never sorted out his convictions. In the same work romantic episodes jostle Spencerian doctrine and socialistic theories.

While he was a student at Harvard, writing under the direction of a remarkable teacher, Lewis E. Gates, he began two novels in the naturalistic vein. *McTeague* is a study of a stupid brute of a man whom sexual passion and greed destroy. *Vandover and the Brute* (published posthumously in 1914) employs another favorite theme of the literary naturalists. Vandover is a man of refinement and an artist, but he starts on the backward path when the brute in him is aroused by lust and drink. In this novel Norris carried the idea of regression to the ultimate. Vandover is finally afflicted with lycanthropy and we leave him at the end growling like a beast, padding around his miserable room on all fours.

McTeague: A Story of San Francisco (1899) is the first avowedly naturalistic novel in American literature. Norris cut it carefully to pattern and was rewarded with the vituperation of the critics. (One reviewer said it should have been called *McTeague: A Study in Stinks.*) McTeague has come a certain distance up the evolutionary scale, having established himself with middle-class complacency as a dentist in San Francisco's Polk Street. But "the evil of an entire race flowed in his veins." By chance his best friend brings Trina Sieppe to his dentist's chair. He desires her and soon marries her. (The gross feeding at the wedding breakfast is worthy of Zola.) Then trouble begins. Trina has won $5,000 in a lottery and its possession turns her natural thriftiness into inordinate greed. Lust and greed grind out the horrible conclusion of the marriage, at the moment when McTeague murders her in the schoolhouse where she is working as a scrubwoman. The rest of the novel is a melodramatic manhunt, ending in death in the desert. Aside from the melodrama of the last sixty pages, there are some other deviations from strict naturalism. The subplots have more than a hint of Dickensian sentimentality in them. And though Norris skillfully describes the milieu of McTeague and Trina, the crowds below them in Polk Street actually serve no functional purpose in the story. But *McTeague* is no doubt an "experimental novel" in that it attempts to study what will happen when two such natures are brought together.

After *McTeague* Norris fell away from his professed creed. *Blix* (1899) is a slick success-story. In the Jack London manner, *A Man's Woman* (1900) mixes romance, love and honor, the struggle for existence in an Arctic expedition, and propaganda for the "new woman." At this point Norris returned to the fold. When he began on his epic of wheat, which was to require three novels in the telling, he wrote to a friend: "Now I think I know where I am and what game I play the best. The Wheat series will be straight naturalism with all the guts I can get into it."

As things turned out *The Pit*, the second novel in the series, was far from straight naturalism, and even in the first novel, *The Octopus* (1901), Norris did not observe all the rules of the game. *The Octopus* has the immense scope required of a Zolaesque novel and in it there are many big scenes full of the vitality characteristic of the genre: the ploughing of the fecund wheat-land in the spring; the gargantuan revels at Annixter's barn; Dyke's mad race, against capture or death, in the stolen locomotive; the bloody jack-rabbit hunt and the feast that follows. Yet the novel breaks apart because Norris was pulled in two directions. Until we come within a hundred pages of the end, we seem to be reading a novel about the class struggle, written in the naturalistic mode. All the elements are there, the hardworking but grasping wheat farmers, the wicked capitalists, and their hirelings who control the railroad Octopus which ruthlessly deprives them of their rights and of the results of their labor. There is even a "Red" who spells this all out for Presley, the young writer who is Norris' observer on the scene. But when Presley faces Shelgrim, the president of the railroad, he meekly listens and learns his lesson. Shelgrim informs him that Wheat is one force, the Railroad another, and the law of supply and demand govern them both. "Men have only little to do in the whole business."

Relying on Herbert Spencer to bring him through, Norris patches up an optimistic conclusion. The power of the Octopus and the maturing of the wheat reveal no malevolence in Nature; only a colossal indifference, a vast trend toward appointed goals. The agony of human defeat sends not the faintest tremor through her prodigious mechanism. Force only, exists, and men fall beside it, mere nothings, mere animalculae. The Wheat, wrapped in Nirvanic calm, grows steadily under the night, "alone with the stars and with God."

With Frank Norris naturalism was an acquired creed, the result of reading and thinking and, certainly, of a revolt, with some guilt in the process, against the gentility to which he had been born. The case was different with Jack London (1876–1916), likewise a son of San Francisco. London's life-story is perfect material for a naturalistic novel, as he himself proved when he transferred it, with few disguises, into his autobiographical *Martin Eden* (1909). As a boy he was forced to be a man. At the age of sixteen he was accepted among the outcast oyster pirates of San Francisco bay and had proved his virility by harboring on his boat the queen of the tribe. He knew all about sex before he had heard of the thing called love, a passion he deals with in his novels as if he had recently learned to kiss by the book. He was inordinately proud of his manhood, which he was constantly testing as a sailor, horseman, slugger, and drinker. At seventeen he was doing a man's work before the mast. During the panic of '93 he joined Coxey's army and saved his division by his power over men, though he deserted the cause at Hannibal, Missouri. In 1897, at the age of twenty, he was again a superman in the Alaska gold strike.

A few months at the University of California disgusted him, but he acquired there the habit of reading and he took down huge though adulterated doses of Darwin and Marx indiscriminately. Success as a writer came almost at once. Soon after the turn of the century he was making thousands a year, but he was always in debt. Two conflicts began to wrack him. He paraded as a Socialist and millions over the world were moved by his belligerent signature, "Yours for the Revolution." But Socialist doctrine cannot be reconciled with the kind of evolutionism which London was forcing on a friend in 1899: "The different families of man must yield to law — to LAW, inexorable, blind, unreasoning law, which has no knowledge of good or ill, right or wrong." A still more agonizing conflict developed in his career as a writer. Magazines were ready to buy any shoddy product from his workshop. Yet he knew that he possessed great talent and was ridden by the hope of producing a masterpiece. Add to these conflicts his disappointments as a lover and father (he begot no men-children and his two daughters rejected him) and one has the clues to his suicide at forty.

What did Jack London make of all he assumed he knew about naturalistic doctrine? He was convinced, most of the time, that the strong survive because they have a drive that is irresistible. The struggle for survival is the theme of one story after another. The settings change from the sea, to the Klondike, to the prize-ring, to the class-war, but the theme is the same in *The Sea-Wolf* (1904), *The Game* (1905), and *Burning Daylight* (1910).

The kind of man who survives and leads is the blond beast, the superman for whom a mate equally scornful of convention usually waits in the next chapter. Sometimes his admirable brutishness sleeps beneath a veneer of civilization and has to be wakened. London's notion of reversion to the primitive is an interesting variation on the naturalistic idea of devolution, for to London it is a wholly admirable transformation. The dog who becomes a wolf in *The Call of the Wild* (1903) is still London's most popular hero.* Socialist though he professed to be, London believed that the mass of men must be ruled by the few — because "most men are fools, and therefore must be taken care of by the few men who are wise." The "few" who were fit to rule were inevitably Anglo-Saxons.

Such was the "inexorable, blind, unreasoning" law which London professed to believe. Actually he compromised most of the time with the conventional morality of his age. His ruthless heroes do not sweep all before them; his mate-women are as chaste as his publishers required. This characteristic pulling back could be illustrated from a dozen stories but the autobiographical *Martin Eden* will serve best since there is so much of London's own life in it. Martin is a natural man, whose maleness attracts the refined and intellectual Ruth Morse. She yields to him because she can't help herself, being a mate-woman by nature. She rejects him when he turns Socialist, however, and then seeks him again when he becomes famous as a writer. What

---

* London was fond of the word wolf. He used to sign his letters "Wolf." The word turns up in titles to his stories, and the ranch house he built at the end of his life was called "Wolf House."

can the next stage be in Martin's struggle upward? An ending like London's own, a sense of futility and unful-fillment, and then suicide.

London's supermen have a habit of fizzling out. The lines of verse which he prefixed to *Martin Eden* are pro-phetic of his own end and a summary of much of his fiction.

> Let me live out my years in the heat of blood!
> Let me lie drunken with the dreamer's wine!
> Let me not see this soul-house built of mud
> Go toppling to the dust a vacant shrine!

Compared with the meteoric rise of Norris and Jack London, Dreiser's career moves at an elephant's gait. As a thinker Dreiser (1871–1945) was seldom to be found twice in the same place. Now that the facts of his life are known we begin to understand why he twisted and turned as he did, and why shortly before he died he became a Communist, and yet commented so oddly on what he had just done: "What the world needs is more spiritual character. The true religion is in Matthew."

The circumstances of his upbringing were decisive. His family was poor; his father's Catholicism ineffectual in teaching him the validity of moral ideas. When he broke away and was on his own in Chicago, he fumbled in business and in love. The pattern of his youthful years was similar to that of many second generation immigrants who tried to reject the culture of their parents. Thus far he re-sembled one of his own weak-willed heroes — groping, uncertain, unequal to life. The newspaper days that fol-lowed opened his eyes to the world of business and political power. Not all people, he discovered, are weak and sub-missive. Balanced against them are strong-willed individ-uals who get what they want. His pity went out to the weak; his admiration to the strong. Years later in a chapter of his *Hey Rub-A-Dub-Dub* (1920), "Equation Inevitable," he tried to make a formula out of what he had observed. He held (for the time, at least) that "there is, on the one hand, inherent in the chemic impulses and appetites of life (which man does not create), an instinct toward individuality which may be for good or for ill, plus, on the other hand, this law of balance or equation but over which neither the humanitarian nor the idealist, any more than the criminal or indifferent or self-seeking realist, has any control whatever." Nature desires equilibrium, and balances a St. Francis or a Buddha against an Alexander VI or a Morgan.

All his life Dreiser was a seeker. When he began to read in earnest, the Social Darwinists held sway over him. When he was working on *The Financier* (1912), he was fascinated by the explanation of human behavior in physiochemical terms which he found in Jacques Loeb's *The Mechanistic Conception of Life*. Towards the end he discovered Thoreau and thought he found an answer in the Thoreauvian fusion of science and intuition. He was also attracted to the quietism of the Friends.

There are several reasons why Dreiser's naturalistic beliefs helped him as a novelist and why they do not seem so antiquated as those which animated the fiction of Norris and London. In the first place they were always for Dreiser "tentatives," as Robert Frost would say. They did not preempt the mysteries of human existence. His predecessors shouted with Whitman "Hurrah for positive science! Long live exact demonstration." As the "scientific" tenets they used have been carried out with the rubbish, the actions or characters which they validated have also gone into the discard. Dreiser does not begin a novel with a flourish of hypotheses about his characters. Generalizations come later, when situations have been established from which they may be drawn.

Dreiser wrote his novels out of conviction and from the best knowledge of human nature with which his endless quest for answers could provide him. Thus when he wrote *Sister Carrie* (1900) he was spellbound by the Spencerian idea of the stage of civilization to which modern man (and woman) had attained. When he wrote *The Financier* he was not only calling on his memories of business leaders and his knowledge of the career of Charles T. Yerkes, who becomes the Cowperwood of the novel. He thought he had found some ideas in Jacques Loeb which helped to explain aggressive and ruthless American individuals of this type, and these ideas he used to buttress his novel. But he seldom made the mistake, as Norris and London did, of using mutually contradictory concepts in a single work. The ideas which inform *Sister Carrie* or *The Bulwark* (1946) work together in each instance and are sufficient for what they are required to do. The worlds they help to explain are wholly different. Dreiser seldom let his different worlds collide, though they did certainly once when he struggled, just before his death, to finish *The Stoic* (1947), the last novel of the trilogy of business. The mood in which he had conceived *The Financier* and *The Titan* (1914) had long since passed. The grand climax of Cowperwood's career, which ends in defeat and not victory, is missed and the novel drifts off into Berenice's conversion to oriental mysticism.

One is obliged to answer the question why Dreiser's fiction offended his fellow-Americans for so long a time. As Mencken observed, few writers have absorbed so much abuse and only a Dreiser could have persisted in the face of it. One can understand this opposition if one will consider how heretical a novel *Sister Carrie* was, a "banned book" that had to wait twelve years for public sale in this country.

Carrie Meeber comes to Chicago from Columbia City.

She finds work but the pay is low and factory life intolerable. She drifts into a liaison with a drummer, then leaves him after a time for an older man, a saloon manager who deserts his wife for her and robs the safe in order that they may escape to New York. As her new lover drifts downward in the social scale, because he is too old to make a new life for himself, she drifts upward and becomes a successful actress. Without compunction she lets Hurstwood drop out of her existence. Too weak of will to struggle further, he turns on the gas in a shabby lodging house. Carrie sits by her window, dreaming of the happiness she may never feel.

What was so deeply shocking here? Though Carrie "sleeps" with two men to whom she is not married, the details of sexual intercourse are never mentioned. Hurstwood, it might seem, is duly punished for his moral lapse. But Dreiser implies that there are many — how many? — Carrie Meebers in America who use their sexuality for provender as naturally as they might use any other natural gift. She had, it is true, a few twinges of conscience and she thinks of herself, now and then, as a married woman. She is not even a courtesan in the grand manner, calculating, professional, and because she is damned, acceptable.

But this is not all. What offended most was the inevitability of Carrie's rise to fame and fortune. Braced by his naturalistic belief in Carrie's tropism, which draws her towards beauty and success, Dreiser lifts her to a higher point on the evolutionary scale than her lovers attained. But he leaves her there, because she can, in the nature of things, go no farther. She can see into the beautiful walled city where Ames, the man of culture, the man who really understands her, lives, but she cannot enter it. Nor can other Americans like her — Clyde Griffiths of *An American Tragedy* (1925) is such another — enter there. The happiness which pulsates within these walls they may dream of, but they can never know it. The "walled city" was Dreiser's discovery, and a very great one it was, for Americans have falsely believed anyone can get to the stars if only he struggles hard enough. Carrie is cheated of her starry victory in the end, but not because she chose to be a bad girl. Nature had interdicted her.

IV

Though Dreiser had admirers in his early, difficult years, he did not have imitators. During the first twenty years of the new century novelists were little influenced by literary naturalism. Occasionally the muckrakers adopted naturalistic techniques in order to make more vivid the social evils they were trying to expose, but their novels were not shaped by any consistent naturalistic theory of life. The two leading novelists of the time, Edith Wharton and Willa Cather, had, of course, no alliances with literary naturalism.

When Sherwood Anderson appeared on the horizon the case was altered. He was an avowed admirer of Dreiser, praising him for his honesty and boldness and as the pioneer and hero in the modern movement in American prose writing. Because he had shown the way, no novelist need hesitate before the task of putting his hands upon his material.

One will not find in Anderson any echoes from the Social Darwinists, nor any techniques learned from Zola but his connections with literary naturalism are none the less clear. One sees this in his sympathy for his "grotesques" who have not been equal to the struggle for life and have become stunted, "regressed," or, as he calls them, "queer." One sees it too in his remarkable studies of the hungers and uncertainties of his adolescents for whom emergence into maturity, particularly sexual maturity, is difficult and painful. To many of these adolescents the horses which they tend as swipes are objects of worship because they are symbols of sexual power. They admire Negroes because they are affectionate and uncomplicated. This admiration for the primitive qualities of the Negro was shown by Anderson most pointedly in "A Meeting South," the story of a veteran of the World War who had been badly injured in an airplane crash. He cannot sleep except out of doors, with the Negroes near, singing and making love.

> I have come out of the big house, me and my bottle, and I creep along, low on the ground, 'til I get up close. There I lie. I'm a little drunk. It all makes me happy. I can sleep some, on the ground like that, when the niggers are singing, when no one knows I'm there.

The most completely naturalistic story Anderson wrote, and one of his few masterpieces, is "Death in the Woods." It is the tale of an old woman who struggles to keep food in the bellies of her worthless husband and son. When she dies, alone and defeated, in the woods, the dogs who have scented the food she carries perform a kind of ritualistic dance around her. But in death she is beautiful again, as she must have been as a young girl. In 1937 Anderson explained what his intention in the story was. His words show where he stands among the literary naturalists.

> The story has its particular form . . . the young man and the German fighting over the girl in the road, the son bringing his mistress to his mother's house, the butcher, half-grudgingly and yet out of pity, giving her the meat bones, the dogs circling in the mysterious moonlit night in the forest, the men and boys of the town hurrying out of the town to find the body. . . . What is wanted is something beyond the horizon, to retain the sense of mystery in life while showing at the same time, at what cost our ordinary animal hungers are sometimes fed.[2]

The last sentence in this explication must hold us for a moment for it provides another key to Anderson's naturalism. He differs markedly from most of the older literary naturalists in that he permits his characters, even the most bewildered of them, at least a momentary flash of self-illumination, a glimpse of the wonder of life. This epiphanal moment is usually the climax of the Anderson story and he concentrates in it all the symbolic meaning which he can command.

In the generation of novelists who flourished in the period between the two wars there are many literary naturalists. In one guise or another naturalism informs the fiction of Sinclair Lewis, John Dos Passos, Hemingway, Faulkner, Erskine Caldwell, Nelson Algren, John O'Hara, and John Steinbeck.[3] To avoid a review of some of the careers discussed in the last chapter and to keep the present chapter within bounds, it will be useful to select three literary naturalists of this later generation and let them represent the rest of the company. Farrell must be one of the three because he is the novelist who carried on most avowedly in the tradition. Thomas Wolfe and Conrad Aiken deserve attention because their careers illuminate the course of literary naturalism in special ways.

James T. Farrell has frequently declared himself the disciple of Dreiser and Anderson and is proud of belonging to what he has called the "bottom dog" school of literature. It is clear that the chief motivation in his writing has been a desire to show what American boys and girls have to face whose lives are spiritually poverty-stricken. Thus his Studs Lonigan and Danny O'Neill (his best creations) and to a lesser degree his other boys and young men, are pictured as bewildered and morally uncertain as they struggle with the urban realities surrounding them. Farrell wishes to speak for them because he once knew the same problems, doubts, and moods. As a boy he often seemed "lost in an inner state of bewildered loneliness," with no realization that other boys were just as confused and bewildered. Out of his conviction that modern urban life isolates and estranges individuals and that this isolation deserved novelistic treatment, came his effort "to present a realism of everyday life, a realism involving the continuity of everyday life, a realism dealing with the conduct of urban childhood and youth." In this respect Farrell is at one with many of the other latter-day naturalists who tend to specialize in a particular segment of society and to confine themselves to a particular scene. Thus Algren takes for his narrow province skid row in Chicago; O'Hara specializes in the country club set in two or three cities in central Pennsylvania.

With few exceptions Farrell stuck to this theme of urban adolescence almost to the point of exhausting it. A prolific writer, in the naturalistic tradition of bigness — Farrell could be counted on for at least a book a year — he seldom strays very far from Chicago's Jackson Park and the Bourbon Palace, Fifty-eighth Street and the Wagon Call Department of the Continental Express Company. The boys attend St. Patrick's Grammar School and the families who can afford it send the older girls to St. Paul's, but are considered snobby when they do. Occasionally Farrell writes a story about Hollywood or Paris or New York, but even then his leading character is likely to be a refugee from the neighborhood of Chicago's Washington Park, and we find him on the last page packing his belongings and heading home, as Bernard Clare does after experimenting with love and novel-writing in New York.

Farrell is not a master of the short story, though his collected stories must be popular since they are frequently issued in reprint editions. He needs the scope which he gives himself in the three Studs Lonigan novels and the four Danny O'Neill novels. The Studs Lonigan trilogy is undoubtedly his best work. The chief reason is that we see all that happens to Studs, and to his friends and his family, through his eyes and consciousness. The point of view does not shift from character to character as it does in the Danny O'Neill series so frequently that the story seems to belong as much to Danny's father as it does to Danny.

Equally important is the fact that Farrell had considered carefully the pressures which form boys like Studs and precisely why he must be the kind of failure that he is. The Studs Lonigan novels originated in a short story, "Studs," which Farrell wrote for a composition course when he was a student at the University of Chicago. When he began working on *Young Lonigan,* he already had in mind what the end would be; how Studs, once a boy with some pride and imagination, would be dead at twenty-six, his dreams and ambitions aborted by the poison of his useless life.

Farrell had found a theme that was new and his technique for presenting it in fiction was equal to his insight. Studs already stands out as a unique character in American fiction, though he is kin to Henry Fleming of *The Red Badge of Courage* and Clyde Griffiths of *An American Tragedy.* Why he is a person and not merely a type can best be understood by noting how Farrell differentiated him from the young delinquent.

He is not really a hard guy. He is a normal young American of his time and his class. His values become the values of his world. He has as many good impulses as normal beings have. In time, because of defeat, of frustration, of a total situation characterized by spiritual poverty, these good impulses are expressed more and more in the stream of his reverie. Here we find the source of Studs's constant dream of himself. Studs's dream of himself changes in character as the story progresses. In the beginning, it is a vision of what he is going to be. He is a boy waiting at the threshold of life. His dream of himself is a romantic projection of his future, conceived in the terms and the values of his world. In time, this dream of himself turns backward. It is no longer a romantic projection of things to come. More and more it becomes a nostalgic image turned toward the past.[4]

The four Danny O'Neill novels are inferior to the Studs Lonigan trilogy — and for several reasons. In the first place Farrell has two households which he must drive ahead in tandem or in parallel. So the reader is moved back and forth between the quarrels and reconciliations of Danny's parents and the goings-on in the flat where he lives with his bawdy-tongued grandmother, his shoe-salesman Uncle Al, and his dipsomaniac Aunt Peg. The details pile up but somehow they do not *add* up. The intent is to show them as the matrix of young Danny O'Neill, but he seems rather to move through events than to be shaped by them. We are convinced that Studs Lonigan fell and we know the process of his fall. It is not clear how Danny rises. The literary naturalist has generally found it easier to describe the process which brings about defeat rather than that which ends in spiritual or moral victory.

Thomas Wolfe (1900–1938) would resent being called a literary naturalist. He disliked labels of any kind and the critics pinned many different ones on him in their efforts to describe this phenomenal man. He was edgy with his friends when they drew comparisons between his work and that of other writers. When Scott Fitzgerald once urged him to be more selective, to take out rather than put in, he answered: "Why does it follow that if a man writes a book that is not like Madame Bovary it is inevitably like Zola?" He said to Sherwood Anderson that there might be better ways to write a novel than to "pour it out, boil it out, flood it out," but he had to work in his own way — "and it would be wrong to worry about doing it Flaubert's way, or Hemingway's way, or Henry James' way."

Whether he admired the naturalists' way or not makes little difference. His manner of working resembles theirs and so, much of the time, do the results he achieved. He was also a romantic. These two conflicting impulses in his life — the naturalist's desire to experience all, especially all that is sordid and gross, and the romantic's search for the way out and the way up — produced many badly muddled passages in his novels. But in the end he succeeded in resolving the conflict and had begun to present a view of life and of America which was his own.

Like the naturalists he had to tell all. It is well known that he and his editors labored for months to get his huge piles of manuscript reduced to book size. Wolfe would set out to cut a chapter only to find that the new version was far larger than the first. His first two novels, *Look Homeward, Angel* (1929) and *Of Time and the River* (1935), were pressed into shape with the expert help of Maxwell Perkins of Scribner's. His other two novels (posthumously published), *The Web and the Rock* (1939) and *You Can't Go Home Again* (1940), would never have reached the printers if Edward C. Aswell of Harper's had not performed the same kind of operation on them. As Wolfe toiled at his bales of pages, characters and episodes multiplied under his hand. When he was at work on his first novel, he was suddenly overwhelmed with the fact that the material he had hoped to deal with in a single book covered 150 years of history, "demanded the action of more than 2000 characters, and would in final design include almost every racial type and social class of American life." Here was stuff, not for a naturalistic trilogy but for a heptalogy! In the four novels which stand complete and in the fragment of a fifth (*The Hills Beyond*, 1941), Wolfe took one hero, Eugene Gant, through boyhood and young manhood, started over again with the life of George Webber (in the posthumous novels), and had begun to turn into fiction the past of his ancestors. Wolfe did have a plan for the whole vast work and he referred to his accumulating manuscripts as "the book." If he had lived beyond his brief thirty-nine years, we might have had a work on the scale of Zola's Rougon-Macquart novels.

In his passion for the details of daily living, occupations, eating, drinking, traveling, Wolfe also showed his naturalistic bias. In *The Story of a Novel* (1936) he tells how he filled his ledgers with vast stores of recollected fact which he might wish to use in *Look Homeward, Angel.*

It included everything from gigantic and staggering lists of the towns, cities, counties, states, and countries I had been in, to minutely thorough, desperately evocative descriptions of the undercarriage, the springs, wheels, flanges, axle rods, color, weight, and quality of the day coach of an American railway train. There were lists of the rooms and houses in which I had lived or in which I had slept for at least a night, together with the most accurate and evocative descriptions of those rooms that I could write — their size, their shape, the color and design of the wallpaper, the way a towel hung down, the way a chair creaked, a streak of water rust upon the ceiling. There were countless charts, catalogues, descriptions that I can only classify here under the general heading of Amount and Number.

Wolfe's first novel is the most naturalistic of the four. The circumstances of his life through his twenty-ninth year gave it this bias. Proud, sensitive, hungry for experience as a boy and youth, loving yet rebelling violently from his father and mother, disgusted with the narrowness of life in the small city of Asheville, the Altamont of *Look Homeward, Angel,* Wolfe poured into his first work all his memories of his life until the time he made his escape. For the most part they were bitter memories, of frightening family quarrels, of his mother's greed for the possession of real estate, of his father's drinking, of friends who betrayed him, of loves which were sordid or cold. The naturalism of the novel is evinced in its smashing scenes (Eugene's first drunken binge, the death of brother Ben), in the grotesque characters (there is only one lovely and lovable person in the novel), in the grossness of Negro life, the lore of brothels, the ruttishness of Eugene's weeks in Norfolk doing war work. It is betrayed on almost every page by apostrophes to chance and fate and humanity's blind striving; and in such constant phrases as "the slow inexorable chemistry of union and repellance" (in the "alignment" of the Gants) and "the terrible destiny of his blood."

Caught though he is in this web of inheritance and environment, Eugene is at heart a romantic, an Apollo in the house of Admetus. He is fascinated but he is also revolted by "the waste, the confusion, the blind cruelty" of the lives to which he is bound. His one will is to escape.

It was also Wolfe's. The rest of his life he spent like Ulysses in wanderings which by good chance brought him home. Having escaped from the south which he hated for its Puritanism and poverty and zeal for making money, he reached out for answers at Harvard, in the ant-life of great cities, in the strangeness and age of Europe, in the houses of the rich and the studios of artists, in a long and tortured love affair. The years of the depression nearly killed his love for America and his faith in its future. He vented his disgust in satire, for which he showed a surprising aptitude. Gradually his feeling for America was purged of despair. He untangled himself from the giant web in which he had been caught, "the product of my huge inheritance." He found at the end "the rock" for which he had been searching. The faith by which he lived in his last months was a blend of naturalism and humanism. Though he may not have realized it, this faith resembles that of the philosophical naturalists of his day (such men as Dewey and Santayana) who stressed events and relations, process and character, essence and flux. In his excellent study of Wolfe (*New Directions*, 1947) Herbert J. Muller defined this turn in naturalistic thought and Wolfe's connection with it.

The fact is that the only religion possible for many men of

good will is a religion of humanity, a natural idealism. And at least a robust faith is possible on these terms. Wolfe is in line with such thoroughly characteristic Americans as William James and Oliver Wendell Holmes, Jr. Far from being dismayed by their acknowledgment of ultimate uncertainty, they were the more devoted to the democratic ideal; for they regarded the good life as an adventure in an evolving, unfinished world, an experiment that is more hopeful as well as more dangerous because its conditions are not absolute and unalterable — an experiment that both permits and demands freedom.

There are few kin of Sister Carrie or McTeague or even Eugene Gant in the fictional world of Conrad Aiken (b. 1889) and when they do appear, briefly, they are used for contrast. Often they are symbolic projections of lust, hate, or vengefulness in the reveries and nightmares of the main characters. Aiken's world is inhabited by sensitive, well-educated people — poets, artists, professors. They belong to clubs and when they were children, their families went to the seashore in the summer. But education, sophisticated experience of the world, hypersensitivity, knowledge of music and art and literature have brought them no peace. In each novel or story by Aiken we are presented with a crisis. When it is resolved the character is purged of his foul dreams and on the way to a cure — or has plunged deeper toward madness.

The epigraph to his *Great Circle* (1933), taken from John Marston's *Scourge of Villanie*, explains Aiken's version of naturalism.

> O can it be the spirit's function,
> The soule, not subject to dimension,
> Should be made slave to reprehension
> Of crafty nature's paint? Fie! can our soule
> Be underling to such a vile controule?

What troubles Aiken's characters is the appalling contrast between their aspirations — to love well, write or paint well, to be good fathers, hold friends close and dear —

and their inner, deeper life planted in them by "crafty nature." There are no morals in the blood stream, "no morals in hand or claw or mouth." Which is reality: "the butcher-shop meat reality of life" (being born, the traumas of childhood, the "foul bitterness of death") or the illusion of well-being brought by a chance love affair?

Aiken was the first American novelist to make full use of Freudian theory. He was already writing "pseudo-psychological" stories (so he once said) for the *Advocate* when he was at Harvard. (He was graduated in 1912.) Committed to poetry for more than a decade, he published his first volume of short stories, *Bring! Bring!* in 1925; his first novel, *Blue Voyage*, in 1927. His long training in poetry made him the better writer of fiction. His stories are notable for their precision of form, subtlety and beauty of expression, and their swift power of evoking scenes and persons. Every few years an oncoming critic rediscovers Aiken. Sometime enough readers to make a public will wake up to the fact that he is a master who has been unaccountably neglected.

A brief synopsis of an Aiken novel can give no indication of his ability to lay bare the hidden impulses, the moods and dreams of his characters, but it can serve to show the kind of themes he chooses. In *Blue Voyage* we see a young writer on his way to England to compel the girl he loves to love him. The discovery that she is on board and engaged to another man sets up such a turmoil in his life that the voyage becomes a nightmare to him. In *Great Circle* (1933), a novel which Freud thought a masterpiece, a professor returns home to Cambridge to spy on his wife's infidelity and punish her for it. Before the story's end he has revisited his childhood (there the trouble lies) and has told his woe to a psychiatrist friend. (This time there is a cure.) *King Coffin* (1935) is a study in egomania. A man sets out to find, follow, and eventually murder some faceless person chosen from the crowd. (The murder does not take place.) A quarrel between husband and wife is the center of *Conversation* (1940). She is punishing him for not appreciating how much she has sacrificed for his career as an artist; he makes her suffer because she insists that he give up his raffish artist friends who believe in his creative powers. The pawn in this tense game of spoken cruelties and bristling silences is their little girl, Buzzer, one of Aiken's most charming characters.

If a pedantic reader wished to take the trouble, he could scribble in the margins of an Aiken novel or short story "projection," "incest motive," "Oedipus complex," "regression," "repetition-compulsion." The Freudian facts of life are there, certainly, but they are named only when the characters would naturally make use of the terms. His characters are people; not "My patient, X" or "A young man who was brought to me for treatment."

In *Great Circle* Aiken permits Professor Cather to come on the important truth which reconciles for him (and apparently for Aiken himself) the lower and the higher halves of man's existence. May it not be true that consciousness itself is a kind of dishonesty, "a false simplification of animal existence," just as the animate must be a natural distortion of the inanimate? Each step, perhaps, is a new kind of dishonesty, "a dishonesty inherent in evolution." If this is so, the fluidity of life can never have the immobile integrity of the rock from which it came. "It will only be honest rock again when it is dead. And in the meantime, if it suffers, if it is aware that it suffers, if it says that it is aware that it suffers, and if it is aware that it cannot say completely *why* it suffers, or in severance from what, that's all you can ask of it. In sum — idiot! — it is only unhappy because it is no longer for the moment rock."

What is permitted to the modern man who is fully conscious and suffers because he is? At least he may enjoy the "minor advantages of the temporary emancipation from rock, the pleasures of dishonesty, or treason [to rock], to which evolution has led us."

v

Literary naturalism refuses to die. The critics who demand its death fail to comprehend why it has in America the ability to renew itself decade by decade. One can predict that it will be with us for some time to come, because of its essential flexibility.

We need to be reminded that naturalism can claim status as a system of thought. It traces its ancestry from Aristotle and the Stoics down through Hobbes and Spinoza to Huxley and beyond. Incapable of being precisely defined in any century before the nineteenth, naturalism at last was able, under the influence of the evolutionary hypothesis, to "put man and his experience squarely into the Nature over against which he had hitherto been set." Naturalism consequently became identified with biological evolution and the descent of man.

But philosophical naturalism moved on, the chief modifiers of the tradition in America being William James, John Dewey, and George Santayana. The earlier rigidities were relaxed. One member of the modern school finds himself warranted in declaring that eternity is not an attribute of authentic Being (of course), "but a quality of human vision; and divinity belongs, not to what is existent, but to what man discerns in imagination." Modern naturalism has a cheerful tone because it finds much good within actual existence. When in 1944 a group of philosophical naturalists put together the symposium *Naturalism and the Human Spirit*, they were frank to say that one of their purposes was to rescue their faith from the corruptions inflicted on it by their nineteenth century predecessors. They declared that the world they sought to explain "is the world of natural existence, since only this world can be empirically authenticated." But they were also intensely concerned "with the aspirations of the human spirit — its love of freedom, its sense of beauty, its hope of creating a better civilization."

Spencer's name was once a household word; today few Americans could list the philosophical naturalists of our time. But nearly every child who has gone to a public school has had the chance of becoming an unwitting follower of John Dewey. The schools of education have attended to this matter well. As a result philosophical naturalism comes nearer to being a universal American belief than any other one might name. And one might expect contemporary fiction to reflect its influence, as it does.

There are many characteristics of modern American life which have helped to keep literary naturalism alive. Americans, by tradition, are environmentalists. Almost from the beginning we have been proud of our regional differences. In spite of the standardization of modern life we still differentiate dozens of regional types: crackers, wool hats, poor whites, Yankees, up-staters (in New York), Down-Easters. We have tribal names and totem animals for our states, often solemnly authenticated by legislation. We want our novelists to tell us how the slums of one city differ from those of another, and more minutely, how to differentiate the particular Chicago *milieu* that shaped Studs Lonigan from the one that produced Nick Romano of Willard Motley's *Knock on Any Door* or Nelson Algren's "man with the golden arm." In time these discoveries may come to an end but the pursuit does not seem to slacken. In *End as a Man* Calder Willingham exercises his naturalistic technique on the American military school; Fritz Peters invades the "world next door" (a hospital for the insane); James Bellah walks "Ward 20" where war veterans who are incurably maimed are trying to learn what kind of adjustment they can make to their future; Oakley Hall registers the pain of growing into manhood experienced by the newest college generation in California (*Corpus of Joe Bailey*). Unless the sociologists and cultural anthropologists eventually make them technologically unemployable, the environmental novelists can probably keep at their work as long as they can find interesting new areas to exploit.

Contemporary literary naturalists are much less concerned with heredity than were the followers of Zola who thought the theory of atavistic reversion could explain why men behaved in such nasty ways. A subhuman ancestor in the family tree is easier to tag than a wayward gene. But Freud helped out here with a new scientific concept which was a godsend. We now have the id which "contains everything that is inherited, that is present at birth, that is fixed in the constitution." Equally inescapable, from the fact of growth in a society, is the superego, the influence of what is taken over from other people; the individual's social *milieu,* if one chooses to consider it in that light. (Freud speaks rather, of "teachers, admired figures in public life, or high social ideals.") What is being shaped between the id and the superego is the ego. And here is the novelist's character if he wishes the help of Freud.

It was Hippolyte Taine's theory of determinism which persuaded Zola to consider carefully the moment of time in which his characters were to move. The requirement has persisted and later American naturalists have been obedient to it. The reason seems to be that as a nation we have grown increasingly conscious of the moment and the age. Signs of this are all around us. Every recent decade or lustrum has its descriptive adjective, sometimes a half-dozen, as the 1920's have. Dos Passos' titles tell us that the year of his novel is 1919 or the era that of *The Big Money.* James Farrell in describing how *Studs Lonigan* was written is explicit about the reasons why his story opens on the day Woodrow Wilson was renominated for a second term and closes in the depths of the Hoover era.

Modern philosophical naturalism avoids bleak determinism.[5] It permits man a large measure of free will, operative in his own life and in the society in which he lives.' Novelists who have availed themselves of this permission have been fortified in their faith (if they chose to seek help in these quarters) by the doctrines of Marxism as well as the concepts of Freudianism, for both are systems which permit man to hope while he struggles toward the revolution and the classless society, along the route mapped by Marx and Lenin, or toward self-awareness and an eventual cure by psychoanalytic therapy, on the other road. Ways to salvation, which permit one to avoid religious authoritarianism on the one hand and despair and cynicism on the other, were thus opened for the modern literary naturalists.

Are there any features of American life which have made the methods of the literary naturalists continuously acceptable? From the beginning they have employed a realism of surfaces. Their canvases are crammed with detail and every detail is rendered with a passionate fidelity. Their novels are museums of objects Americans have stuffed their houses with and used as the tools of their trade.[6] Is there not something distinctly American in all this cataloguing and exhibiting? One of our national recreations is window-shopping and only Americans could believe that a child cannot learn without audio-visual aids.

If one considers the history of American painting one can see even more clearly that we do in truth delight in the realism of surfaces. The art of Copley when New England worthies were sitting for him rendered the sheen of satin and the light on glass and copper with a happy innocence which he lost when he made himself a second career in England. Two of the great painters America has produced, Winslow Homer and Thomas Eakins, went beyond this traditional surface-realism to overt naturalism. In Homer's later work, he shows us man against the sea, dwarfed by the power and beauty of wave and storm. Eakins delighted in the strength of boxers and oarsmen, and two of his finest paintings represent the great surgeon operating before students and other surgeons who look on with admiration as he demonstrates his skill.[7]

There are subtle connections, too, between the desire of some literary naturalists to use a big canvas, to crowd the lives of hundreds of characters into their novels, and the American desire to "get around." We scorn to be provincial. We would know how the other half lives, go to Florida when it is cold and to Maine when it is hot. Some have said that the social mobility of American life is a residuum of our pioneering past when the important news about a man was that he had "gone to Texas" or to California. Since those days the tide has flowed eastward with the "back-trailers" from the middle border. Thus the human tide ebbs and flows in America, with a continent for its ocean floor.

The gregariousness of Americans must also be reckoned with. It is un-American to refuse to mix and join and know a great many people even though one cannot know them well. When two Americans meet, they do not begin their conversation with the give and take of ideas. They establish common ground by asking: "Didn't you room with Dave Jones at Cornell in '39" or "Aren't you one of the Richmond Todds?" None of our novelists has pictured so well as Dos Passos the way American lives converge for a moment and then drift apart.

By prescription, the literary naturalists are obligated to present characters who are more types than individuals. Always implicit in their fiction is the assurance that we can find more than one Sister Carrie or Elmer Gantry or Sergeant Croft. They isolate them at moments from the crowd in order to particularize them, but inevitably the characterization adds up to a case history. The psychologist and sociologist collect case histories in order that they may find the type, hypothesize the norm, and recognize the expected deviations from it. The naturalistic novelist has the same end in view. Just as the supply of *milieus* continues to be abundant, new and interesting types are still discoverable. Two in particular have been anatomized in novels written since the second World War: the homosexual and the neurotic Negro whose sense of injustice drives him to desperate ends. Who will be next?

A note on style is required. It has often been charged that the literary naturalists are imperfect artists because they are contemptuous of form and style. Many of them indeed maintained that since life has no plot or pattern, to attempt to impose one on their characters would be a violation of truth. Back of this was a sincere if naïve conviction. There was unconscious revolt as well, revolt against the contrived novels of the genteel writers.

If Flaubert had been the master of the earlier literary naturalists (as he has been of many of the later ones), this notion might not have developed into a creed. Later naturalists have departed from it. They are ready, as Stephen Crane was, to use irony for their ends. And they have borrowed the symbolist technique from another tradition and grafted it onto theirs. Ernest Hemingway and William Faulkner are the greatest of contemporary literary naturalists. What makes their novels so different from the work of their predecessors is their mastery of form and their bold invention of a new style and new techniques to suit the requirements of their materials and themes. They stand alone because each is a master, even as Flaubert was.

VI

To place Ernest Hemingway (b. 1899) in the tradition

of literary naturalism accomplishes about as much as to identify Poe by calling him a writer of Gothic tales. Yet Hemingway's naturalism is basic and evidences of it turn up on nearly every page. He likes his heroes to be strong and brave, men of action who are little given to reflection. Where he finds them on the social scale makes no difference. Harry Morgan of *To Have and Have Not*, who kills naturally to protect his livelihood and his wife and daughters, is the equal of Colonel Cantwell of *Across the River and Into the Trees*, the beat-up veteran of two wars who loves Venice, its history and its art, as much as he does his nineteen-year old, nobly-born mistress. Both men have *cojones* and a man has nothing if he doesn't have *cojones*. On the other side of the ledger are the supercivilized ones whom Hemingway tolerates only long enough to get them into the story: finicky writers, homosexuals (male and female), the parasitical rich, husbands and wives who are no good in bed.

Uncorrupted, earthy people have Hemingway's respect, and there are scores of them among his minor characters: Alice, the good-natured, 350-pound whore in "The Light of the World"; the Fontans, the honest bootleggers of "Wine of Wyoming"; the done-for jockey of "My Old Man"; Pilar, the earth-mother in *For Whom the Bell Tolls*. He likes and has written admiringly about the Indians he knew as a boy in northern Michigan, the Spanish bullfighters he celebrated in *Death in the Afternoon*, the deep-sea fishermen he has known during his years in Key West and Cuba.

Hemingway's attitude toward nature is not easy to define. When nature is being used for sport — skiing, fishing, big-game hunting, bullfighting — it is beneficent. The joy it can give is so mystical it is beyond naming. (George in "Cross-Country Snow" says of the way it feels when "you first drop off on a long run": "It's too swell to talk about.")

Mountains are good and so are streams to fish in, but the mountain in "The Snows of Kilimanjaro" is a death-symbol and there is a sinister place where the "river narrowed and went into a swamp" that Nick Adams, fishing for surcease, in "Big Two-Hearted River," will not go near. Several animals are to be admired, particularly the bulls who give man the finest sport in the world; others, like the silly-looking hyena, are contemptible. The marlin is one of the great wonders of creation. "But thank God," the Old Man says, "they are not as intelligent as we who kill them; although they are noble and more able."

To say that Hemingway held fast to one attitude toward nature would be untrue. His attitude shifts in accord with the requirements of the story. Two passages, one from *A Farewell to Arms*, the other from *The Old Man and the Sea*, will show on how wide an arc his naturalism swings.

Shortly before Lieutenant Henry and Catherine make their escape to Switzerland (and after a fine night in bed), Henry meditates on their happiness, with premonitions of their fate. The passage is famous and has often been pointed to as the key to the novel's meaning.

If people bring so much courage to this world the world has to kill them to break them, so of course it kills them. The world breaks every one and afterward many are strong at the broken places. But those that will not break it kills. It kills the very good and the very gentle and the very brave impartially. If you are none of these you can be sure that it will kill you too but there will be no special hurry.*

What is "the world" here? Behind the word is Henry's earlier mention of the biological trap which springs shut as a consequence of loving well. Catherine will die in the

---

* In another passage "they" also do the killing. "They killed you gratuitously like Aymo. Or gave you the syphilis like Rinaldo. But they killed you in the end. You could count on that. Stay around and they would kill you."

trap and so will their child. Nature will see to it. Also behind the word is Henry's rejection of the chaos of war and
his willed escape from it. For his refusal "the world" will
make him pay, not with his life but by breaking him. He
has been broken once, by the trench-mortar shell, and he
has grown strong at the broken place. He will be broken
again when Catherine dies in childbirth but he will be
strong enough to survive the second breaking.

Such a view of nature would not have served as a base
on which to build *The Old Man and the Sea*. The Old
Man is a primitive, a Saint Francis who lives by killing, of
necessity, his "true brothers," but he thinks as clearly about
man and nature as Henry does about his "world."

> Then he was sorry for the great fish that had nothing to eat
> and his determination to kill him never relaxed in his sorrow
> for him. How many people will he feed, he thought. But are
> they worthy to eat him? No, of course not. There is no one
> worthy of eating him from the manner of his behavior and his
> great dignity.
> I do not understand these things, he thought. But it is good
> that we do not have to kill the sun or the moon or the stars.
> It is enough to live on the sea and kill our true brothers.

The first task Hemingway set himself as a storyteller
was to "state everything behavioristically" — to let actions
and events educe the reader's emotional response, not force
it from him by description or reflection or direct statement.
His early characters live to act and experience. If life has
meaning beyond the experiencing of it, perhaps you'll
learn as you go along. As Jake Barnes says of his chaotic
world, "I did not care what it was all about. All I wanted
to know was how to live in it. Maybe if you found out how
to live in it you learned from that what it was all about."

According to the Hemingway legend (the most fabulous
attached to an American writer) he was a charter member
of the expatriate band in Paris after the War, only vaguely

aware of his talent and fumbling his way toward a subject and a style. If he had not meekly submitted to the literary chaperonage of Sherwood Anderson and Gertrude Stein he might not have made his debut at all. Actually, from the start Hemingway knew he was headed for something big and in a short time he had his bearings. In high school, in Oak Park, Illinois, he learned to write well and led the busy, happy life of the normal American boy to whom sports and friends and ambition mean everything. At graduation he wanted to get into the War but his father prevented his enlisting. So he got a job on one of the best newspapers in America, the Kansas City *Star*. There, over seven months, his training as a professional writer began under able editors who had faith in their precocious, likable cub reporter. In 1918 he went to Italy with the Red Cross ambulance corps. Two weeks before his nineteenth birthday he was severely wounded near the village of Fossalte di Piave. He brought home with him the Medaglia d'Argento. After a few discouraging months he began to write for the Toronto *Daily Star* and *Star Weekly*, a connection he kept for more than four years. Like Mark Twain, Stephen Crane, and Ring Lardner, whom he admired, he was an excellent reporter. He could have gone on to be a first-rate foreign correspondent but he was determined to write fiction, an art which he had been practicing on the side.

The turning point came between the publication of *in our time* (without caps) in 1924 and the enlarged edition of this work (with caps), issued in 1925. The first volume is a series of sketches, most of them bull-fighting scenes, some from the War, one of a hanging he had witnessed in Kansas City. These tense vignettes go beyond reporting and show Hemingway's power with situation, dialogue, and character. In the 1925 edition they served as interchapters between stories which were soon to make him famous, such as "The

Battler," "Soldier's Home," and "Big Two-Hearted River." The sketches are not the matrix which formed the stories. They stand in the book as a kind of bodyguard to them, as if Hemingway was not quite ready to let the stories go unprotected into the world.

All this — in addition to marriage and fatherhood — had happened to the Doctor's son by the time he was twenty-four.

Eight of the eighteen stories which make up *In Our Time* have to do with Nick Adams, the first Hemingway hero. Two others may be about Nick, though he is not named.* These eight stories, with possibly five others which appeared in later collections, take Nick from a first love-affair and considerable sexual experimentation with the Indian girl Trudy, through the War and the aftermath of his wounding, to marriage and fatherhood. Nick Adams is Hemingway's most engaging hero and many critics have regretted that he was never put into a novel. Possibly the reason is that too much that happened to the young Hemingway is in the Nick stories. Like his creator, he is self-reliant, open to experience, venturesome, in love with sport, sensitive as well as brave. The horrors of the War and the terrible wounds he received in it nearly drive Nick out of his mind ("A Way You'll Never Be") and his psychological recovery is slow and hard.

The *In Our Time* stories show Hemingway as a master who has arrived. He had achieved his ambition of writing terse, economical prose in which more is left out than put in. He never describes emotions but reproduces the events which caused his characters to experience them. The reader, in turn, feels the elation or wonder or depression. Hemingway had also learned how to conjure with only a handful of materials. In "Big Two-Hearted River" Nick does nothing but fish and make camp but these rituals tell

* One of them, "A Very Short Story," is the germ of *A Farewell to Arms*.

us all about his state of mind. Scenes which will turn up in later work are in embryo here and are handled the same way. Hemingway's trick of using verbal rhythms to suggest the ecstasy of sexual intercourse was first tried with Jim Gilmore and Liz Coates in "Up in Michigan." Nick and his friend Bill get wittier (so they think) as they get drunker, much as Jake Barnes and another Bill do on their fishing trip in *The Sun Also Rises*.

Compared with Willa Cather, Sinclair Lewis, and Faulkner, Hemingway has not written much fiction. There are the stories, among the best in the language. (They were collected in 1938 under the title of *The Fifth Column and the First Forty-nine Stories*.) There are five novels — *The Sun Also Rises* (1926), *A Farewell to Arms* (1929), *To Have and Have Not* (1937), *For Whom the Bell Tolls* (1940), and *Across the River and Into the Trees* (1950). There is also *The Old Man and the Sea* (1952), a flawless but static novella. *To Have and Have Not* possesses some brilliant scenes but it is slack in form, little more, in fact, than several juxtaposed short stories. From any angle, *Across the River and Into the Trees* is a failure. Hemingway uses his Colonel Cantwell as a mouthpiece to vent his bitterness towards several persons he disliked. (Even President Truman gets a mouthful of gall.) The Colonel's pliant mistress is a convenience to go to bed with and to feed the Colonel the answers he wants and so turn what is essentially a monologue into a dialogue. These inanities are enclosed in a well-carved frame of duck-shooting scenes. We are left, then, with three novels of indisputable excellence.

In spite of several long waits between appearances, a new Hemingway novel was talked about months in advance of publication and argued over for months afterward. Few important American novelists have had so many detractors (Hemingway the adolescent who never grew up, the man with false hair on his chest, the reveller in sex and violence); few have had so devoted a following, from the readers of *Esquire* (for which he wrote more than thirty pieces) to the eminent critics. In the first six months a half-million copies of *For Whom the Bell Tolls* were sold. When Hollywood paid $125,000 for "The Snows of Kilimanjaro," a record for a short story, it expected to cash in on the Hemingway name and legend, and did.

Hemingway's first novel, *The Sun Also Rises*, was aimed at his generation. He says so in its two epigraphs: one from Ecclesiastes ("One generation passeth away, and another generation cometh; but the earth abideth forever"); the other Gertrude Stein's re-echoed judgment — "You are all a lost generation." In this novel are all the European pleasures of the generation which Hemingway and Fitzgerald (to name only two) were tutoring: how good it feels to be on your own in Paris; knowing the brightest slang in many languages; finding the best bars and remotest night spots; being casual and free with women (and telling them off when you want to); being witty, sober or drunk, a necessity a solemn later generation cannot understand.

Hemingway might have added as a third epigraph Thoreau's "The mass of men lead lives of quiet desperation." No one is really happy except Romero, the handsome young bullfighter, and Lady Brett fixes that when she adds him to her Circe's rout. Jake Barnes, who tells the story, has been made impotent by a war wound. Brett, who has had too many lovers and will have more, loves Jake but there is nothing they can do about it. Robert Cohn can't forget he's a Jew nor learn not to beat up his friends when they offend his sensitive soul. They all hide their desperation behind drinking and talking and being rude to those who don't know the code. They have a fine time at Pamplona watching the bullfights, all except Robert that is, who beats up Romero for sleeping with Brett. The novel ends in the key in which it begins.

"Oh, Jake," Brett said, "we could have had such a damned good time together."

Ahead was a mounted policeman in khaki directing traffic. He raised his baton. The car slowed suddenly pressing Brett against me.

"Yes," I said. "Isn't it pretty to think so?"

In writing *A Farewell to Arms* Hemingway went back to the War to see if what happened to his generation in it was responsible for their being "lost" in the 1920's. For many this is the great novel of the first World War, though the largest part of it is a love story of the most romantic kind. Having shown Lieutenant Henry among his Italian and American comrades at the Austrian front (this part of the War is good), Hemingway starts the love affair with Catherine Barkley, the nurse, in the fifth chapter. It is interrupted twice — when Henry is wounded (Catherine soon contrives to be nursing him) and when he returns to the fighting, only to desert the cause when it goes to pieces in the retreat at Caporetto. The rest is love-making, waiting for the baby to be born, and Catherine's death. It is not a very long novel but Hemingway took great pains with it, using five months for cutting and revising. The war scenes have their counterpart in earlier work but the love story, which Hemingway later called his *Romeo and Juliet*, is a *tour de force*. His skill was equal to the delicate task he had set himself — to write about the intimacies of love-making without being silly.

Instead of a third novel the Hemingway aficionados got in 1932 a book about bullfighting in Spain, *Death in the Afternoon*. Spaniards say it is authoritative. What we see in it, beyond the minute descriptions of the ritual of killing and the life histories of famous toreros, is a Hemingway who is escaping from the psychic wounds of war, from the Paris of the expatriates, and from the America they had renounced. One thing he was not escaping from was death.

There had been plenty of it in his life and in his war and he wanted to go where it was treated ceremoniously and exorcised by the ritual of working to the bull.

Three years later Hemingway carried his pursuit of death into the *Green Hills of Africa.* Ostensibly about the techniques of big-game hunting — there are a lot of animals killed — it is actually a fragment of autobiography. Nine times in the first seventy-two pages Hemingway says he is happy. It's his own damned life he is leading, and "I would lead it when and how I pleased." But the *Green Hills* is full of self-justification and of belligerency toward other writers. America he now sees as "a country that is finished." It had been a good country once but "we had made a bloody mess of it." About all that is left of Hemingway's world is bullfighting, the green hills, and the sea. And even the sea is polluted by the loads of garbage (remnants of history) dumped in it every day. "The palm fronds of our victories, the worn light bulbs of our discoveries and the empty condoms of our great loves float with no significance against one single, lasting thing — the stream." If this nihilism, this *nada* mood, had lasted much longer Hemingway might have been finished as a novelist.

What brought him back to writing about people instead of varieties of killing was the Spanish Civil War and his commitment to the cause of the Loyalists. He raised $40,000 on personal notes to buy ambulances for their armies, and then served in Spain as a correspondent in order to pay off the notes. He was often at the front and came to know well the Loyalist military leaders. Here, at last, was a war he could believe in and wanted to write about affirmatively. *For Whom the Bell Tolls* (1940) was not just about the civil war. "It was," as Hemingway said of it, "everything I had learned about Spain for eighteen years."

On several counts *For Whom The Bell Tolls* is

Hemingway's finest novel. It has a great theme: the tragic sacrifice the American Robert Jordan makes for a cause he knows is doomed in his time but, because it is the universal cause of free men everywhere and in any time, must be fought for whenever it is threatened. The rendering of the Spanish characters, the wise and earthy Pilar, the gentle Anselmo, Pablo, the guerrilla leader who in defeat turns to treason, is true and complete. Possibly Maria, Robert's companion in the sleeping bag, is too good to be true but Hemingway has always wanted his heroines to cosset their men. Hemingway's greatest technical problem in this novel was to make his time sequences believable. The actual time of the whole action is three days. Through flashbacks, conversations, and stream-of-consciousness revery the pasts of several of the characters must be got into the story without loosening the suspense. Hemingway had never attempted so complicated a structure but he built this one without any joints showing.

Everyone knows that Hemingway taught his generation how it might endure a world it had not made and for which it had little liking. It is also acknowledged that he was one of the purifiers of "the dialect of the tribe." His imitators have made some of his famous passages look faded. They were able to reproduce his surfaces but the deeper thing they could not steal from him — his sense of man's mysterious connection with the earth and the sea and God's creatures, the way man is still bound to the cycle of the seasons. In an age when many artists were trying to revive the lost feeling for legend, myth, and ritual (Eliot in *The Waste Land*, Stravinsky in *Le Sacre du Printemps*, Picasso in *Guernica*), Hemingway was the least bookish of the new primitivists. He did not need to write by the book because his wisdom was chthonian.

SIX

Make it New: Poetry, 1920-1950

BY 1920 the poets identified with the "new" poetry move-ment described in Chapter Two — Sandburg, Masters, Lindsay, and Frost — had found a responsive audience. By 1920, also, the generation of poets coming on had broken with this recently established tradition and were effecting still another revolution.

Readers were bewildered by what they considered the willful obscurity of this newest poetry. What were these poets trying to do? Why did they import into their verse symbols which could not be penetrated because they re-ferred to recondite events or were meaningful only in the context of the poet's private life? Why were they so much preoccupied with the recurrence of myth that a reader could not tell whether the poem was about Ulysses of Ithaca (one *knew* with Tennyson) or a modern Ulysses or both at the same time? How were the annoying ironies, ambiguities, and word-plays to be taken? Was the poet hav-ing his little joke at your expense? These new poems seemed, often, to consist only of gists and piths. The dis-course was not continuous. As in the most dissonant of modern music, the melodic line was so broken that it was heard only in brief and widely separated passages.

With each manifestation of the new style in verse — Eliot's *Waste Land* in 1922, Ezra Pound's *A Draft of XVI Cantos* in 1925, Hart Crane's *White Buildings* in 1926 —

the alarm spread. Had poetry become an intellectual parlor game, anagrams or crossword puzzles which could be solved only by young zealots who had the patience to thumb encyclopedias and track down obscure quotations from Cyril Tourneur, Heraclitus, Confucius, and Varchi's *Storia Fiorentina?* (Homer, Ovid, Dante, Shakespeare, and Donne were taken as read.)

What was not understood in 1925, or for some years thereafter, was that these poets were intensely serious in their enterprise. Far from wishing to be private poets, they were deeply concerned to be spokesmen for their community. They knew that the dislocations produced by war had changed their world. One could not go back beyond the line of 1918 but must go forward. All the arts except poetry had moved ahead, had long since broken with nineteenth century gentility and provinciality and cosmicism. What Cézanne and Picasso had done for painting and Debussy and Schoenberg for music they wished to do for poetry. The "new poets" of the 1912–1920 generation freed their art from Matthew Arnold's mandamus of high seriousness but their movement for liberation had not gone far enough. The Chicago poems of Sandburg, the little tragedies of Masters' Spoon River, even the eclogues of Robert Frost touched only a small segment of modern life and made use technically of only the simplest tools from the vast store which poets over the centuries had accumulated. Poetry must again be free "to be applied to any human situation, broadening out then into the freedom characteristic of high cultures." [1] There were to be "no forbidden subjects and no proscribed methods."

We can date precisely the beginnings of this second revolution in poetry. It developed from the quarrel in 1914 between Amy Lowell and Ezra Pound over which of them should captain the Imagist movement. Pound capitulated without a struggle and Miss Lowell carried "Amygism," as he derisively called it, to America and had her way with it. As always, he was impatient to move on to something new. Vorticism was coming up next.

II

Born in Idaho in 1885, Pound had been well educated in the classics and the Romance literatures at Hamilton College and the University of Pennsylvania. Fired from the faculty of Wabash College for having befriended innocently a stranded burlesque girl, he got to Europe on a cattle boat and walked from Gibraltar to Venice where he paused long enough to publish his first book of poems, A *Lume Spento* (1908). Arriving in London in 1908, he was soon well known for his red beard, his voluble opinions on every subject from Chinese ideograms to medieval economics, his versatility as a poet, and his prodigious output. In two years, 1909–1910, he published three volumes of verse, *Personae, Exultations*, and *Provença*, and an important critical work, *The Spirit of Romance*, a study of the pre-Renaissance literature of Latin Europe.

Pound was one of the most powerful forces in English letters between 1910 and 1920. He became so primarily because of the stimulating novelty of his ideas and the example of his verse. But he was also a born promoter and what he wanted to promote was writing which followed his injunction to "make it new." He was a natural teacher and any young poet whom he took on got from him sympathetic understanding of what he was trying to do and patient correction. He was in some measure responsible for Yeats's becoming a "modern" poet by helping him to "get back to the definite and concrete" and away from abstractions. Through his influence the Egoist Press published Joyce's A *Portrait of the Artist as a Young Man* and the American *Little Review* issued installments of *Ulysses*, until the New York Society for the Suppression of Vice got the filthy business stopped.

In 1914 Pound received a visit from T. S. Eliot, a young American who had left Germany when war broke out and had come to England to study philosophy at Merton College. Pound was much impressed by "The Love Song of J. Alfred Prufrock" and immediately shipped it off to *Poetry*. In 1917 he arranged for the publication of *Prufrock and Other Observations*, Eliot's first volume. In 1922 Eliot, so he tells us, placed before Pound "the manuscript of a sprawling chaotic poem called *The Waste Land* which left his hands reduced to about half its size, in the form in which it appears in print." The dedication of this most influential of modern poems reads: For Ezra Pound/*il miglior fabbro*.

When he was not discovering and coaching young poets, Pound was busy editing anthologies, writing critical introductions for his friends, and founding new magazines. The story of the way he moved in on *Poetry* has been told in Chapter Two. In 1914 he helped to transform a feminist magazine, *The New Freewoman*, into *The Egoist* which then became an outlet for the work of poets he favored. In the same year he and Wyndham Lewis started the short-lived *Blast* as "The Review of the Great English Vortex." In America his influence was felt in the *Little Review* and the *Smart Set* as well as *Poetry*. By 1940 he had put his stamp on at least fifty little magazines published on both sides of the Atlantic.

When Pound arrived in London the shadow of Swinburne still lingered over the poets. He was supposed to have carried English prosody to the ultimate, leaving nothing to be discovered. The best a poet could do now was to try the simpler measures of Dowson and Lionel Johnson, unless he wanted to go all the way to vulgarity with Kipling. Pound's earliest verse imitates the mistiness of the nineties, just as Yeats's does, but he was on that road, so he says, only three years. His study of the Provençal poets taught him their witty, chivalric mode and the rhythms of their dance songs and courtly poems. As an Imagist he discarded abstractions, didacticism, and ornament and preached the doctrine that a presented image can be "the perfectly adequate expression or exposition of *any* urge." The next notion Pound seized on, that the image is "a radiant node or cluster . . . a VORTEX, from which, and through which, and into which ideas are constantly rushing," produced the whirling images (suggestive of Cubism) of which there are hundreds in the *Cantos*. His study of Chinese poetry took him deep into the problems of communication and held him entranced before the magic of the ideogram. Paying homage to Sextus Propertius (48–10 B.C.) by making free translations of twelve of his Elegies in 1917, Pound recreated a charming poetic sensibility from hints rejected by cautious biographers.

On all these forays into distant literatures Pound experimented with each new style he encountered. In this way his own style was formed. By 1920 he could make his verse obey his wish. He could move easily from the elegance of Bertram de Born to the wit and self-mockery of Propertius to the mellifluousness of Waller. Their sense he borrowed but the sounds were his own.

By 1920 Pound had had enough of England. He moved on to Paris where he took up sculpturing under the tutelage of Brancusi, championed the American composer Antheil, and had some part in the literary education of Hemingway. He soon found the swarms of expatriate Americans boring and not worth the time they demanded of him. After three years he removed to Rapallo on the Italian Riviera. There he stayed until 1945 when the American authorities carried him off to an army prison-compound at Pisa, to await trial for treason. During the War his broadcasts over the Rome Radio mingled abuse of President Roosevelt with diatribes against "usocracy," an evil which had become an obsession with him. In his barbed-wire cage (without shelter for the first six weeks) Pound wrote the "Pisan Cantos" which now stand as numbers LXXIV–LXXXIV in the still expanding *Cantos of Ezra Pound.*

Before leaving Paris in 1920 Pound spoke his farewell to England in *Hugh Selwyn Mauberley* (1920) which might have taken its place in history as the first important modern poem if the prestige of Eliot's *The Waste Land* (1922) had not obscured it. *Mauberley* is Pound's most lucid and moving poem and shows better than any other work the astonishing technical virtuosity he had achieved. It is not a self-portrait, as some have supposed, but a mask through which Pound speaks. Mauberley is at times the Pound whom the pressures of the age compelled to listen to "neo-Nietzschean chatter" as well as the gratuitous commercial advice of "Mr. Nixon" (possibly Arnold Bennett); he is at other times the Pound who was determined not to give his age the image it demanded ("a mould in plaster," "a prose kinema") but intended to follow "his true Penelope, Flaubert" — a great hero to Pound because Flaubert and Stendhal were the instigators of the "revolution of the word." For one who wishes to make a beginning with this underground poetry written between 1920 and 1950 *Mauberley* is the place to start.

From his Paris days Pound's chief poetic effort has been the *Cantos* which have appeared in installments since *A Draft of XVI Cantos* in 1925. No modern poem has been so much debated. Many who venture into it retreat at once, calling it inchoate, perverse, and opaque; disconnected film-strips of historic scenes and personages and Pound's private woes and hates (which he certainly never kept to himself); and a waste of any sensible man's time. On the other hand, *The Cantos* have become a cult, especially with younger poets and critics, and their scholia have multiplied by the month. No one need be frightened by *The Cantos*. Some of them are not worth struggling with but many yield their meaning easily — for example the Sigismundo Malatesta cantos (VIII–XI) and the scatalogical XIV and XV in which Pound hurls his enemies into an excremental hell. Nothing could be more lucid than the crucial canto on usury (XLV). Perhaps Pound made it straightforward so that no one could miss the point.

> Usura rusteth the chisel
> It rusteth the craft and the craftsman
> It gnaweth the thread in the loom
> None learneth to weave gold in her pattern;
> Azure hath a canker by usura; cramoisi is unbroidered
> Emerald findeth no Memling
> Usura slayeth the child in the womb
> It stayeth the young man's courting
> It hath brought palsey to bed, lyeth
> between the young bride and her bridegroom*

From the beginning Pound had planned to write an epic whose hero should be modern man (Pound himself or the reader), voyaging, not to fight at Troy or found Rome, but to hunt down evil in today's world and salvage whatsoever things are good and beautiful from the wreckage of history. It is ironic that a poet whose name connotes to many only violence and disorder should have chosen as his thirty years' mission bringing his readers to a knowledge of the good life and a desire to emulate those, like Sigismundo and Jefferson and John Adams, who lived it and tried to construct societies in which other men could live it too. Even in the frenetic *Pisan Cantos*, colored with bile as they are, visions of what man can and should be come through, fitfully.

> "Master thyself, then others shall thee beare"
> Pull down thy vanity

* Ezra Pound, *The Cantos of Ezra Pound*, Norfolk, Connecticut, 1948, copyright 1934, 1937, 1940, 1948 by Ezra Pound. Reprinted by permission of New Directions.

> Thou art a beaten dog beneath the hail,
> A swollen magpie in a fitful sun,
> Half black half white
> Nor knowst'ou wing from tail
> Pull down thy vanity
>   How mean thy hates
> Fostered in falsity,
>   Pull down thy vanity,
> Rathe to destroy, niggard in charity,
> Pull down thy vanity,
>   I say pull down. (LXXXI)

In his autobiography, *Life for Life's Sake* (1941), Richard Aldington, one of the Imagist group, contrasts the careers of Pound and T. S. Eliot. By 1920 Pound was well on the way to becoming a literary dictator. He muffed his chances, according to Aldington, "by his conceit, folly, and bad manners." Eliot began as an unknown in "the enormous confusion of war and postwar England," yet by "merit, tact, prudence, and pertinacity" he succeeded in doing what no other American has ever done: he imposed "his personality, taste, and even many of his opinions on literary England." (Aldington might have remembered Henry James.) By 1935 Eliot had become one of the leading men of letters of Europe, standing in the company of Mann, Shaw, Yeats, Joyce, Valéry, and Gide.

In 1927 he was confirmed in the Church of England and became a British subject. He had already won acceptance in university circles. In 1926 he gave the Clark Lectures at Trinity College, Cambridge, and honorary degrees were soon showered on him. The Church of England valued him as its most forceful apologist and lay theologian. In 1948 (the year he won the Nobel Prize) he received the Order of Merit, the highest award the British government bestows on distinguished citizens. He is said to have declined being knighted.

Eliot took care of his reputation along the way, as a

writer or artist should, but his extraordinary climb to fame was due in part to the loyalty of his admirers. Like Pound, but with none of his fanfare, he was a discoverer of talent and was always helpful to younger writers. As editor of the influential *Criterion* from 1922 to 1939 he was in a position to publish and review their work. In 1925 he entered the firm of Faber and Gwyer (now Faber and Faber), the publishing house which has done most in England to encourage oncoming poets.

Until *The Waste Land* began to be talked about as a poem that must be taken seriously, the going was not easy. All the opprobrious adjectives which conservative critics were heaping on the poetry of Pound's disciples now came hurtling down on Eliot. One trait was particularly obnoxious: he borrowed from other writers, and not just occasional phrases but whole lines and a great many of them. Could he be called a poet at all if he never — so it seemed — wrote a line of his own? His allusions and patched-in quotations were bafflingly obscure. Yet one was forced to catch them because Eliot, it was soon discovered, used the emotions associated with them in constructing his poem. The antagonists were especially outraged when he appended brief but learned source-notes to *The Waste Land* (and taught other poets the same practice). If one had to get up quotations from Ovid, Gerard de Nerval, and the Buddha's Fire Sermon before one could begin on the poem, the reward was not worth the effort. So went the argument *contra* Eliot. Meanwhile the younger generation defended their champion's right to his obscurities and delighted in them. It was fine sport to allude casually to the "broad-backed hippopotamus" and Griskin's "friendly bust" with its "promise of pneumatic bliss," and be understood by those in the know.

Before Eliot settled in London in 1914 he had begun to move out on his own road as a poet. His satires of American gentility ("The *Boston Evening Transcript*," "Mr. Apollinax"), his explorations of life in the back streets of cities ("Preludes"), and his studies of tremulous young men who find life and love too much for them ("Rhapsody on a Windy Night") show the influence of writers as diverse as Henry James, Dostoevsky, Laforgue, Charles-Louis Phillipe (a novelist Eliot greatly admired) and the philosopher Bergson (under whom he had studied without admiration). The most notable of the poems which appeared in the 1917 volume, *Prufrock and Other Observations*, was the title-poem itself. J. Alfred Prufrock tells us his story, shyly and in anguish, so the poem is in form a dramatic monologue. Already present are many characteristic Eliot devices — the supple free-verse rhythms, the metaphysical conceits ("Like a patient etherized upon a table"), the use of refrain lines to bring in fragments from other existences, the mythological allusions. In the light of what was to come the most impressive achievement of the poem is the evocation of Prufrock himself. It should not have surprised readers when, in the 1930's, Eliot became a practicing dramatist. For years he had been creating memorable characters and compelling them to reveal their buried life through their speech. What most puzzled the first readers of "Prufrock" was its tone. Was this satire? Was J. Alfred (of the prissy name) merely an oversensitive bachelor who dared not "presume" with the lady? Or was he a tragic figure? Was he, possibly, the Prufrock who is in each of us?

As a poet Eliot has always moved on, like many of the poets he admired, Marvell and Dryden, for example. In the 1920 *Poems* (American edition) a new set of influences can be detected — the Jacobean dramatists, Donne, Gautier, and Rimbaud. Several of these poems, especially "The Hippopotamus" and "Mr. Eliot's Sunday Morning Service," are so thick with allusions that the explicators are still tracking them down. Apeneck Sweeney makes his first appearance here, in "Sweeney Erect" and "Sweeney Among the Nightingales." The finest poem in the collection is "Gerontion." Like "Prufrock" it points ahead to later work. The speaker, "an old man in a dry month," has come to the end. History, with its cunning passages, has betrayed him. He has waited for the sign which never came. ("The word within a word, unable to speak a word.") He has lost his passion. Why should he need to keep it, "Since what is kept must be adulterated"? Here, for the first time, is the Eliotian despair which persisted for seven or eight years in his own writing and colored so much of the literature of the 1920's.

When *The Waste Land* appeared there was no doubt that Eliot had moved up to the front rank. Within the space of 433 lines, half the length of a book of *Paradise Lost*, he had brought to life a score of unforgettable characters in brief vignettes, among them Madame Sosostris, Lil and Albert, Mr. Eugenides, and the young man carbuncular. The poem was filled with moments of sudden insight which Joyce had taught the critics to call epiphanies. Almost every line was quotable and was soon being quoted. The poem's scope and depth were as remarkable as its novel organization. The chief organizing principle was the myth of the Fisher King which Eliot took from Jessie Weston's *From Ritual to Romance*. This widespread myth explains how sterility comes over the land whose king suffers from a sexual wound and is unable to help his people. The myth poeticizes the observed fact of the recurrence of the seasons, the death of the year and rebirth in springtime. Eliot makes his waste land the whole of modern western civilization (with London as its center) from which religious faith has departed and where love has degenerated into sterile lust. For most readers in 1922 the poem seemed to end in utter despair. Actually in "What the Thunder

Said" (Section V) three words are spoken — Give, Sympathize, Control — which might, if harkened to, bring the life-giving rain. *The Waste Land* was a more religious poem than Eliot perhaps intended or his readers knew.

Eliot's despair over the human situation in the postwar time sank to the nadir in "The Hollow Men" (1925). It is the poem of the generation which called itself lost, gloried in its lostness, and had little desire to be found, though this was decidedly not true of Eliot. No words of his have been so much quoted as its final lines. (One year they turned up five times in Hollywood scripts.)

> *This is the way the world ends*
> *Not with a bang but a whimper.*

But in this poem, as in *The Waste Land,* one hears at least a sigh of religious aspiration. Some of the hollow men form prayers to broken stone and some know that the hope of empty men is the "multifoliate rose" of Dante's *Paradiso*.

In the four Ariel Poems * light has begun to break on the darkness. In "The Journey of the Magi" (1927) the wise men, returning from the manger, cannot tell whether it is birth they have seen or the death of their world. But so wonderful was the experience that they would "be glad of another death." Simeon ("A Song for Simeon," 1928) asks his Nunc Dimittis because he is eighty and has no tomorrow. But he has held the Infant in his arms, "the still unspeaking and unspoken Word." "Animula" (1929) is a meditation on the growth of the human soul, from the time of its bold infant joys to the time when the heavy burden of perplexity makes it unable either to fare forward or retreat. "Marina" (1930) alludes to Shakespeare's Pericles and his reunion with his long-lost daughter. To the

---

* So called because they appeared first in the pamphlet series of modern poems thus designated by Faber and Faber.

old king her recovery is like a rebirth of himself, too visionlike to be believed.

In the Ariel Poems the theme of rebirth and the possibility of salvation through it is constant. It is carried over into *Ash Wednesday* (1930). The perplexing allusions persist. Who are the three white leopards who sat under a juniper-tree? Are the turnings of the stair the *scaglioni santi* of Dante's *Purgatorio*? Does the mysterious Lady, several times addressed, merge with the Virgin to whom the poet's prayers, using the words which belong to her in the liturgy, are spoken? The difficulties posed by *Ash Wednesday* arise chiefly, one surmises, from the dubieties of Eliot's religious state at the time the poem was written. One thing is certain: the old mocking tone is gone, and the savage self-torture and the black despair. Many of Eliot's admirers were dismayed by *Ash Wednesday*. The creator of Prufrock and Sweeney had gone churchly on them and they resented the betrayal. He was supposed to be a leader of the lost generation but he had refused to stay lost.

In the 1930's Eliot turned to the writing of poetic drama, beginning with a pageant-play, *The Rock* (1934), written for the Forty-five Churches Fund. He was then asked to furnish a play for the Canterbury Festival of 1935 and responded with *Murder in the Cathedral*. He took for his plot the intrigues leading to the killing of Thomas à Becket before the altar in 1170 and for his theme the theology of martyrdom. Successful productions in the commercial theater encouraged him to continue as a playwright. His next venture, *The Family Reunion*, apparently cost him much effort since it was not ready for the stage until 1939. It proved to be too abstruse for regular theater audiences, but Eliot persisted and in *The Cocktail Party*, first produced in 1949, he had a commercial success. Its triumphant reception in England and America vindicated

Eliot's belief that if poetry was again to be viable in the theater, after a lapse of two centuries and a half, the poet must learn the craft of the dramatist. Meter was not enough.

Meanwhile Eliot had begun work on a series of meditative poems which would be brought together in 1943 under the title of *Four Quartets*. The first of them, *Burnt Norton*, was published in 1936. The others followed in this order: *East Coker*, 1940; *The Dry Salvages*, 1941; and *Little Gidding* in 1942. It was while he was at work on *East Coker* that the idea came to Eliot of composing a group of four poems using the same structural pattern of five sections in each and carrying his themes from one poem to the next. Because of the variety and beauty of the verse, the importance of its themes and its totally adequate structure, *Four Quartets* stands as Eliot's highest achievement. It is undoubtedly one of the great poems of the century.

Four Quartets is a personal poem which brings to a climax Eliot's speculations, over many years, on philosophical and theological problems and on the art of poetry. He no longer speaks through a mask as he did when he made use of Gerontion or Simeon. He also abandons the dramatic monologue, the form in which many of his earlier poems were cast. Throughout *Four Quartets* it is the poet's voice we hear, in the philosophical speculations, in the didactic and gravely meditative passages, and in the lyrics. Eliot achieved magnificently here what the poets of his generation had been striving for, a poetic language which should be conversational in tone yet adequate to carry any thought or emotion. The poem draws on many sources but what Eliot took from St. John of the Cross or Krishna has been completely absorbed. The language is always Eliot's, grave and persuasive, moving easily from the satire of modern soothsayers (in *The Dry Salvages*) who can communicate with Mars or "dissect the recurrent image into pre-conscious terrors" to the magnificent lyric, "The dove descending breaks the air," which is section IV of *Little Gidding*.

Four Quartets is also a poem about places, each of which holds associations for Eliot of a deeply personal kind and around which he could weave his major themes. The places themselves are magically evoked, with a feeling for landscape first voiced in a group of short poems written in America in 1933, "New Hampshire," "Virginia," and "Cape Ann." From Burnt Norton, an English country seat which Eliot visited in 1934, the theme of "movement and stillness, time and timelessness" emerges. East Coker, the village in Somersetshire from which the Eliot family emigrated to America, prompts the meditations on man's beginning and man's end and the poet's constant fight to

> recover what has been lost
> And found and lost again and again. . . .

In *The Dry Salvages* (the place is a group of rocks off the New England coast which he knew as a child), Eliot is concerned with the way man may apprehend — through hints and guesses only — "the point of intersection of the timeless with time." For the saints this is an occupation; for the rest of mankind the moment "in and out of time" comes only in

> The distraction fit, lost in a shaft of sunlight
> The wild thyme unseen, or the winter lightning. . . .

At Little Gidding, in Huntingdonshire, there was in the early seventeenth century a little Anglican community subsequently desecrated by the Roundheads. What was said and done there affected Eliot deeply and undoubtedly helped to sustain him during the months of England's terrible trial by fire. This Quartet turns on the question of

which fire man will choose: the airman's fire of destruction
or the Dove's "flame of incandescent terror." As one critic
has epitomized the difficult theology of this Quartet, it is
given to man to "move in anticipation beyond the searing
flames of purgatory to the radiant sphere of paradise." The
poem ends on a note of hard-won hope.

> All manner of things shall be well
> When the tongues of flame are in-folded
> Into the crowned knot of fire
> And the fire and the rose are one.

III

By 1925 most of the battles of the newest poetic revolution had been fought. Several poets who had given themselves the kind of rigorous training Pound and Eliot had
undergone were sufficiently established to make it clear
that a break with the Sandburg-Masters-Lindsay tradition
had taken place. Already William Carlos Williams
(b. 1883), Marianne Moore (b. 1887), and E.E. Cummings
(b. 1894), to name only three of the successful experi-
menters, had found their own special subjects and, though
the poetry of each was distinctive, each had followed
Pound's injunction to "make it new."

Williams was a medical student at the University of
Pennsylvania when Pound and Hilda Doolittle were also
there. After further study in Europe he returned to his
native Rutherford, New Jersey, where he practiced medicine
and poetry, with vigor and devotion. His second volume,
The Tempers (1913), shows the influence of Pound's
incursions into Provençal poetry (Pound was responsible
for getting it published) and for a time Williams was in
the Imagist camp. But he soon struck out on his own,
having found Imagism incapable of producing the precision he wanted to get into his verse.* He preferred the

---

* Williams was sufficiently loyal to the movement to consent to contribute
to the *Imagist Anthology*, 1930.

"objectivist" approach and later helped to found the Objectivist movement which had as its aim resolving words into a poetic structure so successfully that the mind does not wish to add anything to what has been said. If many of his pronouncements about poetry showed him to be "anti-poetic" (as some of his friends accused him of being), his reasons were sound enough. He wished to transfer to his verses life as he knew it in the drab houses of the humble people whose doctor he was. He was determined to make contact with his readers by eliminating all barriers to the immediate apprehension of the thing seen and felt. He had no use for strained associations, complicated ritualistic forms, or meter as meter. Such devices separated the poem from the reality.

A poem by Williams does its work quickly in a kind of rapid shorthand. He is most difficult, perhaps, in his ambitious long poem, *Paterson*, but the subject is a big one, no less than the history and present life of the city Dr. Williams knows best and loves well. Many of the short poems are accessible at once and are by now well known — for instance, the tender "The Widow's Lament in Springtime," the nostalgic "Burning the Christmas Greens," and "These," full of the desperate loneliness that comes when "the year plunges into night" and one remembers

> the people gone that we loved,
> the beds lying empty, the couches
> damp, the chairs unused —

Marianne Moore came to the critics' attention after the appearance of her second volume, *Observations* (1924), which won her the *Dial* Award for the second time.* From

* This much-coveted award, of $2,000, was given to poets who needed money and deserved the recognition. From 1921 to 1927 the recipients were all members of the new poetry movement: Marianne Moore (1921 and 1924); T. S. Eliot (1922); E. E. Cummings (1925); William Carlos Williams (1926); and Ezra Pound (1927).

1925 to 1929 she was editor of the *Dial* and helped to make it the best American journal devoted to letters and the arts we have ever had.

The fact that Miss Moore's *Collected Poems* (1952) is a book of fewer than 200 pages shows with what deliberation she writes. Ever since she outraged poets who submitted verse to the *Dial* by mending their work, she has been impatient with half poets. What they drag into prominence is not poetry.

> nor till the poets among us can be
>   'literalists of
> the imagination' — above
>   insolence and triviality and can present
>
> for inspection, 'imaginary gardens with real toads in them,'
>   shall we have
> it.   ("Poetry")

A first glance at her titles suggests that she writes almost exclusively about toads and other unpoetic beasts. What, one wonders, can a poet do with such subjects? — "The Buffalo," "The Monkeys," "Snakes, Mongooses," "To a Snail," "The Wood-Weasel." The titles are deceptive, as they were intended to be. She likes to begin with the evocation of an object, in lines as sharp as draughtsman's work. This is followed by seemingly miscellaneous bits of information (often footnoted in the poem itself) about the object's natural history. But the conclusion has left the object behind and always has a moral in it, showing that from the beginning she intended to make an observation about poetry or critics or courage or war or the difference between good and bad manners. When Miss Moore, at W. H. Auden's suggestion, undertook to translate the *Fables of La Fontaine* (1954), she was working in a congenial medium for she is by nature a fabulist. Each of her poems ends with a *haec fabula docet*. Those who admire her verse — and she has become of late something of a pet with the public — enjoy having her tell them what's what with the firmness and wit of a favorite maiden aunt. But within and beyond the wit and the strong statements there is a music which only a great metrist could compose.

For years E. E. Cummings has been the bad boy of poetry, confusing librarians by giving his volumes such uncataloguable titles as *&* (1952) and *is 5* (1926), pushing the parts of speech around, and shattering sonnets into fragments with the end in view of making readers pay attention. Responding to his publishers' request to please explain the why of his verbal acrobatics, Cummings replied, in the Foreword to *is 5*: "It is with roses and locomotives (not to mention acrobats Spring electricity Coney Island the 4th of July the eyes of mice and Niagara Falls) that my 'poems' are competing."

Fortunately the poet's "ineluctable preoccupation with The Verb" gives him one priceless advantage. Nonmakers have to abide by the undeniable fact that two times two is four. The poet can say "is 5" and make people believe him. Cummings' "is 5" world is graced with acres of imaginary gardens but Marianne Moore would agree (she is a great admirer of his work) that there are real toads in them.

Having gone to the War with the rest of his generation and having suffered unjustified confinement in a French concentration camp (he used the experience in one of the best books about the War, *The Enormous Room*), Cummings turned to poetry and was ready with his first volume, *Tulips and Chimneys*, in 1923. Except for side excursions into playwriting and painting he has been a poet ever since, and a prolific one. His *Poems 1923–1954* is a big book of nearly 500 pages.

In *Tulips and Chimneys* the songs and love sonnets

proved that Cummings was already one of the most accomplished lyric poets of his generation. But the characteristic Cummings typographical devices have already begun to appear — the line that is one word or only one letter long, the adroit spacing between words and lines, the sudden capital in the middle of a word, the shaped poems (reminding one of the altars and angels' wings of the seventeenth century poets), the manipulated punctuation. In using these tricks Cummings was not merely trying to divert the reader momentarily from Spring electricity Coney Island. He realized that in this age we take in more by eye than by ear. To make his rhythms felt and his words audible he called on the printers for help. Let the eye see and then the ear might listen. When he mastered this technique he could do just about anything with it he desired. He could paint a portrait, or make a mouse skitter down the page and vanish, or reproduce the pomposity of a bore who has you boxed up in a corner.

Through the years Cummings has remained a lyric poet. No one in our time writes a better sonnet. His songs should be sung by children, though they will not be very innocent children if they understand the words. He is the best writer of erotic verse since the Earl of Rochester. (Possibly this is why his "Sonnets – Realities" and "Sonnets – Actualities" are always charged out to students when one looks for them in a college library.) Cummings does not play the role of Puck or Pierrot unremittingly. He drops his antic mask in such a superb sonnet as "true lovers in each happening of their hearts" and in the beautiful elegy which begins:

> my father moved through dooms of love
> through sames of am through haves of give,
> singing each morning out of each night
> my father moved through depths of height

Of the younger writers immediately influenced by the poetic revolution none was more talented than Hart Crane (1899-1932). Before his suicide, two months short of his thirty-third birthday, he had had time to publish only two volumes, *White Buildings* (1926) and *The Bridge* (1930). Their excellence was unmistakable.

Crane was born to mid-western parents who were divorced when he was seventeen. (The humiliations he suffered as the hostage between them may sufficiently account for his homosexuality.) His formal education was slight. (He could barely translate the French poets Laforgue and Rimbaud he so much admired.) It has been rightly observed that the editors of the magazines to whom he sent his poems were his instructors and their magazines — *Others, The Little Review,* and *The Dial* — his university.

Unlike Eliot, Williams, Marianne Moore, and Cummings, Crane was the veritable romantic poet, ardent, affirmative, intoxicated with words, able to write only when he was at fever pitch. Alcohol and the playing of records at full volume could sometimes induce the fever but there were weeks when inspiration deserted him completely. As the disorder of his life mounted he became less and less capable of sustained work. In his last months when he was in Mexico on a Guggenheim fellowship, he produced only one poem — one of his finest — "The Broken Tower." Yet as his worksheets reveal, when he could get the lines to flow, he knew precisely what effects he wished to achieve. He talked endlessly with friends (Allen Tate, Gorham Munson, and Waldo Frank) about technical problems and his superb letters (collected in 1952 by Brom Weber) are filled with valuable observations about his own poetry and that of his friends.

Crane was a poet of the sea, of the modern city, of

the machine age, of the America of his own time. He suffered none of Eliot's revulsion from modern life and thought it the poet's office to find spiritual values in the world around him. Yet he knew something of the mystic's desire for communion with the Unknowable. Religious metaphors occur with such frequency in his verse that one can imagine that in an age less hostile to religion he might have been a religious poet. All he lacked was a God to believe in. He worshipped heroes instead — Columbus, Melville, Whitman — and Brooklyn Bridge (his bridge, he called it) beside which he lived and to which he turned when he sought a myth to unify his long poem about America.

In *White Buildings*, mixed with many poems that show Crane still working under the influence of Imagism and the French Symbolists, there are at least a half-dozen pieces completely in his own developed idiom — "Lachrymae Christi," "For the Marriage of Faustus and Helen," "At Melville's Tomb," and the group called "Voyages." They are difficult poems. Even on first reading one cannot fail to be moved by the ardor and excitement in them, but in trying to penetrate their meaning one has to struggle with Crane's fused metaphors. Characteristically he extracts one particular significance from a many-faceted symbol and fuses it with the next one in the row. In consequence a line of his poetry is so compacted that a prose explication of it may require a paragraph.*

Crane's long poem, *The Bridge*, is one of the most ambitious works of the decade, challenging comparison

---

* Like most artists Crane was willing to explain patiently what he was trying to do. When Harriet Monroe was troubled by what she took to be mixed metaphors in "At Melville's Tomb," he wrote her a detailed account of his method. Their correspondence was published in the October, 1926 issue of *Poetry*. It is reprinted in the Appendix to Brom Weber's *Hart Crane*, 1948.

with Eliot's *The Waste Land*. He attempted to fill it with his admiration for the strong beginnings of America, for our conquest of a continent and our voyaging into far seas and distant skies. It contains some magnificent lyrics — "Ave Maria" (Columbus' prayer), "The Harbor Dawn," "The Dance" — but in spite of Crane's effort to unify his work by the use of historical, biographical, and geographical themes, the parts of *The Bridge* do not cohere. His bold attempt to make Brooklyn Bridge into " the Myth of America" failed because he did not understand how myth can be made to work in poetry or fiction. Either it must have been believed in by many people and still be accessible for belief or, if the artist invents a new myth, as Melville did in *Moby-Dick,* he must make it believable. The apostrophic poem, "To Brooklyn Bridge," is one of Crane's finest lyrics, but this "harp and altar, of the fury fused" does not in the rest of the poem vault the American seas and "the prairies' dreaming sod"; nor does it, as Crane hoped it would,

> descend
> And of the curveship lend a myth to God.

During the 1920's a number of excellent poets marched under the banners of the new movement. Some were the age of Eliot and Pound and had helped them make the break with two traditions; others, like Crane (ten years their junior), were converts to the new fashion. Among the older poets the one whose work would eventually prove to be the most distinguished was Wallace Stevens. He had been writing verse since his undergraduate years at Harvard, from which he was graduated in 1900, and his poems had appeared in the *avant-garde* magazines of the years 1915-1920. His first collection was *Harmonium* (1923), as remarkable a first volume as the decade produced.* Conrad

---

* Stevens' work will be considered in some detail in the last section of this chapter.

Aiken was another recruit from the older generation, though not a very partisan one. Still, the award of the Pulitzer Prize to his *Selected Poems* (1929) showed that the newest poetry was getting a hearing with the public.

Distinguished first volumes published in this decade were Louise Bogan's *Body of this Death* (1923), Léonie Adams' *Those Not Elect* (1925), and Horace Gregory's *Chelsea Rooming House* (1930).

One of the most remarkable features of the new movement is the fact that it was both international and regional in character. As expatriates, Pound and Eliot had been in touch with each successive revolution of the word in European cultural capitals, but after the War the younger poets followed the currencies downward in France, Italy, Germany, and Austria. Many of the little magazines journeyed with their editors. *Broom* (1921-1924) was issued successively in Rome, Berlin, and New York; *Secession* (1922-1924) in Vienna, Berlin, Florence, and New York.

At home groups of poets began to gather around experimental magazines issued in various regions. In the beginning *Poetry* was partial to the "Chicago school" but it soon took on an international character. In Iowa City there was *The Midland* (1915-1933); in Richmond, *The Reviewer* (1921-1925); in New Orleans, *The Double Dealer* (1921-1926).

Of these many regional magazines the one which had the most far-reaching influence was *The Fugitive*, published in Nashville from 1922 to 1925. In the beginning, when they were studying or teaching at Vanderbilt, the poets in this remarkable group, John Crowe Ransom, Donald Davidson, Allen Tate, and Merrill Moore, read and criticized one another's work minutely.* Even when most of them scattered to different parts of the country, they re-

---

* The contribution of the Fugitives to the renaissance of letters in the South is discussed in the next chapter.

mained close in spirit. Three extremely influential literary reviews were later edited by Fugitives or their disciples: the *Sewanee Review* by Allen Tate; the *Southern Review* by Cleanth Brooks and Robert Penn Warren; and the *Kenyon Review* by Ransom. These journals were hospitable to the work of the newest generation of poets.

Of the many poets who became identified with particular regions in the 1920's Robinson Jeffers (b. 1887) is the one who defies the categories of critics and literary historians. He belonged to no school. He made no alliances with other poets and he was as indifferent to criticism as the rocks and surf of the Carmel Coast in California which the murders and suicides in his long narrative poems should by now have unpeopled. He is introduced at this point only because he belongs to the generation of Pound and Eliot.

Jeffers' first volume in his characteristic vein was *Tamar and Other Poems* (1924). From then on he has published a volume of verse almost yearly. His beliefs are as simple as his form and style are uncomplicated. Influenced early by Nietzsche's *The Birth of Tragedy*, he has been elaborating its doctrine ever since: "What is best of all is beyond your reach forever: not to be born, not to *be*, to be *nothing*. But the second best for you — is quickly to die." Nature, though harsh, is pure; man has been corrupted by turning in on himself (allegorized by the recurrent theme of incest in the poems), by self-deification, and by his lust for destruction. Once the fuse of destruction has been fired in a Jeffers poem (by an adulterous seduction, a rape, a murder), a train of terrible explosions follows until a whole family is wiped out.

Jeffers believes in his own nihilism, of course, but his violent plots are deliberately chosen because he thinks them appropriate to his time. He remarked in the Foreword he wrote to L. C. Powell's study of his work (1940) that in earlier eras a poet might turn to war or to religion, but "in times of high civilization war becomes too specialized and inhuman, and religion too vague or incredible, for poetry to fix its roots in." The one theme continuously available has been family relationships, as the Greek dramatists and Shakespeare dealt with them. "These relationships are always unhappy and often vicious, not because the poets prefer vice and sorrow, but because happiness makes no story, and but calm emotion."

IV

In the depression years when there was much talk of the need for a proletarian art, a number of poets turned to the Left, or tried to. Their effort parallels that of such dramatists as Odets and Miss Hellman and the playwrights of the Federal Theatre and such novelists as Grace Lumpkin and Albert Malz. These poets had before them the example of the Russians Andrei Bely, A. A. Blok, and Mayakovski who learned how to be revolutionary poets and glorify the Soviet regime though their early work had been in the Symbolist or Futurist manner. There were difficulties. For more than a decade young poets, following Pound and Eliot, had been inventing techniques for projecting complicated emotional states and were content with the small audiences which could understand their verse. Now, suddenly, if they were to reach "the people," their work must be extraverted and deal in a straightforward, exhortative manner with dynamos, tractors, the tragedies of jobless men, and the blight which had descended on farm and field.

The work of the poets who tried to meet this challenge was meager in quantity and less successful, either as art or propaganda, than that of the dramatists and novelists. Samples of proletarian poetry appeared in the three *Unrest* anthologies (1929, 1930, 1931) and in *Proletarian*

Literature in the United States (1935), designed to present the best work of the leftist writers, in fiction and criticism as well as poetry. Two poets whose verse is distinguished were claimed for a time by the leftists, Kenneth Fearing and Muriel Rukeyser.

Recently graduated from Wisconsin, Fearing arrived in New York in 1924. He loved his adopted city and knew its juke joints and all-night-eateries, its taxi drivers and tabloid journalists, and especially what was happening around Union Square, New York's temporary equivalent of Moscow's Red Square. Though Fearing had sat in the school of Pound and Eliot, Sandburg's long, loose line and crowded verse paragraph formed his style. By the time he published his second volume, *Poems* (1935), he had made it into an excellent vehicle for satires of the flashy rich and the inert middle class and portraits of the worn-down people of a city scarred by the depression. There is a sense of doom in many of his poems, but readers of the *New Yorker*, where he frequently appears, ignore his signals because he is thought to be just a writer of light verse, though somewhat more cynical than his peers, Dorothy Parker and Ogden Nash.

There is more anger at injustice and more compassion in the verse of Miss Rukeyser. Leaving Vassar at a time when many college graduates intended to go out fighting into a society which had hardened its heart against the Negro and the worker and was indifferent to the threat of Fascism, she promised in her first volume, *Theory of Flight* (1935), that she would never re-enter the old, easy life.

> I have left forever
> house and maternal river
> given up sitting in that private tomb
> quitted that land   that house   that velvet room.

She has been a fighter for causes in her verse ever since.

The Left was full of pride when it believed — for a few months only — that it had made a convert of Archibald MacLeish. In his first eight volumes (1915–1929) he had followed the new fashions in verse and his heart was oftener in the Europe he had fought for in 1917 than in America. By inclination a lyric poet (and an excellent one), he had defended the poet's right to keep clear of politics. "Invocation to the Social Muse" (*Poems, 1924–1933*) asks in scorn

> Besides Tovarishch how to embrace an army?
> How to take to one's chamber a million souls?

Answering his own question, MacLeish declared that poets are persons of

> Known vocation following troops: they must sleep with
> Stragglers from either prince and of both views:
> The rules permit them to further the business of neither:

MacLeish finally emerged into the arena. He was provoked to anger and spoke out when the Rivera murals commissioned by the Rockefellers for their skyscraper Center in New York were effaced. (An offending portrait of Lenin had been detected in one corner.) In *Frescoes for Mr. Rockefeller's City* (1933) he scarified the monopolists, the Mellons, Morgans, Harrimans, Rockefellers, who move in and take over from the true pioneers who opened up the land and discovered its hidden resources. The poem ends, however, with a nasty satire of American revolutionaries who tell the Starvers all they need is Dialectical Materialism. In *Public Speech* (1936) MacLeish made amends in such poems as "The lost speakers" and "The German girls! The German girls!" But he warns the thunderers on the Left, in "Speech to those who say

Comrade," that true brotherhood comes only through shared labor and shared danger. It is "Not to be had for a word or a week's wishing." MacLeish had not joined up. The second part of *Public Speech* is a group of ten very personal lyrics, "The Woman on the Stair," which are among his finest.

Of the younger poets who began publishing during the second World War, three achieved a distinctive idiom in a remarkably short time: Karl Shapiro (b. 1913), Randall Jarrell (b. 1914), and Robert Lowell (b. 1917). Shapiro and Jarrell published the first collections of their verse in 1942: *Person Place and Thing* and *Blood for a Stranger*. Shapiro's poetry ranges widely in theme and is varied in style. Much of his verse is personal and speaks unaffectedly to the reader about his childhood and coming of age, his thoughts on war (he served in the South Pacific), and what it means to be a Jew. His collected poems appeared in 1953 (*Poems, 1940–1953*). Jarrell likes to surprise his readers by choosing unexpected themes. A more "literary" poet than Shapiro, he finds his subjects in books or painting as often as in personal experience. Many of his poems are soliloquies uttered by children or soldiers or prisoners of war. For his *Selected Poems* (1955) he cheerfully provided unpedantic notes to help his readers find their way through his wit and learning. Robert Lowell's *Lord Weary's Castle* won the Pulitzer Prize in 1946. It is filled with the New England to which he was heir as a member of the famous Lowell family and many of the poems in it reflect his conversion to Roman Catholicism. His next volume, *The Mills of the Kavanaughs* (1951), confirmed the judgment of those critics who had seen him as one of the most accomplished poets of his generation.

Other younger poets who had begun to make names for themselves by 1950 are William Meredith (*Love Letter*

from an Impossible Land, 1944; *Ships and other Figures,*
1948; *The Open Sea,* 1958); Reed Whittemore (*Heroes and
Heroines,* 1946; *An American Takes a Walk,* 1956); Louis
O. Coxe (*The Sea Faring,* 1947; *The Second Man,* 1955);
and Richard Wilbur (*The Beautiful Changes,* 1947; *Things
of this World,* 1956). Though differing widely in their
choice of themes, these four poets had this in common:
they were trying to write more simply and directly than
their elders of the generation of Pound and Eliot and they
did not seek to escape from emotion. In general this
return to direct and lyrical expression was true of other
poets who came to notice after the second World War.

v

Of the poets writing between 1920 and 1950 none followed more deliberately than Wallace Stevens (1879–
1955) the call by Pound to "make it new." Not that he was
in any degree a follower of Pound. It was just a fact that his
vision and his way of expressing it were new, so new in
fact that years elapsed before readers in any number were
able to understand and take delight in what he was saying. Until 1950 (he was then past seventy) he was a poet's
and critic's poet. In the next decade he had a following
among the young which can only be compared to the
Eliot cult of the 1920's.

The outward events of Stevens' life were not in the
least dramatic. After graduating from Harvard, where he
wrote for the *Advocate,* he studied law and practiced for
a time in New York. William Carlos Williams testifies
that after Stevens moved to Hartford, Connecticut, in
1915, he kept up his acquaintance with "the entire New
York group" (which included Marianne Moore, Cummings,
and Williams), came to their parties "but always in a
distant manner, shyly, unwilling to be active or vocal.

Everybody knew him, knew him well — but he never said much."

While working in the legal department of an insurance company, of which he later became vice-president, Stevens continued to write poetry, and a great deal of it. Harriet Monroe claimed to have discovered him when she published four of his poems in the War Number of *Poetry* (November 1914). She was not the only discoverer. Between 1914 and 1923, when his first volume of verse was issued, such magazines as *Others, Secession, Broom,* the *New Republic,* and the *Little Review* took about one hundred of his poems. A few of these — "Peter Quince at the Clavier" and "Le Monocle de Mon Oncle" in particular — became anthology pieces. He experimented briefly with poetic drama and two of these plays — *Carlos among the Candles* and *Three Travellers Watch a Sunrise* — received productions in little theaters. The drama reviewers either ignored or damned them. Critics and fellow poets continued to cry up his verse — in 1929 Allen Tate called him "the most finished poet of the age" — but readers beyond his circle were few. This we know from the reception of *Harmonium* in 1923. It is said to have sold fewer than a hundred copies. Critics who admired Stevens commended his verse for its "delicately enunciated melody," its "sonority," "verbal elegance," and the "riot of gorgeousness" in which his imagination "takes refuge." The opposition objected to the "verbal morasses that utterly blind and baffle the reader" and a wit that was "tentative, perverse, and superfine."

Possibly because of the unsuccess of *Harmonium* Stevens published only two poems between 1924 and 1930. In 1931 *Harmonium* was reissued with a dozen poems added. During the 1930's, again prolific, he published three volumes: *Ideas of Order* (1935), *Owl's Clover* (1936), *The Man with the Blue Guitar* (1937). There were four volumes in the next decade: *Parts of a World* (1942), *Notes Toward a Supreme Fiction* (1942), *Esthétique du Mal* (1945), and *Transport to Summer* (1947). To celebrate Stevens' seventy-fifth birthday, Alfred Knopf (who had been Stevens' devoted publisher from the beginning) issued the *Collected Poems* in 1955. Additional poems and other writing which had not been printed or collected were gathered in *Opus Posthumous* (1957). A volume of Stevens' critical essays, *The Necessary Angel, Essays on Reality and the Imagination*, had appeared in 1951.

Why did it take so long? What was so new that readers had to wait for the scholiasts to annotate and unravel? There is no question that Stevens is and will continue to be a difficult poet. In the early verse the reader was hung up by strange, though precisely used, words. Before he could get on with the sense of a passage he had to run to the dictionary (a small one would not do) to find such words as brune, effendi, panicles, selvages, princox, fisc, funest, fubbed, clickering. (The strange words were not always to be found because Stevens had coined some of them.) Many of the early poems resembled what painters call collages, artifacts made by pasting fragments of newspapers, bits of string, wire, and cloth to a board, then painting color into the interstices. How did these odd fragments fit together or, if they did, would the whole thing add up to a joke sprung on the reader? At times Stevens seemed to be a very serious poet indeed but how could one be sure when the titles to his poems were often whimsical or nonsensical? "The Emperor of Ice-Cream" gave no hint that the poem to follow would be about death and how we should deal with it. How was one to guess that "Metaphors of a Magnifico" would ponder the way the mind works when it concentrates on an abstract idea? "Le Monocle de Mon Oncle" was an odd lens through which to study the theme of death's subordination to life. "Asides on the Oboe" seemed to be a trifling way to introduce one of Stevens' most interesting ideas: the concept of his fictive hero who sums us up.

> In the end, however naked, tall, there is still
> The impossible possible philosophers' man,
> The man who has had the time to think enough,
> The central man, the human globe, responsive
> As a mirror with a voice, the man of glass,
> Who in a million diamonds sums us up.

One difficulty was — and it was major — that Stevens' view of modern man differed markedly from that of the influential poets contemporary with him. Unlike Eliot and Tate (one can add Ransom and Auden), he expressed no sorrow over the loss of a tradition or the collapse of religious faith. (Where could one find any reference in his poetry to Original Sin or the Fortunate Fall?) They lamented. Stevens rejoiced. Where they found tragedy, he found delight, joy, exuberance, hope, uttering them with a *sprezzatura* which might have shocked if it had not been undeniably beautiful. When the reluctant lady in "Sunday Morning" demands a heaven of some kind — "some imperishable bliss" — the poet answers her need with another faith, which was his.

> Supple and turbulent, a ring of men
> Shall chant in orgy on a summer morn
> Their boisterous devotion to the sun,
> Not as a god, but as a god might be,
> Naked among them, like a savage source.
> Their chant shall be a chant of paradise,
> Out of their blood, returning to the sky;
> And in their chant shall enter, voice by voice,
> The windy lake wherein their lord delights,
> The trees, like serafin, and echoing hills,
> That choir among themselves long afterward.
> They shall know well the heavenly fellowship

> Of men that perish and of summer morn.
> And whence they came and whither they shall go
> The dew upon their feet shall manifest.

But the greatest difficulty was that Stevens was a philosophical poet, an exponent of ideas which only gradually became clear. These ideas in themselves, having to do chiefly with the nature of reality, the imagination, the kind of world the poet's imagination creates, do not constitute a dense esthetic. What makes them seem difficult is the way they emerge in the poetry. They are the flowering in the upper, final, conclusive reaches of his verse, but the flowers have their roots in reality, in "things as they are" which the "man with the blue guitar" sings of.

Stevens never lost delight in the world of the senses, in color, light, waves, clouds, exotic flowers, scents, shadows, the strong sun — "that brave man" who gives his energy to the world. The seasons' changes, from the summer of "bright & blue birds & gala sun," on through the auroras of autumn, to the winter of the snow man, were profoundly meaningful to Stevens. The summer is the sun's time, the season of inspiration and creativity. In that gay time the "world is larger" and the poet most readily transforms "things as they are," just as the sun's light, "by giving itself and taking nothing, absorbs the world in itself." In the vision of autumn are seen the world's imperfections, man's disillusionment and bitterness. Premonitions of winter crowd the imagination.

> The scholar of one candle sees
> An Arctic effulgence flaring on the frame
> Of everything he is. And he feels afraid.

Winter is the time of terror. Reality contracts to nothingness. But at the lowest point come stirrings of new life. The cycle is soon to revolve again and there will be a new reality.

In the cycle of the seasons, with all the things seen, people known, experiences lived through, Stevens found enough reality for a poet's lifetime. But what was the poet's relation to these inexhaustible things as they are? Without his imagination to work on them they would be inert, unformed, devoid of meaning. This weight of reality exerts a pressure on the poet which he can be rid of only by transforming it. In his constant "rage for order" he seeks "to abstract himself and also to abstract reality, which he does by placing it in the imagination." He must "create his unreal out of what is real." "There is, in fact," Stevens said in "The Noble Rider and the Sound of Words," "a world of poetry indistinguishable from the world in which we live, or, I ought to say, no doubt, from the world in which we shall come to live, since what makes the poet the potent figure that he is, or was, or ought to be, is that he creates the world to which we turn incessantly and without knowing it and that he gives to life the supreme fictions without which we are unable to conceive of it." The "supreme fictions" of the true poet satisfy both the reason and the imagination. Such poetry is at least the equal of philosophy; it may be its superior.

Because Stevens believed so passionately in the supremacy of art, some considered him an escapist, a reincarnation of the art for art's sake poet of the nineties. Where were his poems about evil, social injustice, war, it was asked? (He did take account of these matters but in poems which are about other things as well.) In "The Noble Rider" he met the charge that he was an escapist and answered it firmly.

The chatter about escapism is, to my way of thinking, merely common cant. My own remarks about resisting or evading the pressure of reality mean escapism, if analyzed. Escapism has a pejorative sense, which it cannot be supposed that I include in the sense in which I use the word. The pejorative sense applies where the poet is not attached to reality, where the imagination does not adhere to reality, which, for my part, I regard as fundamental.

Earlier, in "Notes Toward a Supreme Fiction," he had said this another way, in verse.

> The freshness of transformation is
>
> The freshness of a world. It is our own,
> It is ourselves, the freshness of ourselves,
> And that necessity and that presentation
>
> Are rubbings of a glass in which we peer.
> Of these beginnings, gay and green, propose
> The suitable amours. Time will write them down.

The novice who opens Stevens' *Collected Poems* * for the first time will do well to begin with such short but electrifying poems as "Anecdote of the Jar," "Thirteen Ways of Looking at a Blackbird," and "The Idea of Order at Key West." In these reason and imagination meet on such friendly terms that the reader is scarcely aware that they are philosophical poems. But in time he must go on to the long and difficult poems and puzzle them through: "Chocorua to its Neighbor," "Esthétique du Mal," "Notes Toward a Supreme Fiction," and "The Auroras of Autumn." Baffled at times, at times angry with a poet who would not simplify because his vision could not be diminished, he will be rewarded often by such superb lines as these which conclude "Esthétique du Mal."

> One might have thought of sight, but who could think
> Of what it sees, for all the ill it sees?
> Speech found the ear, for all the evil sound,
> But the dark italics it could not propound.
> And out of what one sees and hears and out
> Of what one feels, who could have thought to make

* Copyright 1954 by Wallace Stevens.

So many selves, so many sensuous worlds,
As if the air, the mid-day air, was swarming
With the metaphysical changes that occur,
Merely in living as and where we live.

SEVEN

Southern Renaissance

I

UP TO THIS POINT the method of presentation has been
mainly chronological, with emphasis in particular chapters
on the genres which flourished over a period of two or three
decades. The general narrative has been interrupted all
along in order that at least rough justice might be done
to the best writers and their work. This chapter is a
diversion, in that it will discuss what happened to writing
over a fifty-year period in one region, the south. Though
there would be distortions, one could tell the story of
American literature in this century by concentrating on the
regions which were fortunate enough to have an abundance of poets, novelists, and playwrights as their spokesmen. The renaissance in southern writing is only one,
although it has been the most continuous and extensive, of
the literary reawakenings in various parts of the country.
From 1890 to 1920 there was an "Indian summer" of New
England writing. In the 1900's there was a Hoosier
"school." From 1910 to 1930 Chicago magnetized writers
as Philadelphia had done in the late eighteenth century
and Boston in the 1840's. The story of writing in California, from Norris and London to Henry Miller and
"Howl" has yet to be written.

But there are reasons why the upsurge of writing in
the south should be singled out for special consideration.
In the first place, the south has produced in this century

more writers and more good writers than any other region. At least a dozen have international reputations and there are dozens more on whom we have depended for enlightenment and entertainment. The list is longest in fiction: Ellen Glasgow, James Branch Cabell, Elizabeth Madox Roberts, Stark Young, Caroline Gordon, Thomas Wolfe, Katherine Anne Porter, T. S. Stribling, Marjorie Kinnan Rawlings, Lyle Saxon, Hamilton Basso, Robert Tallant, Erskine Caldwell, William Faulkner, Hervey Allen, Julia Peterkin, Margaret Mitchell, Andrew Lytle, Jesse Stuart, Eudora Welty, Richard Wright, Arna Bontemps, and Ralph Ellison. Among the poets are Donald Davidson, Merrill Moore, John Gould Fletcher, John Peale Bishop, and Randall Jarrell. The dramatists are fewer in number but the contributions to the American theater of DuBose Heyward, Hatcher Hughes, Paul Green, and Tennessee Williams are very considerable. Robert Penn Warren has played in five sections of this regional orchestra, biography, fiction, poetry, criticism, and drama; John Crowe Ransom in two, poetry and criticism; Allen Tate in four, biography, poetry, fiction, and criticism. The line shows no sign of thinning out. In the younger generation — all of them born since 1916 — are Peter Taylor, Carson McCullers, Truman Capote, Flannery O'Connor, William Goyen, James Dickey, William Styron, and George Garrett.

Many of these writers specialized in particular states. Miss Glasgow is identified with Virginia; Wolfe with North Carolina; Heyward and Mrs. Peterkin with South Carolina; Mrs. Rawlings with Florida. Kentucky can claim Miss Roberts and Jesse Stuart. The setting for many of Caroline Gordon's novels is the Kentucky-Tennessee border. Caldwell and Margaret Mitchell offered contradictory versions of life in Georgia, as Stark Young and William Faulkner did for Mississippi. Warren's characters are to be found burning up the roads anywhere between Kentucky and New Orleans.

The causes of this remarkable flowering have been much debated. It should be remarked that it was part of the general literary renaissance taking place in many sections of the country. Some of the inducements which made writers of Sandburg, Anderson, and Frost appealed to Miss Glasgow and Branch Cabell as well. In the next generation such writers as Allen Tate and Katherine Anne Porter mingled with the other temporary expatriates from the north and west who were taking postgraduate work, so to speak, in Paris.

Nevertheless, the situation in the south was special. For one thing, writers there were conscious of the fact that they were establishing the profession of letters in their region. In the hierarchical society of the Old South there had been no place for the writer. Lawyers and preachers, overseers and house servants, fitted into the niches God had ordained for them. There was no niche reserved for the artist or writer. If a gentleman composed sonnets and elegant essays as one of his accomplishments, this was as laudable as excelling in field sports, but earning one's living by writing was not acceptable. Most ante-bellum southern writers who eventually made names for themselves studied for one of the professions and practiced law or medicine for a time. The poets Edward Coote Pinkney, Philip Pendleton Cooke, and Henry Timrod made a try at the law but found they had no taste for it. The Virginia novelist William Caruthers was a doctor. John Esten Cooke practiced law before the War and wrote his first novels between the visits of clients. Even William Gilmore Simms, the most distinguished southern author of his generation, was trained for the law and evaded the practice of it by hack writing before the sales of his novels were sufficient to bring him a livelihood.

This state of affairs the southern writers born between 1890 and 1910 deliberately set out to alter. The south had produced, it is true, several professional writers after

Appomattox — Thomas Nelson Page, Joel Chandler Harris, James Lane Allen, G. W. Cable, and Mary Noailles Murfree — but too often they were isolated and their professional connections were with their admiring publishers in the north. By the time the newer writers came along their families had recovered sufficiently from the War and Reconstruction so that sons and occasionally daughters could be sent to college. At Vanderbilt and the University of North Carolina they met others of their kind and they argued constantly among themselves and with their professors about the state of letters in the south and the need to make writing a respectable occupation in their region.

Though they faced discouragements (who, at home, would read them?) they enjoyed some advantages. For the novelists there was an inexhaustible subject matter at hand in the history of the south and its recurrent economic and social dilemmas. They also had a great resource in their knowledge of the lives of members of their families, reaching back for generations. To turn into fiction the stories of kinfolk they had heard since childhood was a congenial task.

Novelists and poets alike faced the question of what to do with the past of their region. Should they, reverencing the ordered society of their grandfathers, its sense of honor and Christian piety, turn back and idealize life in the lost years? Or should they repudiate the memory of the dreamed of Confederate empire and side with the leaders of the New South who rejoiced in the whir of cotton spindles and the flaming sky over the iron city of Birmingham? The necessity of deciding provided tensions which helped their work, since a good poet or novelist writes from conviction. Most of these writers came out into the modern age, though they dissented from the boosters who were taking their south down the road to the standardized industrial society of the north. What had been good in the life of the Old South they tried to preserve.

In the 1920's, when most of these writers were making names for themselves, the south was subject to unusually scurrilous attacks from the north. The Scopes trial, reported to the world from the hill-village of Dayton, Tennessee, seemed to confirm the northern view of an unprogressive south, fundamentalist in religion and reactionary in politics, Here was a cause: the defense of the region the writers loved but whose shortcomings they acknowledged. The best defense was to tell the whole truth. So thoroughly did they do it that novelists like Faulkner and Caldwell were thought, in their home states, to be defaming rather than defending their kin.

II

The first writer of stature to emerge was Ellen Glasgow of Richmond, in many respects an heroic figure, though the younger writers who knew her in her later days (she was born in 1874) were reluctant to admit that this imperious lady-novelist had inaugurated anything. They forgot that in the 1900's she had waged a one-woman battle against prudery and sentimentality in fiction. The going was not easy, and for a time she deserted her region and lived in New York. A kinsman of hers, having read her first story, whose central character is an illegitimate poor white, found it incredible "that a well-brought-up Southern girl should even know what a bastard is."

Early in her career Miss Glasgow set herself the task of telling the story of the Commonwealth of Virginia in a succession of novels, truthfully and with a comprehensive view of all levels of society. Six of the thirteen novels in the series treat the "Commonwealth at large" and range in time from the period just before the Civil War (*The*

Battleground, 1902) to the outbreak of the first World War (*Life and Gabriella*, 1916). The other seven novels she divided into a country group and a city group — the city being, of course, Richmond. The last two novels in the country group, *Barren Ground* (1925) and *Vein of Iron* (1935), are her best-known works, the reason being, possibly, that she wrote so much of herself into them. Each is dominated by the kind of courageous woman who possesses the "vein of iron" Miss Glasgow admired and which she invariably discovers only in her women.

The four novels of the city would seem to have been less deliberately planned as part of the grand scheme. Covering the years between 1910 and 1939, they are all novels of manners. Two of them, *The Romantic Comedians* (1926) and *They Stooped to Folly* (1929), are in the vein of high comedy in which Miss Glasgow excelled, though unfortunately she experimented with it only late in her career. In *They Stooped to Folly* she developed in detail a situation which had always fascinated her, the plight of women who have "gone wrong" — once. For good measure she introduces three of them, from different generations — Aunt Agatha, who did not recover from her disgrace until she could redeem herself by making Red Cross pajamas during the War; Mrs. Dalrymple, who recovered immediately to enjoy a fortunate marriage and an even more fortunate widowhood; and militant Milly Burden, who, having discovered that "being ruined is only a state of mind," stops sniveling about her limp lover and goes in search of substantial happiness.

Miss Glasgow was probably late in discovering that irony and high comedy were her best weapons against sentimentality because she was for thirty years faithful to the realism preached by W. D. Howells and his disciples. She believed that her *Voice of the People* (1900) was the "first work of genuine realism to appear in Southern fiction" and was proud that Stuart Sherman recognized this years later when he remarked: "Miss Glasgow's democratic fight in realism is incarnate in the little red-haired hero of *The Voice of the People*. Realism crossed the Potomac twenty-five years ago going North."

When one tries to square Miss Glasgow's social philosophy with the actions of her characters, some paradoxes are observed. Her intellectual sympathies were with the New South. She hoped to see strong leaders arise — and where could they come from except from the "stock" of the "plain people"? — who would bring economic prosperity to her region and rebuild it into a genuinely democratic society. And yet, though she several times takes such a potential leader for her hero, we are never shown in detail how he rises to power or what it is precisely that he is attempting to accomplish. Was it lack of knowledge or lack of conviction that made her withhold the obligatory scenes which would have shown by what "tedious processes" the triumphs of her leaders from the plain people had been achieved?

However ardently Miss Glasgow wished for a New South she was frequently dismayed by what economic progress was doing to her region. Some of her most despicable characters are men who have made money since the Civil War but are without principles or manners or taste. Though she had tried to imagine a new order in which men would dare to go forward with faith in the future, in reality she saw little to admire in what the new century had brought to the Commonwealth.

Compared with "Miss Ellen," the great lady of Richmond, Elizabeth Madox Roberts, twelve years her junior, seems like a country cousin who has come in from the knob region of Kentucky. She had none of Miss Glasgow's fondness for the big scene and the sententious passage, but nearly every quiet page she wrote was masterly. She published only seven novels, the first written when she was forty, the last, twelve years later. Two of them, her first, *The Time of Man* (1926), and her one historical novel, *The Great Meadow* (1930), are among the classics of our literature.

Her settings are the region she knew best, the fertile lands south of Lexington. Yet she makes no effort to describe this region in detail, preferring to let it build up for us in the daydreams of her characters. Her plots are simple in the extreme, sometimes turning on a single incident. Her narrative method is oblique, symbolic, poetical. (She was a practicing poet.) The excellence of her fiction does not lie in the detailing of an action but in the responses of those who are acted upon. One remembers chiefly in her novels the emotional states of her characters, as in the early chapters of *The Time of Man* which are filled with the reaching toward life of the young girl, Ellen, her anguish because of the poverty of her parents, her envy of the girls who have lovers and know how to hold them. Seldom has the "perpetual sadness of youth" been so movingly evoked.

Most of Miss Roberts' characters are lonely and isolated. They are in awe of cities and crowds and before elegant people. They keep their secrets. They know little of what is happening beyond the horizon which is blocked by a Kentucky mountain. The outer world moves across the mirror of their imagination and disappears into it. Yet they are not shadows but people of a passionate intensity, capable of being hurt deeply, but of enduring hurt, and of triumphing over circumstance.

Like Sarah Orne Jewett and Willa Cather, Miss Roberts invariably maintains a right relationship with her characters. If the event is tragic, she convinces us that it is tragic. Her comedy is true folk comedy. Her pathos is never mawkish. The tone is right because she knows the worth of her creatures. The reader perceives at once that she formed their idiom and speech cadences, in some degree, from the ballads of the region. The question of literal accuracy is, of course, irrelevant. The people of her region ought to talk this way, if they do not, for her characters know their own thoughts and the names of the things in their world and utter them simply and accurately.

III

During the first years of the century the leaders of the southern renaissance did their work in comparative isolation. Suddenly, in the early twenties, there was a burst of literary activity in many cities where groups of writers were banding together to help one another by sharing ideas and critical comment. Most of these groups issued little magazines, chiefly as outlets for their own work or that of other writers of the region. The first of these groups was the Poetry Society of Charleston whose leaders were DuBose Heyward, Josephine Pinckney, and Hervey Allen. The Fugitives of Nashville began to publish their magazine (*The Fugitive*) in 1922. In 1921 two other magazines had come into existence: the witty and conservative *Reviewer* in Richmond and the more experimental *Double Dealer* in New Orleans. Other little magazines which nurtured regional writing were the *Lyric* in Norfolk, the *Nomad* in Birmingham, and the Texas *Buccaneer*. With the founding of the *Virginia Quarterly Review* in 1925 the south had at last a well-subsidized literary journal which rivaled the best of its kind in the north.

It was a momentous decision for American literature when in the fall of 1921 a group of Nashville friends who called themselves Fugitives turned from their discussions of literature and philosophy to the writing of poetry. From their sessions evolved one of the most influential movements in our literary history, suggesting in its pervasiveness the energy radiated by Boston's Transcendental Club of

1836 which included in its informal membership such movers and shakers as Emerson, Margaret Fuller, and Orestes Brownson. So great has been the influence of the Fugitives and their disciples that in discussing the revival of letters in the south during the past forty years it is difficult to get them out of the foreground long enough to focus on other writers who had no connections with them and may have disliked all they stood for.

There are several reasons which will account for the extraordinary influence of the Fugitives. In the first place, there were a number of excellent writers among them, real professionals, such as Davidson, Ransom, Tate, Warren, Andrew Lytle, Caroline Gordon, who would soon have a national reputation. Many of them became university teachers and so helped to train a succession of writers. They were remarkably hospitable to young talent. The story of their generosity on this score may never be told, but if it is, we shall learn of house-room given, money lent, imperative letters written to publishers and patrons. Uniting them was a loyalty to their region, anxiety over its problems, and a steady determination to make southern writing something to be proud of. Though they differed among themselves they were loyal to their common purposes.

In the first years their interests were almost entirely literary. As Fugitives they were in flight from the vacuity of earlier southern writing and from the social optimism of the New South. Citizens of Nashville were puzzled to know what they were up to but were proud of *The Fugitive* as a sign of the city's cultural maturity. (Among the magazine's patrons were the Associated Retailers of Nashville.) In the late twenties some of the Fugitives began to investigate the connections between southern economics and politics and southern writing. Out of their discussions came *I'll Take My Stand: The South and the Agrarian Tradition, By Twelve Southerners* (1930), a book which provoked one of the hottest literary controversies of the century. Only four of the contributors, Ransom, Davidson, Tate, and Warren, had been members of the group in its Fugitive stage. They were now joined by a southern historian, Frank L. Owsley, and an economist, H. C. Nixon. Among the other men of letters who participated were John Gould Fletcher, Andrew Lytle, and Stark Young. The volume contains essays on the state of southern letters, education, religion, and economic development. It was doubtless the introductory "Statement of Principles" which evoked the violent criticisms of the book. The authors stood together in decrying the evils of an industrialized society and in advocating that the south remain faithful to its agrarian tradition. For their pains these twelve Southern Agrarians (the designation stuck) were attacked as neo-Confederate reactionaries and poets who were meddling in matters they knew nothing about. But their theses were brilliantly argued and converts were not slow in coming to their defense.*

It has been said that every southern boy who heard veterans' tales of the War between the States dreamed at some time of leading the charge which would have turned defeat into final victory. Donald Davidson (b. 1893) must have been visited often by this dream. His writing abounds in images of surrenderless retreat. He has defended his region and his state like a Confederate general falling back but never capitulating.

It is easier to say what Davidson dislikes about modern America (dominated by hustling Yankees) than what he approves of. With the rhetoric of a Calvinist preacher he thunders against science, industry, gadgetry, machine-reproduced art, Teachers College education, reconstructed southerners, sociologists, bureaucrats hell-bent to build the

* In 1936 eight of the Agrarians joined with a group of Distributists to issue a second symposium, *Who Owns America?*

Leviathan state, and integrationists. He admires the Old Southern way of life (and describes it believably), shape-note singers, the Tall Men of Tennessee, and, oddly enough it might seem, Brother Jonathan in Vermont where he finds that the New England of Whittier and Webster miraculously survives.

Davidson has published only three volumes of verse. The third, *Lee in the Mountains* (1938), constitutes his selected poems. Most of them are verse narratives, little affected by modern techniques. In another age he might have written epic poetry, the verse form he most admires. He has been prolific as a critic, historian, and commentator (or denunciator). His selected essays — *Still Rebels, Still Yankees* (1957) — suggests the range of his interests and his leading ideas. His most enduring work may prove to be *The Tennessee* (1946, 1948), his contribution to the Rivers of America Series.

After the other Agrarians departed from Nashville, re-treating north, Davidson stood alone on the ramparts. He must feel at times, like his Robert E. Lee (in "Lee in the Mountains"), that he is "a voice commanding in a dream where no flag flies."

One has to read only a little way in the writings of the Fugitives and Agrarians to realize that John Crowe Ransom was their leading strategist. Born in 1888, he was older than the others; five years older than Davidson, eleven years older than Tate. Having taught so many of the group — Tate, Warren, Lytle, Brooks, and among their disciples, Randall Jarrell and Peter Taylor — he was naturally de-ferred to. In turn, in the early days, his students did much for him. If it had not been for the stimulus of their com-pany, he might have continued to be the superb teacher that he was, without playing any part in the movement he helped them initiate. He had been slower than the other Fugitives to recognize the changes wrought in the south by the first World War. He wrote no poetry until he was twenty-eight and most of the poems in his first volume, *Poems about God* (1919), were old-fashioned. As Randall Jarrell has remarked, they are "full of reapers and sermons and blackberry pie, quite as country as anything in the early Frost." The midnight conclaves in Nashville changed the direction of his life.

Ransom's career as a poet was brief. He published two further volumes in the twenties, *Chills and Fever* (1924) and *Two Gentlemen in Bonds* (1927); only five poems thereafter. In compiling his *Selected Poems* in 1945 he pruned so rigorously (taking nothing from *Poems about God*) that the volume is stripped down to forty-two poems. It would be difficult to name a single volume by an American poet in which the quality is so consistently high. Only a handful are "southern" in theme or reference — "Dead Boy," "Conrad in Twilight," "Old Mansion," "Antique Harvesters" — but we know their place of origin by other signs. There are sudden glimpses of southern landscape, the names of Tennessee things, the momentary rhetoric of the southern preacher or orator, and fine old words like theogony and bruit, carried from England to the southern mountains and remembered there, though forgotten by most of us. There are frequent echoes of the King James version of the Bible which remind us that Ransom was brought up in a parson's family.

Though his output was small, Ransom's poetry is as idiosyncratic as that of Marianne Moore or Allen Tate. The metaphysical influence is visible but there are no echoes of Donne or Marvell. In the human tragedies, large or little, which he writes about, life is always in a state of crisis: ambition forewarned of defeat, appearance deceiving reality, the trustingness of youth overborne by the discovery of death, small passion which feigns large. But the wit is never bitter nor the irony cruel.

In the 1930's Ransom became one of the most influential of American literary critics. Many of the essays in his first collection, *The World's Body* (1938), deal directly with particular authors and their work, but others indicate that he had been pondering the state of literary criticism in this country and the need for precise formulations of terms and concepts. In such essays as "Poets without Laurels" and "Poetry: a Note in Ontology" he was already at work inventing new terminology. His next volume, *The New Criticism* (1941), reveals him in search of the kind of critic demanded by our age. Having found I. A. Richards, Eliot, and Yvor Winters wanting, he advertises for an "ontological critic." With his usual modesty and good manners Ransom does not claim the job for himself.

After he went to Kenyon College in 1937 as Carnegie Professor of Poetry and Editor of the *Kenyon Review*, Ransom became even more devoted to criticism as a guide in an age which had lost its faculty "for the rule of action which is positive and life-giving." In his Introduction to *The Kenyon Critics, Studies in Modern Literature from the Kenyon Review* (1951) he asserts the primacy of the critical function. The one authority left us which is still universally reputable is literature, but literature in our time has become, perforce, cryptic and Delphic. "It is the critic who must teach us to find the thing truly authoritative but hidden."

Allen Tate's part in the southern renaissance is paradoxical. A friend of Eliot, Spender, Alexis St.-Leger ("St.-John Perse"), and Jacques Maritain, quoted and written about by men of letters in London, Paris, Rome, and even the Orient, he is the member of the Fugitive group who is most certainly an international figure. He was the first to leave the Nashville nest. In 1924 he came to New York, determined to make his way as a poet, and was soon of the company of Fitzgerald, Hart Crane, and John Peale

Bishop. Like them he made the pilgrimage to Paris. Though he has returned to the south at intervals, he is now identified with the larger movement of modern letters. One would suppose that images of his region might long since have faded from his poetry. But they have not. The unifying episode of one of his latest poems, "The Swimmers" (1953), recalls the aftermath of a lynching he witnessed as a boy.

In the early Fugitive days Tate (b. 1899) was more oppressed by the weight of the southern past than were his associates. In his contribution to *I'll Take My Stand* he could not assume the somewhat jaunty pose taken by Ransom in "Reconstructed but Unregenerate" or praise unreservedly the yeoman south as Lytle did in "The Hind Tit." In his "Remarks on Southern Religion" Tate was searching for the roots of failure rather than defeat. What had brought about the collapse of the Old South, he maintained, was the inadequacy of its religion. Hag-ridden with politics and so believing that the "ends of man are sufficiently contained in his political destiny," the south after the War had no defense against "the post-bellum temptations of the devil, who is the exploiter of nature." Industrialism, scientism, positivism might well triumph in the south as they had done, long since, in the north.

It was impossible for Tate to move into the modern world without coming to terms, somehow, with his past. In such early poems as "The Mediterranean" and "Aeneas at Washington" he pursues the themes of willed exile and alienation from ancestors. He found the symbol he needed for these poems in the figure of Aeneas, setting forth from ruined Troy, carrying the old man, his father, upon his back. From the wreck there was little that Aeneas (or the poet) could save, except "a mind imperishable" and

> a love of past things tenuous
> As the hesitation of receding love.

In 1926 Tate completed the first version of his best-known poem, "Ode to the Confederate Dead," which he continued to revise over the next ten years. Here he faces the Fugitives' problem anew and states it definitively. The narrator stands at the gate of a Confederate cemetery, looking out on row after row of headstones and listening to the dirge of the plunging leaves. Memories of the "immoderate past" and of the inscrutable infantry which once rose "demons out of the earth" turn the narrator in on himself. What can we do who bow "our heads with a commemorial woe"?

> Shall we take the act
> To the grave? Shall we, more hopeful, set up the grave
> In the house? The ravenous grave?

The narrator gives no answer, for there can be no answer except to shut the gate and leave time, the gentle serpent, as "sentinel of the grave who counts us all!"

This fine poem, one of the finest written in this century, is "about" a southerner and his past. It is also about something else more universal, as Tate obligingly tells us in an explanatory essay published in 1938, "Narcissus as Narcissus": It is about solipsism or Narcissism "or any other *ism* that denotes the failure of the human personality to function objectively in nature and society."

In this sentence Tate gives us a key to his critical prose as well as his poetry. He has been obsessed continuously with the evil which results because modern man "wastes his energy piecemeal over separate functions that ought to come under a unity of being." Means have become divorced from ends, religion from moral agency, "poetry from thought, communion from experience, and mankind in the community from men in the crowd" ("The Man of Letters in the Modern World"). Tate's poetry shows us instances of this fragmentation. In "Last Days of Alice" we see the folly of our elevation of science to a religious cult. In "Sonnets at Christmas" the theme is the impotence of modern religion within its easy forms. In "Winter Mask" the poet asks "the master Yeats" why man hates his salvation and finds his last safety

> In the self-made curse that bore
> Him towards damnatiòn.

In his criticism Tate has been chiefly concerned with the relation between the dissociated sensibility of modern man and the condition of letters. Among his critical essays there are many excellent pieces on individual writers (Hart Crane, Pound, Hardy, Poe) and Tate, like Ransom, has made contributions to literary theory ("Tension in Poetry," "The Angelic Imagination"), but a mere listing of some of his titles will show how constantly he has bent his mind to the function of literature in this "time of illiberal specializations": "The Present Function of Criticism," "Literature as Knowledge," "The Man of Letters in the Modern World," "To Whom is the Poet Responsible?" He has believed with an undiminished passion that literature furnishes us "the complete knowledge of man's experience." The only cure for our present ills is to restore literature to its rightful place among man's activities. Tate is not very hopeful of the outcome but he does venture to assert, in "The Present Function of Criticism," that literature is tough; "and after the dark ages of our present enlightenment it will flourish again."

Though Caroline Gordon Tate (b. 1895) never signed any manifestoes issued by the Agrarians, she has been present in their councils. She has fed and lodged their protégés, and reshaped many a neophyte's prose. All of her eight novels, except *The Malefactors* (1956), deal with southern life. Northern readers who wish to learn about southern ways should go to school to her fiction. She knows the life cycle of the quail, how a house grows from a dog-trot cabin to a mansion with a portico, how the Tennessee walking horse is trained, how often the boys at Sawney Webb's school were birched, how crops and animals were bred out of the land, and how nature had to be propitiated if there was to be fertility.

From the beginning Miss Gordon experimented with form. Each new novel was a challenge to her technical competence. In *Penhally* (1931) she orders the manifold life of three generations in one plantation house by committing the events to the consciousness of the three men who, in successive generations, care most deeply for the land and the house. Technically, *Aleck Maury, Sportsman* (1934) is a tour de force. Here her problem was to interest the reader continuously in an old man telling his life story, a story which is essentially one prolonged fishing trip. Though her next two novels, *None Shall Look Back* and *The Garden of Adonis* (both published in 1937), have structural faults, they are much more ambitious than the first two. *The Garden of Adonis* is significant because she was searching for new ways to relate two levels of experience and experimenting for the first time with the uses of myth.

In *Green Centuries* (1941), one of the few first-rate American historical novels, Miss Gordon brought substance and form into perfect harmony. The story concerns two brothers who join the pioneers heading west from North Carolina to settle on the new lands between the Watauga and the Holston. Archy is captured by Indians, learns to revere their ordered life, and never returns to white civilization; Rion makes a clearing but his life ends in tragedy when his child is killed in an Indian raid and his wife dies, driven mad by grief. The means by which the two stories, with their pictures of two opposed societies, are united gives the novel an extraordinary depth. As the wandering white

men follow the sun towards its setting, the plans and movements of the Indians are always present in their consciousness. In the councils of the Indians the white invaders are
never forgotten. We see the one society through Rion's
eyes, the other through Archy's; each among his people,
they make the reader see.

With *The Women on the Porch* (1944) Miss Gordon
turned to a different kind of novel, concentrating on a
few characters and the modern scene. Catherine Chapman,
married to a young historian, discovers his infidelity, and
flees instinctively to her childhood home in the south, Swan
Quarter, where three women sit rocking on the porch, waiting for nothing. (Are they the three Fates?) What she
has really fled to is a modern southern hell, and as the
story unfolds she moves deeper and deeper into its blackness until at the end Jim, her husband, comes to rescue
her. Informing the novel, as one soon guesses, is the myth
of Orpheus and Eurydice, not the classical version, but
the story as Gluck transformed it, permitting Eurydice
to return to the land of the living.

Miss Gordon's *The Strange Children* (1951) is another
parable for our time, its main theme being the search for
a way out or a way up by the "strange children," these still
not grown up children of the modern world. Because Lucy,
the child in the house, is at the age when children are avid
to know what their elders are really up to, it is possible for
Miss Gordon to project her story through and beyond her.
Because Lucy is innocent, she has no names for the
strange things she witnesses — adultery, madness, and religious ecstasy. She has only wonder and compassion. But
her heart has guessed what cannot be said by either mind
or mouth.

The setting of *The Malefactors* is an estate in Pennsylvania, and the south enters it only through the reveries of
some of its characters. Essentially it is a religious novel,

the story of a marriage which has gone to smash and is pieced together by the intervention of a saintly woman, friend of the unhappy pair in the days of their first love.

It is too early to say whether, because of Miss Gordon's conversion to Roman Catholicism, religion will replace the south in her fiction. It is clear, however, that as the south has faded from her novels, religion has taken its place. The way, it would seem, is no longer back, but up.

The careers of Allen and Caroline Tate and Robert Penn Warren (b. 1905) are linked in many ways. Warren was born in Guthrie, Kentucky, near the Tennessee border and was brought up in that region, known as the Black Patch because of the dark-fired tobacco grown there. It is the same region that figures in Caroline Gordon's early novels because it was also her country. Tate and Warren were students together at Vanderbilt.

Warren is best known as a novelist, but he has written excellent criticism and is a distinguished poet. From 1951 to 1956 he taught play-writing at Yale. His most admired novel, *All the King's Men* (1946), was first drafted as a play (*Proud Flesh*); and his *Brother to Dragons* (1953) is an interesting experiment in casting the long narrative poem in a pageantlike form which permits the author to introduce R.P.W. as one of the speakers, as well as Thomas Jefferson and other historical figures (Place: *No Place* Time: *Any time*).

Like the other Fugitives, Warren writes from deeply-rooted principles. He is as much concerned as Tate with man's failure to function objectively in nature and society though he does not find this a particularly modern phenomenon. (Original sin has a long history.) He believes, with Ransom, Davidson, and Caroline Gordon, that the Old South achieved in some degree a balanced social order because (as he says in an essay on Faulkner) it allowed "the traditional man to define himself as human by setting up codes, concepts of virtue, obligations, and by accepting the risks of his humanity." But Warren does not blink the failures of this society, as Davidson does, nor does he follow Miss Gordon in idealizing it.

Two particular themes are constant in Warren's fiction: the inevitablility of violence and the need for self-fulfillment which can be achieved only through self-recognition. Some critics have objected that the violence which erupts in a Warren novel degrades his fiction to the level of melodrama. It is present for two reasons. In the first place Warren wishes to be realistically faithful to the tradition of violence in the south which persists because the south inherits the vigilantism of the frontier and a code which taught men to take the law into their own hands when personal honor was involved. But violence also functions in the moral and psychological structure of Warren's fiction. Some men are naturally evil, like Tiny Duffy, the "city-hall slob" of *All the King's Men*. Some, like Willie Stark (modeled on Huey Long), are corrupted by a vanity nourished by the subservience of their followers. Others, like Percy Munn in *Night Rider* (1939), compromise with evil in the hope of doing good and are thus led, step by step, to destruction. Still others, like Jack Burden, in *All the King's Men*, hope to escape the violence and the evil by standing cynically at one side or, like Dr. Adam Stanton in the same novel, by turning their backs on it. But what Jack Burden learns, as do all the Warren heroes who come to self-fulfillment, is that "the world is like an enormous spider web and if you touch it, however lightly, at any point, the vibration ripples to the remotest perimeter and the drowsy spider feels the tingle and is drowsy no more but springs out to fling the gossamer coils about you who have touched the web and then inject the black, numbing poison under your hide."

There is no way a man may escape the contamination of

the world. All that the good man can do is to help worldly decency conspire with unworldly truth. The recognition of our complicity in the common lot of our kind is the beginning of innocence and the recognition of the necessity which compels our complicity is the beginning of freedom. As R.P.W. himself says, speaking for his heroes, in *Brother to Dragons,*

> The recognition of the direction of fulfillment is the death of the self,
> And the death of self is the beginning of selfhood.
> All else is surrogate of hope and destitution of spirit.

IV

That the south in this century should be supplying the nation with a large part of its fiction, whether written by Agrarians or novelists of some other persuasion, is, of course, no new phenomenon. In the years between 1870 and 1910 the "southern novel" ranked with cotton and tobacco as a staple commodity, Thomas Nelson Page and Mary Johnston sending northward supplies from Virginia, James Lane Allen and John Fox, Jr. from Kentucky, and Miss Murfree from Tennessee. Many of these novelists were born in the upper south so that one hears the voice of the plantation aristocracy in their writing. As a result of the immense popularity of their fiction they must have persuaded many readers of the rightness of the Lost Cause. But they were nationalists as well as southerners; Lincoln was a greater hero to them than Jefferson Davis. Their novels, in consequence, did much to heal the wounds of the Civil War.

The later generation of southern novelists went much farther afield for subjects and uncovered aspects of southern life which would have horrified Mary Johnston or Allen if they had been willing to acknowledge their existence. Despite this new range and variety certain subjects are conspicuously absent or have been only lightly touched. No southern novelist has done for Atlanta or Birmingham what Herrick, Dreiser, and Farrell did for Chicago or O. Henry and Dos Passos for New York.[1] Aside from a few proletarian novels of the 1930's (e.g. Grace Lumpkin's *To Make My Bread*) there are almost no fictional treatments of the industrialized south. Politics, one of the most engrossing of southern occupations, occasionally enters a southern novel by the side door but Warren's *All the King's Men* is the only full-scale fictional study of the southern demagogue of the Tillman-Talmadge-Long variety.[2]

It is also surprising that so few southern novelists have sought their materials in the sweeping social changes taking place in their region. There are almost no novels which deal extensively with the destruction of the power of the planter aristocracy and the rise of the trading class, the effect of the migration of the hill people to the cities, the coming of northern capital, the Yankeefication of such centers as Charlotte, Birmingham, and Houston. Some of the Agrarian novelists deal with one aspect of this swiftly changing scene: the delusive hope of the progressives of the New South that a poultice of industrial and commercial wealth could cure all the ills of the region. Hamilton Basso, in *Cinnamon Seed* (1934), *Courthouse Square* (1936), and *The View from Pompey's Head* (1954), concerned himself with the impact of social change at various levels, but his novels tend to slide over into melodrama or to concentrate on one individual or one family. T. S. Stribling's trilogy — *The Forge* (1931), *The Store* (1932), *Unfinished Cathedral* (1934) — stands as the most ambitious attempt to depict social change in one area of the south (northern Alabama) between 1850 and 1930. Stribling's skill as a novelist did not equal his ambition. His trilogy is plot-ridden and his characters are case histories. As with Sinclair Lewis, it is sometimes difficult to tell whether he is reporting fact or attempting satire. He is best when he deals with the secret relations between Negroes and whites and the tar-brush tragedies which are perpetuated from one generation to the next.

As the attitude of many southerners toward the Negro and the Negro problem changed from paternalistic benevolence to bewilderment and despair to a sense of direct moral involvement, several younger novelists moved with the times. The treatment of race relations in such novels as David Westheimer's *Summer on the Water* (1948), Jefferson Young's *A Good Man* (1953), and Elizabeth Spencer's *The Voice at the Back Door* (1956) is forthright and compassionate.

If modern southern novelists have avoided cities and factories, they have specialized so thoroughly in certain other subjects that the term "southern novel" has a particular significance to critics in Paris as well as to the pocketbook trade at home. History is one of the subjects.

In New England, history has dwindled in the dingy streets of the milltowns. Megalopolis sprawls over the past in the middle states. In the far west the memory of Indian and Spanish days clings to a few scattered mission churches and "restored" forts and mining towns. A sense of the past has likewise faded from the fiction of these regions. But in modern southern fiction one seldom comes on a man who does not carry a past with him. And he cannot move forward into the future without his burden. As the narrator says in Warren's poem "History,"

> We are
> But doom's apparitor
> Time falls, but has no end
> Descend!

This preoccupation with time past is not confined to novelists like Hervey Allen and Margaret Mitchell who made the writing of historical fiction their chief business. Ellen Glasgow worked at her series of novels on the "Commonwealth at large" for twenty years. Three of Warren's six novels are historical as are two of Caroline Gordon's eight. (Possibly her novel of the generations in one family, *Penhally*, should count as a third.) Allen Tate's *The Fathers* (1938) depicts the disintegration of a Virginia family under the pressures caused by the oncoming of the Civil War.

Southern novelists journey back in time as easily as Dos Passos moves along the 42nd parallel. Even when they are not concerned with the great moments of southern history and do not require General Lee or President Davis to make an entrance, the time of the action is as often 1850 or 1880 as the present. Such novelists as Warren and Lytle seem more at home on the Natchez trace or in cities beleagured by Federal troops than in the years of their own lifetime.[3]

Another variety of southern fiction carries on the nineteenth century tradition of "local color" writing, though in their confrontation of the realities of life the stories of Eudora Welty, Jesse Stuart, Marjorie Kinnan Rawlings, and Katherine Anne Porter have little in common with the tepidities of a Miss Murfree or a James Lane Allen. Like them, however, these newer regionalists specialize in the folkways, codes of behavior, inherited feuds, the misfits and rebels of a particular subregion. Miss Welty is at home in the Mississippi Delta region of her *Delta Wedding* (1946) and *The Golden Apples* (1949). Jesse Stuart seldom ventures down from the Kentucky hills which shape the *Head O' W-Hollow* (1936). Mrs. Rawlings' stories of the hammock and scrubland of Florida (*South Moon Under*, 1933; *The Yearling*, 1938) prove that a regionalist does not have to be born to the trade. A journalist for many years in the north, in 1928 she deliberately made for herself a new life in this primitive, semi-frontier region and set to work to know its roads and creeks, its people and their ways, a process she delightfully describes in the auto-biographical sketches in *Cross Creek* (1942). Katherine Anne Porter is a roving regionalist. She has lived in many parts of the south (as well as Mexico and Europe) and she understands the lives of Mexican and German colonists in Texas, the Cajuns of Louisiana, and the Creoles of New Orleans. The varied settings of the stories in her first volume, *Flowering Judas* (1930; 1940), confirm the aptness of her remark that she has known "a borderland of strange tongues and commingled races."

In the 1920's many white novelists turned to Negro life for their subjects. This development coincided with the upsurge of interest in Negro culture, here and abroad, though how much the movement in literature was influenced by the popularity of jazz, the spirituals and the blues, and African primitive art would be difficult to say. This interest has grown and become so diversified that in almost any new novel by a southerner one may expect to find Negro life and the relations between the two races treated extensively.

Some southern novelists — the Agrarians for example — were little affected by the turn to Negro themes.[4] Miss Glasgow had treated her incidental Negro characters sympathetically but with one exception she did not attempt to penetrate their psychology. In her last novel, *In This Our Life* (1941), she made the anguish of a young Negro, on whom one of the white characters tries to shift the blame for accidentally killing a child, the focus of her last chapters. One of Miss Roberts' novels, *My Heart and My Flesh* (1927), is concerned with Negro-white relations. Its action turns on Theodosia Bell's devastating discovery that her father has had three Negro bastards who are living in the same village with her and that one of them is the son of a half-witted Negress whose hovel is in the alley behind the jail.

Two novelists of aristocratic Charleston, DuBose Heyward and Julia Peterkin, reached a wide public with their novels on Negro themes. Heyward's *Porgy* (1925) tells the story of a crippled beggar living in Catfish Row and his mistress, Bess, whom he tries to rescue from drink and dope. It was phenomenally successful as a novel, later as a play, and then in the operatic version, *Porgy and Bess,* for which George Gershwin wrote the music. Heyward's *Mamba's Daughters* (1929), a more ambitious work than *Porgy,* attempts to portray fully three different types of Negro women: Mamba, an untraditional mammy; Hagar, an illiterate giant of a woman who does a man's work in the phosphate mines; and her talented daughter Lissa who becomes a famous concert singer — in the north, of course. Heyward's pages are spotted with purple prose but Negro critics agree that his understanding of Negro life was remarkable. They are less enthusiastic about Julia Peterkin whose best-known work, *Scarlet Sister Mary* (1928), won a Pulitzer Prize. As the wife of a plantation manager, Mrs. Peterkin knew the Negroes of her region well, but in her later work she condescends to them and falls back on the legend of the happy, childlike Negro, content with a clean cabin and plenty of fat-back and pot-liquor.

The liberalism of T. S. Stribling and Hamilton Basso is evident in their treatment of Negro themes. Though Stribling's *Unfinished Cathedral* (1934) was a successful novel, one doubts if it was much liked in the south. The scene in which the old quadroon, Gracie, taunts Colonel Milt Vaiden (who had his first sex with her) with the sins of the white Vaidens is melodramatic but believable. Two little-known collections of stories by E. C. L. Adams, a white physician of Columbia, South Carolina, *Congaree Sketches* (1927) and *Nigger to Nigger* (1928), are admired by Negroes for their faithful recording of the Negro's covert thoughts about white folks. Artistically one of the best of these southern novels on Negro themes is Lyle Saxon's *Children of Strangers* (1937). The setting is a social island in Louisiana populated by mulattoes descended from a French planter who left a fortune to his yellow son. The novel's tragic heroine, Famie (Euphémie), is cast out from the group when, alone and in dire poverty, she turns to the blacks for help. She has sacrificed everything so that her near-white son may escape and pass.

Meanwhile Negro novelists were beginning to find publishers and an audience. The first novel written by an American Negro, William Wells Brown's *Clotel, or the President's Daughters*, was issued in 1853. It imitated, naturally enough, the tears and sunshine romances of the decade. At the turn of the century Charles Waddell Chestnutt was writing boldly and successfully about the white man's injustice to the Negro, facing at the same time the weaknesses of his Negro characters. But until the late 1920's the Negro novelist's difficulties were almost insurmountable. What could he write about? If he attempted to depict white society, he had little first-hand experience to go on. If he wrote exclusively of Negro life (except in such exotic places as Harlem and New Orleans, the city of jazz), his episodes and characters seemed commonplace. A publisher who accepted a novel by a Negro often concealed the fact that his author was colored. As educated Negroes increasingly made their way in the society of their white fellow-writers or turned with confidence in their search for stories to the life of their own people, the situation improved. Louisiana-born Arna Bontemps, librarian of Fisk University, traced the sporting life of a Negro jockey in *God Sends Sunday* (1931) and more ambitiously in *Black Thunder* (1935) built an exciting historical novel on the facts of Gabriel's slave rebellion in the Virginia of 1800. Zora Neale Hurston, trained as an anthropologist, brought to life the Negroes of her native Florida in *Jonah's*

Gourd Vine (1934) and *Their Eyes were Watching God* (1937).[5] James Weldon Johnson's fictional *Autobiography of an Ex-Coloured Man,* published anonymously in 1912, prefigured the kind of novel many Negro writers would later attempt. (Johnson's authorship was acknowledged in the reissue of 1927.) The theme of "passing" was boldly treated and, as Carl Van Vechten notes, the hero "either discusses (or lives) pretty nearly every phase of Negro life, North and South and even in Europe, available to him at that period."

Best known of southern-born Negro novelists is, of course, Richard Wright, whose first work, *Uncle Tom's Children* (1938), contained the most violent and recriminating stories of race relations in the south thus far published. Wright, who fought his way up from poverty with his fists and his brains, hated the south, the black south as well as the white, as his autobiography, *Black Boy* (1945), reveals. As soon as he could, he escaped to Chicago which is the setting of his best-known novel, *Native Son* (1940). Wright's hegira from the south to the supposedly more hospitable north and then onward to Europe has been the course of many Negro writers. (Ralph Ellison is the latest fugitive.) This is part of the price America, and the south especially, pays for its rejection of the Negro. But what sympathetic American would ask of a Wright or an Ellison that he should endure outrageous fortune in order that he might stay, humbly and subserviently, close to his people and write about them when there is a world to win, the world of millions of people of color in Asia and Africa?

For every American who has read a novel by Elizabeth Roberts or Eudora Welty there are 10,000 who read Erskine Caldwell. The man in the street who steps in to buy his fiction from the rack of paperbacks in the drug store or supermarket must believe that the south is entirely populated by characters out of Caldwell's stories. And a pretty lot they are: Jeeter Lester and Sister Bessie; Ty Ty Walden and three-hundred-pound Sheriff Jeff McCurtain; an itinerant evangelist whose side line is lechery; an easy-loving waitress in an all-night restaurant; a widow-woman (size 44 with her girdle on) who feebly tries to save her daughter from a life of sin.

Like Jack London a half century ago, Caldwell is our most read novelist, abroad as well as at home.[6] 'He thinks of himself as a serious writer, as his autobiography, *Call It Experience* (1951), shows, and for many years competent critics also took him seriously. Possibly the reasons why are obvious enough. In *Tobacco Road* (1932) — his fourth book — he seemed to stand forth as the champion of the poor-white, a realist who told the whole truth, and a humorist who could make us laugh at the itchy sexuality of the members of the Lester household, their sole remaining possession and pastime. The verdict was confirmed when *God's Little Acre* appeared the next year. At last America had a writer of fabliaux.

Caldwell seems never to have noticed what his paperback success did to him. From the beginning he wanted to be a writer and he slaved at the job for many years, an expatriate in Maine from his native Georgia. But the promise of the early books was not fulfilled. The inevitable Caldwell novel or collection of stories (there is a new one on the racks every few months) repeats the earlier shootings and shack-ups. He has long since lost his sense of locale. He no longer hears the cadences or the idiom of southern speech. The goods he has to sell are as standardized as the cigars and face-creams with which they compete.

The poor south! The genteel novelists of the 1900's sentimentalized it beyond recognition; Caldwell has vulgarized it in a version which France, Russia, and Japan accept as the sober (and welcome) truth.

V

William Faulkner (b. 1897) must have been aware of the fact that a remarkable renaissance in southern writing was taking place in his lifetime and that, the world over, he was known to be playing the leading role in it. But he belonged to none of the groups or cliques working self-consciously to bring about this revival. He did not theorize about it or sign manifestoes or praise the work of his fellow-writers in the south. He was indifferent to the literary goings-on in Richmond, Charleston, and Nashville. For six months in 1925, while writing sketches and stories for the New Orleans *Times-Picayune,* he knew the men who edited and contributed to the *Double-Dealer,* but this was the only time he has ever been identified with any group of writers. Pressed in an interview, years later, to say whether he read any of his contemporaries, his answer was No.[7] He declared he read only the books he knew and loved when he was young: "The Old Testament, Dickens, Conrad, Cervantes — *Don Quixote,* I read that every year, as some do the Bible, Flaubert, Balzac." He confessed to rereading the Elizabethan and Romantic poets and some of the Russians. Elsewhere he has praised Thomas Wolfe and Hemingway. (The inquisitive Japanese, when he lectured at Nagano in 1955, edged him into recalling that he had looked into a few other contemporary writers.) The Faulkner legend, which he does nothing to disturb, maintains that he is not a literary man at all, but a rustic fellow, fond of hunting, shooting, storytelling, horse-breeding, and whiskey. He is just another man trying to do a job well, like a house-builder or an airplane pilot.

Yet from the year of his first novel, *Soldiers' Pay* (1926), Faulkner has been talking about the south. He has brooded over his region, its history, its present condition, and its possible destiny. Sooner or later most of his characters have something to say on the subject, as young Quentin Compson does at the end of *Absalom, Absalom!* (1936). He has been reviewing and re-creating with his Harvard roommate, Shreve McCannon (a Canadian), the long and involved story of Thomas Sutpen's effort to build a great house and found a dynasty to inherit it, a tale full of violence and sin. When they finish, Shreve says, "Now I want you to tell me just one thing more. Why do you hate the South?" Quentin answers quickly. "I don't hate it. *I don't hate it,* he thought, panting in the cold air, the iron New England dark; *I don't, I don't hate it! I don't hate it.*"

Far from hating the south, Faulkner loves it intensely and with pride. He told his Japanese interrogators, who could not understand how he could love it and still write about the evil and the baseness to be found there, that just to write about the good qualities "wouldn't do anything to change the bad ones." He had to make people angry enough or shamed enough to want to redeem the evil.

In the "proletarian" thirties several misguided reviewers took Faulkner's depiction of such evil characters as Popeye (in *Sanctuary*) and Jason Compson (in *The Sound and the Fury*) and his compassion for the Negro as social criticism. They hoped Faulkner was on his way over to the Left. Nothing could have been further from his intention. Like any one in love, he just wanted the object of his love to be worthy. As Malcolm Cowley says, in the Introduction to the Viking *Portable Faulkner*, there are two sides to Faulkner's feeling for the south: "on the one side, an admiring and possessive love; on the other, a compulsive fear lest what he loves should be destroyed by the ignorance of its native serfs and the greed of traders and absentee landlords."

Faulkner does have a "theory" about the south and though it exists in fragments of recorded conversations, a few scattered magazine pieces, and the speeches of his characters, it is a coherent theory. One could summarize it in this fashion.[8]

"This land, this South, for which God has done so much, with woods for game and streams for fish and deep rich soil for seed and lush springs to sprout it and long summers to mature it and serene falls to harvest it and short mild winters for men and animals" is a doomed land with a curse upon it. The curse was put on it by slavery. The men who settled the Deep South, which is Faulkner's south, were of two kinds, aristocrats like the Sartorises and new men, the Sutpen kind, whose ambition was to be like them. In taking the land from the Indians and making it flourish, the instrument of both kinds of men was chattel slavery. This evil they inherited and with it came the curse upon the land. "The Civil War began the fulfillment of the doom."

When the attempt was made to rebuild the old order after the War, there were new plagues in the land. The carpetbaggers swarmed over it and the era of Yankee exploitation began. The south was once more a colony, owned and directed by bank managers and insurance men who lived hundreds of miles away. The sons of the old order were not the men their fathers were. After the nightmare of Reconstruction was over they held political power once more but had no use for it. Meanwhile the Snopeses, the homeless ones, had begun to seep into the crevices of society, turning up first in remote places like Varner's Crossroads, then moving boldly into the county seat itself, spawning more of their kind, blackmailing their way in. To old Ike McCaslin this land, for which God had done so much, man had "deswamped and denuded and derivered in two generations" so that

White men can own plantations and commute every night to Memphis and black men own plantations and ride in jimcrow cars to Chicago and live in millionaires' mansions on Lake Shore Drive, where white men rent farms and live like niggers and niggers crop on shares and live like animals.

More than any other southern white writer Faulkner has tried to do justice to the Negro. In his early fiction he pictured his Negroes without sentimentality or stereotype. As his understanding of their psychology increased and he continued to brood over the curse brought by slavery, his Negro characters were given larger roles in his stories. Finally, in *Intruder in the Dust* (1948), a Negro and his fate occupy the center of the stage. Lucas Beauchamp, whose grandfather was white, is willing to be lynched for a murder he did not commit, as a gesture of contempt for white folks. The real murderer is found, and Lucas saved, by a sixteen-year-old boy, an aristocratic old lady, and lawyer Stevens, the boy's uncle. Faulkner seems to be saying here, and he speaks explicitly through Stevens, that the south may yet escape its doom. If this does come about, it will be accomplished by the young, by the old who are compassionate, by thinking men, and by the Negro himself, if like Lucas he endures, asking nothing of anybody.

The end papers of the Viking *Portable Faulkner* are a map of "Jefferson and Yoknapatawpha County, Mississippi 1945 — Surveyed and mapped for this volume by William Faulkner." Like Hardy's half-actual, half-mythical Wessex, this is Faulkner's domain of which, as he said on an earlier map, he is "sole owner and proprietor." At the center is Jefferson, the county seat (the Oxford of the actual county). The county roads cross at Jefferson and the Sartoris railroad enters it from north and south. Novel by novel, story by story, Faulkner settled and peopled his county, sometimes going far back in time to single out an ancient wrong, sometimes telling a story of his own day, until a whole society had grown under his writing hand. In the county's northwest corner is Sutpen's Hundred, the locale of the evil deeds of *Absalom, Absalom!* Over to the east, near the Tallahatchie River, is the country of The Bear who roamed the woods in *Go Down, Moses*. Lena Grove, hunting for the father of the child in her belly, leads us into Jefferson and the events of *Light in August*, and to Jefferson the sad procession of the Bundrens bears the stinking corpse of their wife and mother. On a diagonal road in the southeast section is Varner's Crossroads where the insatiable Snopes tribe makes its first depredations before moving on up the road into the Town. Not far away is the Old Frenchman Place where Popeye (in *Sanctuary*) murdered Tawmmy and performed other vile and horrible acts.

Between 1929, when *Sartoris* was published, and 1957, the year of *The Town*, Faulkner recited the history of Yoknapatawpha County in more than a dozen books and three dozen short stories. But *Sartoris* was Faulkner's fourth book. What had preceded it and how, at this stage, did he come to take possession of his Yoknapatawpha domain? Having returned from service in the War, Faulkner studied for a time at the University of Mississippi and then held various odd jobs until he migrated to New Orleans in 1925. Meanwhile he had written a good deal of verse and had succeeded in getting a volume published, *The Marble Faun* (1924). In New Orleans he completed *Soldiers' Pay* (1926), the story of an invalided veteran who returns to the cold comfort of home. Sherwood Anderson, whom Faulkner admired and was seeing frequently, helped him to find a publisher. The next novel, *Mosquitoes* (1927), was written in Paris in the fall of 1925. The weakest of his novels, it mirrors the life of the *Double-Dealer* crowd whose company he had enjoyed in New Orleans. When Faulkner was asked in the interview for the *Paris Review* why in his next novel he made an abrupt departure to Yoknapatawpha County, he gave a straight answer.

With *Soldiers' Pay* I found out writing was fun. But I found out after that not only each book had to have a design but the whole output or sum of an artist's work had to have a design. With *Soldiers' Pay* and *Mosquitoes* I wrote for the sake of writing because it was fun. Beginning with *Sartoris* I discovered that my own little postage stamp of native soil was worth writing about and that I would never live long enough to exhaust it.

With Faulkner's invention of Yoknapatawpha County came a surge of creative energy. Between January 1929 and February 1931 he published four novels. The first of these, *Sartoris* (1929), is a respectable job; the others, *The Sound and the Fury* (1929), *As I Lay Dying* (1930), and *Sanctuary* (1931), are among his best. He had already assembled a large cast of characters, many of whom would reappear in his later fiction.

Sartoris covers three generations of the family which represented for Faulkner the best of the Old South. Its method and style are straightforward and give no hint of the complexities readers would encounter in *The Sound and the Fury*. The first three of the four sections of this novel use the stream of consciousness technique to present the story of the degeneration of the Compson family. In the opening section the clouded lens is the feeble consciousness of Benjy, a thirty-three-year-old idiot. The going is somewhat easier in the next section in which his brother, Quentin, a student at Harvard, broods over his father's futility, his mother's fecklessness, his sister Caddy's promiscuity, and his own vaguely incestuous love for her. The horror is too much for him and he commits suicide. Jason's section, which is easier to comprehend, reveals one of the most despicable of Faulkner's characters. Jason is now, "April 6, 1928," the head of what is left of the Compson family. Obsessed by money, in the end he is robbed by Caddy's daughter of what he has been secretly stealing from her. In this tale of disorder and disintegration Dilsey, the Negro servant, is the only force for good. Her strength comes from her love.

In *As I Lay Dying* Faulkner again uses the stream of consciousness method to take us into the minds of the Bundren family as they toil towards Jefferson, obeying

Addie's request to give her burial among her people. Each is shut up in his world: Darl, the son with the best mind and imagination, who is driven crazy by the journey; Jewell, the wild one; Dewey Dell whose one aim is to be rid of the child growing in her; Cash, who carpenters the coffin as true and straight as he does everything; and Anse, the husband who, as soon as the duty is done, presents his family with a new Mrs. Bundren. How was this novel to be taken? The characters were poor whites and the story, read one way, was sordid. Did Faulkner intend his readers to dwell on the horrors or the humor, for the novel is grimly humorous? Actually it is one of the most compassionate of his works. Here was something new in American fiction, a story of soil-bound people who suffer proudly and ask no help.

Sanctuary was another puzzle. Faulkner declared he wrote it in about three weeks just to make money. If it was a trick, the trick worked. *Sanctuary* soon had a reputation because of Popeye, the impotent bootlegger, who holds the flapper Temple Drake prisoner, rapes her with a corncob, and then keeps her in a brothel in Memphis. There is enough power in *Sanctuary* for a half-dozen novels. A few readers were shrewd enough to see that here was a master in the swift drawing of character, in the use of a quite un-American bawdy humor (the scenes in Miss Reba's Memphis establishment could make a preacher laugh), of plotting, and the construction of suspense-filled scenes.

Looking back now to Faulkner's beginnings, one is puzzled to understand why his reputation grew so slowly. For many years only those in the know cared much for him. His novels did not sell well and were frequently remaindered. As late as 1945 all seventeen of his books were out of print. Yet these four remarkable novels should have established him at once. There is perhaps one explanation why they did not. Notwithstanding their power and the novelty of the life they portrayed, there was a certain modishness about them. *Sartoris* is a novel about a returned war-hero and, as well, a novel about three genera-tions in one family. Both kinds of novels were in vogue at the time. Difficult and unusual as *The Sound and the Fury* was, still one could say of it that Faulkner had just carried Joyce's stream of consciousness technique a step farther. (Joyce had never tried to get inside the head of an idiot.) Before *As I Lay Dying* came along there had been many attempts to picture life among the lowly in America. Just how unusual Faulkner's excursions into the lower depths were remained to be proved. On the surface *Sanctuary* was a gangster novel and the prohibition era had made the gangster as ubiquitous in fiction and on the screen as the cowboy.

In these four novels there were signs of things to come. It could have been foretold that Faulkner would go on writing about some of his characters and about the families to which they belonged. He had already drawn the lives of the Sartorises and the Compsons, but he was by no means done with either family. Not until he completed the cycle of stories which were welded into *The Unvan-quished* (1938) was he ready to dismiss the Sartorises from his imagination. The Compsons were to reappear often, most notably when in 1936 the task was given to Quentin Compson of piecing together the story of Thomas Sutpen (in *Absalom, Absalom!*). But that was not the last of the Compsons. Faulkner has said that *The Sound and the Fury* was the "book I feel tenderest towards. I couldn't leave it alone, and I never could tell it right, though I tried hard and would like to try again." In the *Portable Faulkner* (1946) he did try again, in a way, by furnishing a biographical appendix entitled "1699-1945 — The Compsons," which begins with the first Quentin who fled to Carolina from Culloden Moor and ends with Luster and Dilsey who "endured." The Snopes family was to have its day much later — in *The Hamlet* (1940) and *The Town* (1957), with one more novel to come, *The Mansion* — but in *Sartoris* a Snopes (Flem) has already installed himself in the Jefferson bank and the tribe is following him into town. Faulkner's characters turn up again after they have been quiet for years. Their names are sometimes changed and their actions have been moved about in time. Faulkner had not forgotten them. They were just resting until such time as they were needed for the newest addition to the Yoknapatawpha saga.

After *Sartoris* Faulkner would never again take the easy way in writing a novel, just because he could not be faithful to his material if he did so. A Faulkner novel is enormously complicated because it has to be. Too much of the past bears on the present, too many lives are involved to permit a simple narrative line. His plots therefore defy synopsis. One single-sentence effort to suggest what happens in *Light in August* (1932) declares that it is about "a pregnant girl's violent adventures searching for the lover who has deserted her." So it is — in part — but one of the "adventures" (in which she is a distant spectator) is the murder of an aging spinster, Miss Burden, by her lover, who fears he may be a Negro. But is this statement a more accurate version of the plot? What does it suggest of the anguish of Joe Christmas (the murderer), trapped between the worlds of the Negro and the white man, or of the Reverend Hightower, another isolated one, to whose house Joe flees and where he is caught and castrated, "his eyes open and empty of everything save consciousness"? Or how is one to summarize the primary symbolism of the novel, which is not in the "plot" at all — the gentle, life-bringing natural force of Lena Grove placed beside, or above, or wherever it is but anyway over against the fanaticism and body-hunger of Miss Burden and the drawn-out violence of Joe's life?

Serious readers of Faulkner soon discovered that he had no invariable formula for telling a story. Each new situation had to be worked up as the materials dictated. From the time of *The Sound and the Fury* form was of the greatest concern to him. This is why the first fifty pages of a Faulkner novel are always the hardest. The reader has to learn to find his way again. How can he discover the story hidden in Benjy's idiotic mumblings and cries? What connection will there be between Lena Grove's slow entrance into *Light in August* and the scenes of violence which are to follow?

Possibly Faulkner's most elaborate and complicated use of form to express meaning is to be found in *Absalom, Absalom!* At times it seems to be a huge Chinese nest of boxes, with the last one always still to be disclosed. Why must the novel unfold this way? In the first section young Quentin Compson gathers fragments of the story of Thomas Sutpen — of his coming to Sutpen's Hundred to build his great house, of his marriage into a primly respectable Jefferson family, of the mysterious appearance at Sutpen's Hundred of Charles Bon (his son by a former wife who had been put away because of the taint of Negro blood), of Bon's murder by Henry Sutpen, his friend (and, as Quentin will learn in time, his half-brother), of the shooting of Sutpen by Wash Jones, and so on to the end of this story of toppled pride, miscegenation, incest, and murder, the sole heir to which is a Negro idiot who is left "to lurk around those ashes and howl." What Quentin learns from his father and grandfather and from Rosa Coldfield, Sutpen's sister-in-law, comes in fragments which do not fit. Too many of the pieces are missing. Nor does Rosa Coldfield's soliloquy (the middle section) make the contours plain. Though she knows most, perhaps, she has "demonized" Sutpen into an ogre's shape. In the last section Quentin and Shreve, his Harvard roommate, talk their way through the maze of details, using imagination and sympathy where fact is not enough. The story was given to Quentin to resolve, in the words of one critic, because "the career of Thomas Sutpen is the most persistently disturbing element in the history of his native region, and one in which all of his family have been involved. Indeed, his preoccupation with the meaning of the story is so distressing that he can see no respite from it even in the future." The story was his to resolve, of necessity.

In the *Paris Review* interview Faulkner remarked: "In my opinion, if I could write all my work again, I am convinced that I would do it better, which is the healthiest condition for an artist. That's why he keeps on working, trying again; he believes each time and this time he will do it, bring it off." There is no doubt — as the manuscripts of the novels show — that it was an enormous labor, requiring much rewriting, to bring off one of these complex novels. Possibly this is why many of the later novels are collections of stories which belong together but were extensively revised to make a unified work.[9] This development in his writing has led some critics to assert that Faulkner is most at ease and excels in the long short story. Many would agree that there are no finer episodes in all of his writing than "The Peasants" in *The Hamlet,* and "The Bear," in *Go Down, Moses.* Both were short stories before they were fitted into place in the novels.

We can enter at least one demurrer to Van Wyck Brooks's charge, made in 1921, that with us "the blighted career, the arrested career, the diverted career" are the rule. Faulkner's devotion to his craft has been as steady and may prove to be as long in use as Henry James's. He went his own way, trying to satisfy himself, teaching himself by his own errors, and so gave new life to the novel. He became the best and truest historian of his region, and has from the beginning been its conscience. His version of the Deep South prevails. If some time passed before readers sensed his compassion for his characters and his belief in the dignity of man, this was because the evil and the tortured ones in his novels, Popeye and Jason and Joe Christmas, make the most powerful impression on first reading. But there are Dilsey, who endures; Quentin Compson, whose suicide must have grieved his creator; Miz Rosa Millard, the unvanquished, who steals mules from the Yankees to feed and clothe her own people; Ratliff, the sewing-machine man, who can outguess a Snopes; and — to end a list which has only begun — Cash Bundren, who is no thinker but can think this straight:

Sometimes I aint so sho who's got ere a right to say when a man is crazy and when he aint. Sometimes I think it aint none of us pure crazy and aint none of us pure sane until the balance of us talks him that-a-way. It's like it aint so much what a fellow does, but it's the way the majority of folks is looking at him when he does it.

Some were surprised by the idealism in Faulkner's speech of acceptance when he received the Nobel Prize in 1950. They should not have been. He spoke for many of his characters as well as for himself when he said on that occasion:

I believe that man will not merely endure: he will prevail. He is immortal, not human because he alone among creatures has an inexhaustible voice, but because he has a soul, a spirit capable of compassion and sacrifice and endurance.

EIGHT

Off to the Critical Wars

REMARKABLE as have been the achievements of the American poets, dramatists, and novelists in the past half century, the Cinderella of the literary arts is criticism. In 1900 there were only two or three American literary critics worth mentioning. By 1950 so distinguished were our critics that we excelled in this kind of writing as the French had in the days of Taine and Sainte-Beuve. In John Crowe Ransom's opinion the depth and precision of contemporary critical writing is "beyond all earlier criticism in our language." (The English are invited to take some of the bows.)

For the most part American writers in the nineteenth century struggled along without critical guidance or support. In the time of Emerson and Melville there was no professional criticism to speak of. Only a very few journals — notably the *North American Review* and Duyckinck's *Literary World* — made any attempt to review books at length and with discrimination. For the rest, the reviews, particularly of American works, were perfunctory and often shockingly partisan. Poe was the only critic of distinction the age produced and he was so deeply involved in personal and literary quarrels that much of his criticism is splenetic.

By 1900 the situation was very little improved. In the colleges the traditional instruction in rhetoric and belles

275

lettres (so ably professed at Harvard by Edward Tyrell Channing, teacher of Emerson, Thoreau, and Holmes) had died out. The practitioners of the new German scholarship, putting their emphasis on philology and the older Germanic languages, had driven criticism out of the curriculum or abandoned it to the dilettantes and the "appreciators." Professional reviewing was no longer venal but those who practiced it were little esteemed. The contemporary attitude toward the craft is well summed up in three sentences in Francis W. Halsey's *Our Literary Deluge*, published in 1902: "Criticism in itself is not a high form of literature, and it is proper that it should not be. When it shines at all, it shines by a borrowed light. It must always be an ephemeral thing."

How far from being "an ephemeral thing" criticism is today can be tested by a glance at the display racks of Vintage Books, Anchor Books, Meridian Books, *et al*. Alongside novels by Wolfe, Hemingway, and Faulkner (and not far from Caldwell and Mickey Spillane) one finds such esoteric works as Kenneth Burke's *The Philosophy of Literary Form* and R. P. Blackmur's *Form and Value in Modern Poetry*. These critics are hardly household names but their newest essays are read and argued over by thousands. Their collected essays are prestige items on publishers' lists as poetry once was. The one-time Cinderella of the literary arts is queen of the ball and no one hints that there ever will be a midnight.

How this extraordinary reversal of the state of affairs took place will be the subject of this chapter, but it will be well to pause for a moment to seek some of the reasons *why* it took place. Possibly most important is the fact that by the time of the first World War it had become evident that American as well as European writers were creating works that could not be described and evaluated by using terms and concepts derived from Aristotle, the Renaissance critics, Coleridge, and Arnold. New modes demanded a critical vocabulary adequate to their definition. Unlike their "Victorian" predecessors, who despised Zolaesque naturalism and the colloquial verse of Kipling, the younger critics were eager to foster the new movement in letters and to do battle for it. While defending the contemporary American writers they were also soon led to a re-evaluation of the whole tradition of American literature in their search for a usable past.

In their quest for new techniques of analysis critics here and abroad began to discover that they had at their command a great body of new knowledge about man's behavior which was relevant to their pursuits. They borrowed freely and with admirable results from psychoanalysis, from the social sciences, from anthropology, from philosophy, and semantics. To them Freud, Jung, Marx, and Sir James G. Frazer were authorities who ranked with Aristotle and Coleridge.

As criticism abandoned its routine preoccupation with standards and the ranking of literary works, it began to ask a multitude of questions induced by the widened concept of what a poem or novel is and what it does to the reader. These questions have been aptly summarized by Stanley Edgar Hyman in *The Armed Vision, a Study in the Methods of Modern Literary Criticism.*

What is the significance of the work in relation to the artist's life, his childhood, his family, his deepest needs and desires? What is its relation to his social group, his class, his economic livelihood, the larger pattern of his society? What precisely does it do for him and how? What does it do for the reader, and how? What is the connection between those two functions? What is the relation of the work to the archetypal primitive patterns of ritual, to the inherited corpus of literature, to the philosophic world views of its time and of all time? What is the organization of its images, its diction, its larger formal pattern? What are the ambiguous possibilities of its key words, and how much of its content consists of meaningful and provable statements? [1]

II

When the new century opened, the leading critics were William Dean Howells and Henry James, fellow-novelists and friends since the 1860's. Howells' literary career stretched from 1860 to 1920 and in most of those years he practiced criticism. As editor of the *Atlantic* from 1871 to 1881 and opinion-giver from "The Editor's Study" (1886-1892) and "The Editor's Easy Chair" (1900-1920) of *Harper's Magazine*, Howells exercised a strong influence on American writing. As a critic he was receptive to experiment, though his tastes were in the main conservative. A champion of the kind of realism he practiced in his novels, he suspected the new literary naturalism and charged that it had "possessed itself of the good name of realism to befoul it." When the poets turned to free verse, he went as far with them as he could, though he called their poems "shredded prose" and was pleased to note in 1917 that the movement was coming to an end. Yet Howells deplored the state of criticism as he found it in his earlier years, its lack of principles and its frequent malevolence. Criticism, he maintained, "must concern itself with ascertaining currents and tendencies, and not proposing to direct or stop them; more and more it must realize that it is not a censorship."

In his youth Henry James was a constant reviewer for the *Nation*, the *Galaxy*, and the *North American Review*, taking everything — the bad with the good — that came to his mill. Later, while he was moving as a novelist beyond the straightforward realism of *Roderick Hudson* and *The American*, he gave himself and his readers a thorough course in the theory and practice of the English and Continental novelists. As these essays piled up, he collected them in *French Poets and Novelists* (1878), *Partial Portraits* (1888), and *Essays in London and Elsewhere* (1893). Together with the prefaces he wrote for the New York Edition of his novels and stories (1907) they form the most remarkable body of writing on the theory of fiction that we have. What Aristotle did for dramatic theory in his *Poetics*, James accomplished for the art of the novel.

In his lifetime James's career as a critic was overshadowed by his reputation as a novelist. Much of his periodical criticism remained uncollected at the time of his death. His full critical stature has been realized only in the last twenty years, but he stands now as one of the half-dozen great critics who have written in English.[2]

Much admired in the 1900's by those who hoped America was developing a literature worthy of its achievements in other realms, was the criticism of William Crary Brownell (1851–1928). For many years a journalist, Brownell became in 1888 adviser to Charles Scribner's Sons, a post he held the rest of his life. In his spare time he worked at the carefully reasoned essays which constitute *French Traits, an Essay in Comparative Criticism* (1889), *Victorian Prose Masters* (1901), and *American Prose Masters* (1909). An avowed disciple of Arnold, Brownell was a foe of impressionistic criticism and sought to apply the criterion of reason "to the work of ascertaining values apart from mere attractiveness." He agreed with Sainte-Beuve that "we need to know whether we are right or not when we are pleased." Brownell's judgments are often acute, yet there were defects in his theory that would have prevented him from dealing with the new literature of his time even if he had been so inclined. He disparaged, for example, the technical aspects of a work of art (Bouguereau was a superb technician but a poor artist) and consequently thought it was no concern of the critic to study a writer's "technic." Brownell's later works are essays in theory rather than criticism. His

Criticism (1914), *Standards* (1917), and *The Genius of Style* (1924) were written with only passing references to the new literature growing up around him.

Only nine years younger than Brownell, James Gibbons Huneker (1860-1921) wrote as if a gulf of half a century separated them. Philadelphia-born, trained as a musician but from 1878 a journalist-reviewer who often turned out 10,000 words of copy a week, Huneker loved all the arts with an equal passion. An impressionistic critic by temperament and conviction, he nevertheless possessed a creditable knowledge of the techniques of the seven arts. His reviews and articles were like his conversation at Lüchow's restaurant on New York's 14th Street, voluble, anecdotal, never resting for long on one particular idea, above all exciting and informative. The first American critic to write with due appreciation of Ibsen, Shaw, Strindberg, Nietzsche, Wedekind, Wagner, and Schoenberg, he was always on the trail of the exotic and the revolutionary.

Huneker's critical principles were few and he never bothered to elaborate them as Brownell persisted in doing. "To spill his own soul; that should be the critic's aim." It was as simple as that — if one added the injunction "humbly to follow and register his emotions aroused by a masterpiece." One can read out of Huneker's essays his preference for the aristocratic genius, his dislike of propagandistic and "democratic" art, his belief that what American criticism lacked was catholicity: "Because of our uncritical parochialism America is comparable to a cemetery of clichés."

Huneker was an idol-breaker and a ground-clearer. He did not live long enough to see the triumph of the new music and literature he had championed but he helped to make the triumph possible. One can read him with pleasure today, not only because his enthusiasms are still infective, but for the soundness of his taste and judgment.[3]

Around the time of the first World War a number of literary magazines came into existence which defended and supported the new poetry and the new fiction: the *Masses* in 1911; the *New Republic* in 1914; the *Dial*, moved from Chicago to New York in 1918 and converted from an organ of conservative opinion into a first-rate literary monthly; and the *Freeman*, founded in 1920 by Van Wyck Brooks and others. What further distinguished these journals was the vigor of the criticism they printed.

The critics of the new generation who were appearing in these magazines, men like Randolph Bourne, Conrad Aiken, J. E. Spingarn, Van Wyck Brooks, Edmund Wilson, and H. L. Mencken, were dissatisfied with the state of American criticism. It was still too much preoccupied with questions of moral and aesthetic standards, too academic to cope with the new writing, and too humble. Howells was too hesitant, Brownell, George E. Woodberry, and Paul Elmer More too reactionary. Even Huneker's eclectic impressionism seemed to lack substance and weight.

III

The first call for reform was issued by Joel Elias Spingarn (1875–1939) in "The New Criticism," a lecture delivered in 1910. Spingarn was an able literary historian and a specialist in the history of criticism. He spoke as a professor at Columbia, but his soon-to-be-famous lecture was anything but an academic exercise. By the time he finished he had demolished nearly every existing school of criticism and stood on the ruins, calling for a rebuilding based on the aesthetic of Benedetto Croce.

He began by attacking the impressionists, saying to them: "We are not interested in you, but in 'Prometheus Unbound.' To describe the state of your health is not to help us to understand or to enjoy the poem. Your criticism constantly tends to get away from the work of art, and to centre attention on yourself and your feelings." But the "objective and dogmatic" forms of criticism which were endeavoring to fight this modern heresy of impressionism were engaged in no new battle. The opposition of the two points of view was as old as the earliest reflections on the subject of poetry. "Modern literature begins with the same doubts, with the same quarrel." Yet, if they would only realize the fact, the two schools could meet on common ground and resolve their useless struggle. This common ground is "the theory of expression, the concept of Literature as an art of expression." Modern criticism must get to its real concern: "What has the poet tried to express and how has he expressed it?" With the asking of this question we shall have done with finical arguments over the genres, with theories of style, with moral judgment as the criterion of literary value. We shall have done with the "evolution" of literature, a concept first developed in the seventeenth century but given a new impulse by a false analogy to science advanced in the nineteenth. Most important, the asking of this question will free criticism from its age-long self contempt. "How can the critic answer this question without becoming (if only for a moment of supreme power) at one with the creator? That is to say, taste must reproduce the work of art within itself in order to understand and judge it; and at that moment aesthetic judgment becomes nothing more or less than creative art itself."

In a later essay, "The American Critic" (1917), Spingarn charged the critic with the task of making sure "that Plato's dream of banishing poets from the ideal Republic does not come true."

It is your chief duty, against moralist and hedonist and utilitarian alike, to justify the ways of the artist to Americans. In a land where virtuous platitudes have so often been mistaken for poetry, it is your task to explain the real meaning of the esthetic moment for the higher lives of men. But no one knows better than I that you cannot rest satisfied even with this. For the modern critic has learnt to distinguish clearly between art, philosophy, history, religion, morals, not for the purpose of denying but of establishing their essential unity in the life of the spirit. Those who deny this unity and those who would substitute for it a muddle-headed if well-meaning confusion are alike the Enemy. Though you reject the criticism in which art is forever measured and tested by the moralist's rigid rules and justified by virtues that are not her own, still less can you be satisfied with the criticism in which "ideas" are struck out in random and irresponsible flashes like sparks from the anvil of a gnome.

Spingarn did not care to lead the exodus into the promised land. In his stead Van Wyck Brooks (b. 1886) assumed leadership in the years between 1915 and 1920. Brooks's early works are primarily cultural history in which his main concern was to find explanations for the artistic poverty of the American past and to navigate American writing out of the "vast Sargossa Sea" of conflicting doctrines and emotions.

Brooks propounded his first thesis in *The Wine of the Puritans* (1909) in which he charged the Puritan tradition with having abetted the innate materialism of American society. In *America's Coming-of-Age* (1915) he maintained that there have been only two levels in American life, highbrow and lowbrow, the one typified by the Puritan and the Transcendentalist and the other by the business man: at one extreme Jonathan Edwards, at the other Franklin. There had never been any middle ground. What was not abstraction, theory, idealism was plain, vulgar, practical money-getting. We have only the rudiments of a middle tradition "that effectively combines theory and action." The progenitor of this feeble tradition was Whitman and his real significance is that he gave us for the first time "the sense of something organic in American

life." But Whitman failed us in the end. "With him originated the most unifying of native impulses; but he failed
to react upon them, to mould them, and to drive them
home."

Brooks's next work, *Letters and Leadership* (1918), was
even more pessimistic. He now saw America as a burnt-out
country disfigured by the ashes of our pioneering and the
waste-heaps of industrialism. "Old American things are
old as nothing else anywhere in the world is old, old without majesty, old without mellowness, old without pathos,
just shabby and bloodless and worn out." We have developed swiftly but there has been no ripening. Our life,
on all levels, is "in a state of arrested development." It has
lost, if indeed it has ever possessed, the principle of growth.

Who could lead us out of this waste land? Not the
pragmatists and the sociologists who had sought to pre-
empt leadership. Not the older critics. They belonged to the
same "cultivated class of old" which never "assumed the
existence of, and never attempted to create — how could
it have done so? — a common ground of experience in the
American people." There was only one group to which we
might turn for true leadership — the artists.

But certainly no true social revolution will ever be possible
in America till a race of artists, profound and sincere, has
brought us face to face with our own experience and set working in that experience the leaven of the highest culture. For it
is exalted desires that give their validity to revolutions, and
exalted desires take form only in exalted souls. But has there
ever been a time when masses of men have conceived these
desires without leaders appearing to formulate them and press
them home? We are lax now, too lax, because we do not realize
the responsibility that lies upon us, each in the measure of
his own gift. Is it imaginable, however, that as time goes on
and side by side with other nations we come to see the inadequacy of our own, we shall fail to rise to the gravity of our
situation and recreate, out of the sublime heritage of human
ideals, a new synthesis adaptable to the unique conditions of our
life?

Here is the unmistakable Brooks signature — his iterated belief in the American writer's responsibility for ordering and leading his society, a belief to which he would hold through the many turns of his subsequent career. In the light of this passionately held belief we can understand his later savage rejection of almost all of the literature of the twenties and thirties.[4] They had all failed him, these leaders who would not lead or who led men down rats' alley: Joyce, Eliot (whose John the Baptist was I. A. Richards), Pound, the "spoiled child" Proust, Gertrude Stein — all the creators of "coterie-literature" and the coterie critics who encouraged them.

Brooks's belief in the artist's responsibility was argued further — and on a shriller note — in *The Literary Life in America* (1921). Here he advanced a new hypothesis which soon became a law to his followers.

The blighted career, the arrested career, the diverted career are, with us, the rule. The chronic state of our literature is that of a youthful promise which is never redeemed.[5]

Yet there were some glimmerings of hope on the horizon. On second glance Brooks had discovered that a few earlier writers (Hawthorne, Emerson, Motley, and perhaps a half-dozen others) were held in high esteem by their countrymen. How had they won this status at a time when America, in every other department of life, was more distinctly colonial than it is now? The answer was far from simple but now that Brooks had found it he sought to apply it to his own time. These earlier writers were men of unusual power. By this fact they built up a public confidence in themselves and the literature they represented. Here, then, was the way out.

If the emerging writers of our epoch find themselves handicapped by the skepticism of the public, they have only to remember that they are themselves for the most part in the formative stage and that they have to live down the recent past of their profession.

Having gone this far into the future, Brooks faltered and turned back. After a silence of several years he began to publish his series of laudatory studies of our literary past (to be called *Makers and Finders*), the first volume of which, *The Flowering of New England* (1936), was a great popular success. He had found the cases in the waste land of America for which he had earlier vainly sought. Careers he had once termed blighted now turned out to have been very fruitful indeed and there were scores of them.

About the time when Brooks was cautiously venturing to hope that the writers would boldly seize leadership (as Hawthorne, Emerson, and Motley had once dared to do), H. L. Mencken (1880-1956) was declaring in "The American Novel" (*Prejudices Fourth Series,* 1924) that the creative writer in this country was "quite as free as he deserves to be."

He is free to depict the life about him precisely as he sees it, and to interpret it in any manner he pleases. The publishers of the land, once so fearful of novelty, are now so hospitable to it that they constantly fail to distinguish the novelty that has hard thought behind it from that which has only some village mountebank's desire to stagger the wives of Rotarians. Our stage is perhaps the freest in the world — not only to sensations, but also to ideas. Our poets get into print regularly with stuff so bizarre and unearthly that only Christian Scientists can understand it. The extent of this new freedom, indeed, is so great that large numbers of persons appear to be unable to believe in it; they are constantly getting into sweats about the taboos and inhibitions that remain.

As Edmund Wilson has remarked, Mencken "did more than anyone else in his field to bring about that 'coming of age' for which Brooks had sounded the hour." His

Book of Prefaces (1917), with its assault on Puritanism as a surviving force in our literature and its forthright defense of Dreiser, was a landmark in American criticism. If no one else would lead, Mencken would — and with a full brassband to delight the bystanders.[6]

Mencken raised more welts on sensitive hides than any critic of his generation, but his approval was worth having and was not easy to get. His critical method was empirical and he was probably glad to have Spingarn's doctrine of "creative criticism" to lean on for philosophical support. He applied the term "catalytic critic" to himself and ventured a little theorizing to explain the term. It is the business of this kind of critic "to provoke the reaction between the work of art and the spectator."

Mencken's denunciations of prudery, of insipidity and gush, month by month, in the *American Mercury*, were great fun. No one was sacred and readers rushed to see who was getting a trimming in the woodshed now. Was it Paul Elmer More or Prof. Dr. William Lyon Phelps of Yale or Irvin S. Cobb (the Ersatz Mark Twain)? Too often, it is true, Mencken's rhetoric got out of hand. Scattered through his six series of *Prejudices* (appearing between 1919 and 1927) such revisable statements as the following are preserved in amber for the ages.

Frost? A standard New England poet, with a few changes in phraseology, and the substitution of sour resignation for sweet resignation. Whittier without the whiskers. Robinson? Ditto, but with a polite bow. He has written sound poetry, but not much of it.

IV

Meanwhile two friends from Harvard days, Irving Babbitt (1865-1933) and Paul Elmer More (1864-1937), watched with increasing alarm as the ideas of Spingarn and Mencken and the younger critics gained acceptance.

Both men were advocates of a classical restraint in life as well as literature, but on one subject they were immoderate — the degeneration of modern literature and the way the critics were abetting its indecencies. In the 1900's Babbitt and More could go about their business of reform by persuasion in a tone of sweet reasonableness but as the enemies of light sprang up on all sides, their voices grew harsher. By 1918 they were in the ring slugging it out with Mencken and the rest.

In a charming tribute to his friend written just after Babbitt's death, More tells of the high seriousness of their talks together after their first meeting at Harvard in the fall of 1892.[7] At twenty-seven Babbitt was already a man of settled convictions which were "knit together into a system by logical bonds which were perfectly clear to his mind, so clear, indeed, that he tended to take them for granted as equally obvious to others." More had found in his new friend one "who never changed or faltered in his grasp of principles, whose latest word can be set beside his earliest with no apology for inconsistency, who could always be depended on." Babbitt would have preferred to teach the Greek and Roman poets at Harvard but the Classics department was then, as always, wary of him and he turned to French literature, a choice which, as More observes, was unfortunate because there were very few French writers he could admire.

Babbitt's leading ideas were set forth in his first book, *Literature and the American College* (1908). The first two chapters — "What is Humanism?" and "Two Types of Humanitarians: Bacon and Rousseau" — contain the germs of much of his thought, and he would spend the rest of his life sowing the seeds gathered in this early harvest. To Babbitt a return to humanism was the only possible cure for the diseases and heresies of our society. Modern man "has gained immensely in his grasp on facts, but in the meanwhile has become so immersed in their multiplicity as to lose that vision of the One by which his lower self was once overawed and restrained." The true humanist recognizes (with Emerson) that there is the "Law for man" and the "Law for thing" and that these "two laws discrete" cannot be reconciled. The man of today must do inner obeisance to something higher than his ordinary self. "Without this inner principle of restraint man can only oscillate violently between opposite extremes." This principle of restraint — the *frein vital* — became Babbitt's leading idea. In contrast to the fashionable Bergsonian idea of the *élan vital*, Babbitt saw it as "the highest reality and the supreme factor in that which we know as our individual character."

In the essay on Bacon and Rousseau Babbitt hunted down the enemies of humanism. False notions of progress, largely engendered by the new science of Bacon, had spawned in turn humanitarianism, Rousseauistic romanticism, and finally naturalism. During the next twenty-five years Babbitt ranged up and down modern literature driving from their secure positions writers who had been corrupted by these heresies. His most substantial work, *Rousseau and Romanticism* (1919), is the most prolonged diatribe in the history of literary scholarship. Rousseau had become for him the head devil.

With his thunderbolts in hand Babbitt was ready for the attack on the latter-day disciples of Rousseau among the critics. Spingarn was annihilated as a receiver of stolen goods from Croce and Oscar Wilde ("Genius and Taste," *Nation*, Feb. 7, 1918). The total effect of Mencken's writing is "nearer to intellectual vaudeville than to serious criticism" ("The Critic and American Life," collected in *On being Creative*, 1932). But as a critic himself Babbitt was deficient. Indeed he was not actually a critic but rather an historian of ideas. When he does pause for a sentence or two of analysis, what he has to say wings straight to the writer's moral position or lack of it. Contemporary writers were not even allowed the virtue of contemporaneity. Dreiser was Zola all over again. The much-admired technique of Dos Passos had been anticipated by the Goncourts. The free-verse writers followed in the wake of Whitman and the French symbolists.

More's intellect was subtler than Babbitt's and his personality more complex. For one thing there was a strong religious strain in him though he never submitted to orthodoxy. In contrast, Babbitt seems at times to be on guard lest Christianity proselytize members from his cult of humanism. There were spiritual crises in More's life, as we know from his Thoreau-like retreat to Shelburne, New Hampshire, in 1897.[8] He would not have done with the question of faith until he had explored in five volumes (1921–1931) the relations between the Greek tradition and the origins of Christianity.

For many years a literary editor, on the *Independent* and the New York *Evening Post*, More was from 1909 to 1914 editor-in-chief of the *Nation*. Leaving New York (which he had never liked), he became Lecturer in Greek Philosophy at Princeton. There, in his last years, a loyal group of younger scholars, brought into the humanist camp by him, listened to his essays as they were completed and delighted in his wide-ranging conversation. In their circle he was affectionately known as "the Buddha."

As Babbitt and More had once had in common their graduate studies in Sanscrit and Pali, they continued to share remarkably similar views on literature and life. At times they seem to be following each other around the treadmill. In 1908 Babbitt wrote on the imperative need for the revival of humane learning in the colleges ("Literature and the College"); in 1915 More explored the same theme in "Academic Leadership," in the ninth series of the Shelburne Essays. In the eighth series (1913) he had collected the essays in which he had dealt with the "drift of Romanticism." In 1919 Babbitt was ready with his *Rousseau and Romanticism,* plans for which he had announced nine years earlier.

As a critic More is unvaryingly judicial but he found much to admire in the literature of the past and many of his essays stand up well. (In particular those on Thoreau and Poe.) In his early years he was not given to denunciation as Babbitt was almost from the beginning. When he turned at last to the literature of his own day — in the time of his retirement at Princeton — he rapidly caught up with his phrenetic friend in Cambridge. His "Modern Currents in American Literature," written at the request of the *Revue de Paris* (collected in *The Demon of the Absolute,* 1928), is as stern an indictment of modern American writing as anything Babbitt ever uttered. (It contains his famous description of Dos Passos' *Manhattan Transfer* as "an explosion in a cesspool.")

Nevertheless More continued to make an effort to understand even if he could not enjoy. He admired at least one modern writer, T. S. Eliot, and it made him somewhat uneasy that the younger critic found so much to praise in contemporary literature. Prompted by Eliot's observations on heresy in *After Strange Gods,* More sat down to have another try at Joyce. The effort produced only further shock. More's reconsidered view of *Ulysses* might stand as his general conclusion about most of modern writing.

Here I will for once fling caution to the winds and speak out what I feel, though it subject me to the retort of ribald laughter. In this art I see at work not the conviction of sin, but the ultimate principle of evil invoked as the very enemy of truth.

"What else is this exploitation of the subconscious," More goes on to say, "but an attempt to reduce the world and the life of man back to the abysmal chaos out of which, as Plato taught, God created the actual cosmos by the imposition of law and reason upon the primaeval stuff of chance and disorder?"

As the ideas of Babbitt and More took hold — they found lodgement principally in the minds of English professors — a critical war over humanism broke out. Norman Foerster (then a professor of American literature at North Carolina) took command of the troops. He decided in the late 1920's that the time had come for a frontal attack on the disintegrative forces of modernity and that it should take the form of a symposium designed "to consider the requirements of humanism in the various activities of modern thought and life, to determine the special tasks that confront humanism in this latest moment of time," and to enlist the efforts of the considerable leaven of intelligent people who cannot view with indifference "the chaos into which our intellectual and moral life has been plunged." In 1930 the book appeared, under the title of *Humanism and America, Essays on the Outlook of Modern Civilization.*

Foerster had pressed into service several professors of English (G. R. Elliott of Amherst, Robert Shafer of Cincinnati, Harry Hayden Clark of Wisconsin, and Stanley P. Chase of Bowdoin), an art historian, Frank Jewett Mather, Jr., of Princeton, a scientist, More's brother, Louis Trenchard More, two or three critics, including T. S. Eliot (who almost at once deserted the humanist camp), and a Bowdoin college senior (an athlete as well as a humanist). Of course Babbitt and More contributed.

In his preface Foerster diagnosed one further symptom of the modern illness: the materialism and cynicism of the Harding-Coolidge era. Otherwise he did not add to the Babbitt-More inventory of the diseases of modern life. One passage in his preface came in for a good deal of ridicule from the reviewers. In noting that humanism was not new but rather that it was new "when human wisdom was new," Foerster offered a list of eminent persons who had clarified its doctrine and discipline. He admitted that it was "a strange assortment of names" but he gave them nevertheless: Homer, Phideas, Plato, Aristotle, Confucius, Buddha, Jesus, Paul, Virgil, Horace, Dante, Shakspere, Milton, Goethe, Arnold, Emerson, and Lowell. Foerster's effort to register Christ and St. Paul as partisans for humanism was considered a violation of the Geneva Convention.

Looking back at them now, one must conclude that the essays in *Humanism and America* added little to the arguments Babbitt and More had developed in the preceding twenty years. More himself seemed not much interested in the venture. His contribution — "The Humility of Common Sense" — had already appeared in print as part of the title essay of *The Demon of the Absolute*. Babbitt's "Humanism: an Essay at Definition" concentrated chiefly on the strategy needed to placate those who believed that humanism was antireligious.

The humanists' symposium was effectively attacked by a group of younger critics who were enlisted as contributors to C. Hartley Grattan's *The Critique of Humanism* (1930). One is not surprised to note in the table of contents the names of a half-dozen writers who would seize the leadership in criticism: Edmund Wilson, Malcolm Cowley, Allen Tate, Kenneth Burke, R. P. Blackmur, and Yvor Winters. Grattan's contributors reproached the humanists for the narrowness of their sympathies, their social and aesthetic snobbery, and their antipathy toward contemporary writing. Burton Rascoe called them "pupils of Polonius." Burke was suspicious of their antidemocratic allies abroad. Tate declared that their kind of humanism was merely "a mechanical formula for the recovery of civilization." Blackmur found their criticism defective because none of them knew anything about the arts at first hand. The most devastating essay was Wilson's "Notes on Babbitt and More." With an erudition matching theirs he examined a number of crucial passages in their writing and marked them as defective in logic and scholarship. Had anyone before dared to point out that Babbitt sometimes mistranslated his Greek authorities and wrenched their meaning to suit his purpose?

The critical war over humanism might have lasted longer if a more immediate issue had not pressed for attention — the function of the writer in an age of revolutionary ferment. As the depression deepened and many novelists and dramatists turned to social themes, a new criticism was called for which would direct those writers who were obedient to the "party line" in literature and admonish "fellow travelers" who might be inclined to stray too far from it. This leftist criticism had to be run up in a hurry. The cause was urgent and everything had to be done at once. Correct canons of criticism had to be extracted from the writings of Marx and Engels and promulgated. American literary history needed to be rewritten to show that our best writers had belonged to the "great tradition" of resistance to social injustice and had looked forward to a new order in American society.

As for theory, the primary question was what Marxism-Leninism demanded of the writer. Must he be a member of the Party? To what audience should the American leftist writers try to appeal? Granville Hicks, one of the Party's leading authors, was very certain of the answers when he wrote "The Crisis in Criticism" for the *New Masses* of February, 1937. The chief function of an ideal Marxist work of literature, he maintained, must be to "lead the proletarian reader to recognize his role in the class struggle." It must therefore "directly or indirectly show the effects of the class struggle." The author "must be able to make the reader feel that he is participating in the lives described" and his point of view must "be that of the vanguard of the proletariat; he should be, or should try to make himself a member of the proletariat."

But the vexed question of correct theory was not so easily settled. The revolution had not yet taken place in America and most Americans looked on themselves as members of the middle class. Where was the American proletariat to which the proletarian writer could address himself?

There were further difficulties. In Russia the Party's official attitude towards literature changed constantly. It was impossible to adapt these changes to the American situation rapidly enough. As a result many a leftist critic who considered his views thoroughly orthodox suddenly found himself charged with "deviationism" or "revisionism." Any attempt to formulate Marxist theory was certain to be attacked and discredited as soon as it was printed.[9]

Reviews by leftist critics followed one of three lines. The novelist or dramatist might be dismissed as hopelessly bourgeois or reactionary. Or, if he seemed to be headed towards the Party, the carpet would be rolled out for him. If he were a C. P. member or a fellow traveler, he got the designated treatment: a scolding or a sharp rap over the knuckles or a bouquet, depending on the degree of orthodoxy his work displayed.

Neither in literary theory nor in the analysis of particular works did the leftist critics make any very substantial contribution. Those who attempted a revision of the history of American literature on Marxist lines were more successful. Despite the distortions to be found in them, the works of this kind are still useful: V. F. Calverton's *Liberation of American Literature* (1932); Granville Hicks's *The Great Tradition: an Interpretation of Ameri-*

can Literature since the Civil War (1933; rev. ed., 1935); and Bernard Smith's *Forces in American Criticism* (1939). Two excellent critiques of the ineptitudes of Marxist criticism are James T. Farrell's *A Note on Literary Criticism* (1936) and Edmund Wilson's "Marxism and Literature" (collected in *The Triple Thinkers,* 1938).

The leftist interlude in American writing reached its high point in the mid-thirties. From then on a series of events in Russia convinced most American Marxist writers that revolution, Russian-style, would never take place in America. The first defections were caused by the trials of the "old Bolsheviks" (1936–1938). For a brief time Russia's intervention on the Loyalist side of the Spanish Civil War revived faith in the Russian "experiment." Two years later the final blow came when Stalin signed the Russo-German pact with Hitler. As the poets and novelists deserted in droves, so did the critics. Today one would search in vain for a literary Marxist in America. But the controversies over leftist writing — particularly the wars within the group itself — left many wounds. Even now when one comes on a startlingly savage critical article, there may be reason to suspect that an old quarrel, first aired years ago in the *New Masses* or the *Partisan Review,* is being revived. Though he uses new terms, the critic is really calling his victim a Stalinist or a "Bohemian renegade."

v

During the thirties a new group of critics, only a few of whom were involved in the leftist controversies, were producing important collections of essays. Edmund Wilson's important study of the Symbolist movement, *Axel's Castle,* appeared in 1931. Malcolm Cowley's *Exile's Return* (1934) discussed from first-hand knowledge the American literary expatriates of the 1920's. In the same decade appeared Kenneth Burke's *Counter-Statement*

(1931), Richard Blackmur's *The Double Agent* (1935), Allen Tate's *Reactionary Essays on Poetry and Ideas* (1936), Yvor Winters' *Primitivism and Decadence* (1937), John Crowe Ransom's *The World's Body* (1938), and Cleanth Brooks's *Modern Poetry and the Tradition* (1939). Though these critics differ in their theories of literature, they are uniformly polite to one another, as are their many disciples, and they share in common a leadership in criticism which has lasted for nearly a quarter of a century. Without conspiratorial intent they have achieved a solidarity which is probably unique in the history of criticism.[10] Their detractors — and they have many — regard them as a monopoly that should have to pay taxes as Criticism, Ltd.

Most of the members of this group have come to be known, inescapably, as the "New Critics." Since Edmund Wilson (b. 1895) has never marched under the banner of the "New Criticism," it will be useful to consider him first.

As a critic Wilson is closest to Taine and Sainte-Beuve. Like Taine he studies a writer's ideas in the light of the conditions which helped to form them; like Sainte-Beuve he seems to enjoy most writing psychographic portraits of his subjects. He has always been a journalistic critic, working up his reviews and travel pieces in such a manner that they could later be collected (*Travels in Two Democracies*, 1936; *The Triple Thinkers*, 1938; *Europe without Baedeker*, 1947; *Classics and Commercials*, 1950; *The Shores of Light*, 1952).

Wilson has evinced his faith in the richness and validity of modern literature in many ways. For one thing — and this may be his most valuable service — he has taken the trouble all along to translate, as it were, the modern writers he reviewed, hoping by this means to make them understood and appreciated. He is a gifted summarizer and, in the best sense of the word, a popularizer. Proust, Yeats, Joyce, and Eliot owe some of their present high reputation to his detailed exposition of their work, undertaken when they were still considered too difficult to be worth one's time. Wilson takes pride in his discoveries, counting among them Hemingway's *In Our Time*, Malraux' *La Condition Humaine*, Dos Passos' *Manhattan Transfer*, and the early work of Henry Miller and John O'Hara.

Wilson is the most versatile of modern critics and he has never specialized, as do most of the New Critics, in one theory or one appraoch. His knowledge of the literatures of Germany, France, and Russia fitted him to use the comparative method. He is as capable a cultural critic as Van Wyck Brooks or Constance Rourke. In the essays in *The Wound and the Bow* (1941) he used psychoanalytical and mythological approaches.

What places Wilson farthest from the New Critics is his optimism — or at least his dauntlessness — in confronting modern society. What he does not like he can usually defeat by ridicule or burlesque. Thirty years ago in reviewing Eliot's *For Lancelot Andrewes* he stated the position from which he has never retreated. Eliot had asserted that "it is doubtful whether civilization can endure without religion." Wilson answered flatly: "We have got to make it endure."

Nobody will pretend that this is going to be easy; but it can hardly be any more difficult than persuading oneself that the leadership of the future will be supplied by the Church of England or by the Roman Catholic Church or by any church whatsoever.[11]

To Wilson it seemed "sadly symptomatic of the feeble intellectual condition of a good many literary people" that they were unwilling or incapable of coming to terms with the world they lived in.

One cannot say of the New Critics that they came to terms with the world they lived in, at least not in the sense that Wilson by implication was advocating here. Rather they discovered or created a world in which they could live and keep busy without much reference to the American scene or to world affairs. They would be attacked repeatedly for thus cutting themselves off not only from economic and political man but from the social content of the literary works they discussed.

What is the New Criticism and who are the New Critics? In the 1940's these questions were debated again and again in reviews, articles, and symposia. Lists of the members of this new order were drawn up, but no two lists matched, name for name. Those cited for membership never banded together to issue an official white-paper or a statement confounding their enemies. But as the articles accumulated in the journals which the New Critics were alleged to have founded or captured — the *Southern Review* (1935–1942), the *Kenyon* (1939–   ), the *Sewanee* (under Tate's editorship, 1944–1946), and the *Hudson* (1948–   ) — and these articles were collected into books, the suspicion grew that something like a secret order was taking over. When William Elton prepared his "Glossary of the New Criticism" for *Poetry* (Dec. 1948, Jan. and Feb. 1949), he was certain that he could name all the members. His list was not given the *imprimatur* but neither have any of those he named repudiated their inclusion.

The Father of the New Criticism is probably I. A. Richards, who performed two functions: (1) showed the necessity for considering the semantic operation of poetry as a unique form of discourse, and (2) in *Practical Criticism*, demonstrated the need for training, even of advanced literary students, in the reading of a poetic text. The Name-giver is Kenneth Burke, whose brilliant abstraction helped classify techniques and forms of literature; his primary concern, however, is not with aesthetic judgment but with symbolism and symbolic action, in general. The Apostle is Ransom, who has keenly refined and consolidated the leading concepts, adding important ones of his own. The Prophet is Yvor Winters, who has excellently analyzed and classified poetic structures, but whose moral preoccupations pervade his aesthetic judgments. Cleanth Brooks is the Proselytizer in the Streets, effectively spreading, with his former colleague, R. P. Warren, the gospel of close textual analysis. William Empson, a disciple of Richards, is the Dissector of Ambiguities, and has probably performed the best job of practical criticism in exposing the complex meanings of poetry. Eliot is the Influence, whose general, rather than specific, effect is felt by all the critics. And R. P. Blackmur and Allen Tate, among others, independent critics of much sensitivity and ability, apply the principles of the New Criticism in their own ways.

The increasingly widespread influence of the New Critics frequently drove the opposition to frenzied attack. One such explosion was Robert Gorham Davis' "The New Criticism and the Democratic Tradition" (*American Scholar*, Winter, 1949–50). As a liberal, Davis was shocked by the New Critics' subserviency, as he thought, to the antidemocratic ideas of T. S. Eliot and his French ally, Charles Maurras. By the terms they constantly used Davis was certain he could divine what they really stood for. Their "related terms of honor" were authority, absolutes, dogma, truth; their "terms of rejection and contempt" were liberalism, naturalism, scientism, individualism, equalitarianism, progress, protestantism, pragmatism, personality. Davis admitted that the New Criticism had done some service but it had "completed its corrective purpose" and should be shown up for what it had become.

Noting that Davis' article had raised a storm of replies from their readers, the editors of the *American Scholar* resolved to get to the heart of the mystery by inviting a group of disputants to a symposium. They met at the home of Hiram Haydn, the Editor, and labored until midnight to delineate the New Criticism. Those present were William Barrett (an editor of the *Partisan Review* and pretty far over on Davis' side), Kenneth Burke (by his own admission a "side influence" on the New Critics, if not one himself), Malcolm Cowley (friend to both parties and a critic of eminent good sense), Mr. Davis, and Allen Tate (rightly suspected of belonging to the order). A stenographic record of the conversation was kept so that it might be published in the next issue of the *American Scholar* (Winter, 1950-51). This symposium is by all odds the wittiest of all the debates over the New Criticism. It is also one of the most conclusive.

Always one to carry the argument beyond the immediate point to a remote and novel point he wishes to make, Burke attempted to lead the debate to a searching redefinition of the terms (authority, hierarchy, etc.) which Davis had contended were always "good" words to the New Critics. But the genial host insisted on a discussion of origins. What had the New Critics attempted to do in the first instance and what called into being their particular approach and method? Malcolm Cowley was certain he knew the answer. It began as *explication de texte*, and "from there people went in many different directions."

The first time I read Cleanth Brooks in the *Southern Review* I thought that I was running into something new in American criticism. I had seen something very much like it in French criticism, but it was new in American criticism. It was a close, a very close reading, and I think "close reading" would be a better phrase than New Criticism.

The debate might have ended there, on the conclusion that there had been, indeed, New Critics but no New Criticism, definable as such. Mr. Barrett had a further point to make which opened up a new line of argument.

Was it not all John Ransom's fault (because he had published an influential book in 1941 called *The New Criticism*) that this "bogus entity" was created which now "operates in the minds of a good many people?" Cowley could answer this. Yes, these critics do coalesce, not, however, in their own personalities but in their disciples.

Where Mr. Ransom and Mr. Tate, for example, are miles apart in many of their judgments, young Mr. X, who has listened to both of them and read both of them, seems to be a conglomeration or coagulation of Ransom and Tate. Young Mr. X represents the school — not Ransom, Tate or Blackmur.

Further discussion led to the conclusion that the great debate had begun when the critics of the new persuasion challenged the professors because they were teaching literary history or biography or tracing social influences rather than showing their students how to read a poem or a novel. By their insistence on the primacy of the work of literature and on analysis, the influence of the New Critics had worked down so far that graduate students were now talking about literature exclusively in new critical terms. Mr. Barrett contended that this narrowness resulted in "a kind of separation of literature from life and the use of an elaborate apparatus to reach a point which I find usually trivial, even banal, when you grind down and reduce the apparatus that they have used."

"Mr. Tate: I partly agree with you — about the disciples."

In the course of one evening's conversation the disputants could only allude to many other matters which deserved to be discussed. Several important considerations were not touched on at all. Something might have been said about the relation of the New Critics to the Humanists. Quite as much as Babbitt and More they have been foes of romanticism and naturalism. They are equally disturbed by the encroachments of science and technology in modern society, with the consequent weakening of the authority and influence of the writer. They are as much aware of our loss of a spiritual order.

But several all-important differences set them in opposition to Babbitt and More. They have persistently and with devotion sought to understand and induce others to understand what is best in the literature of our time. If they have helped to build a cult around certain writers, as Cowley asserts (he instances Hart Crane, Pound, Eliot, Yeats, Joyce, Hopkins, Proust, Gide, Mann, Rilke, and Kafka), it should be borne in mind that they are partly responsible for a revival of interest in the Jacobean dramatists, Donne, Marvell, Dryden, the French Symbolists, Melville, Emily Dickinson, and Conrad, to name only a few. More and Babbitt possessed a limited number of critical ideas and they hammered away with them so constantly that the reader becomes insensitive to the blows. The New Critics, so their detractors believe, have *too* many ideas about literature and are always advancing new ones. (Wallace Stevens was content with thirteen ways of looking at a blackbird. A New Critic could find thrice thirteen ways of looking at the poem Stevens wrote about his ornithological observations.) But in all fairness, admitting that their super-refinements are sometimes hard to follow, one must grant that they enormously extended the province of criticism. Jests can be made about the proliferation of the new-critical terms — Eliot's "objective correlative," Ransom's "ontological criticism," Tate's "tension in poetry," Winters' "pseudo-reference," Empson's "seven types of ambiguity," I. A. Richards' "stock response," Wimsatt and Beardsley's "intentional fallacy," and everyone's "sensibility," "tact," and "strategy" — but most of these terms are good sharp tools and we had need of them.[12]

In their discussion the members of the symposium might

have said more about T. S. Eliot as the first New Critic and the way he set the pattern, in the essays in *The Sacred Wood* (1920), for the exploration of method. And there should have been at least a glance at the influence of T. E. Hulme and Pound. Some time might also have been spent on the international aspects of the movement.

One other matter deserved attention: the way the New Critics moved on from explication to theory. Kenneth Burke was a theorist from the beginning and so was Yvor Winters but the others only gradually developed a theory of criticism. It is not true, as one of their uneasy allies, Irving Howe, has said, that any one of their essays "might just as well have been written by six other people, so depersonalized is it." Their individual positions as theorists are distinct and have been stated. Ransom presented his ideas on the subject in the last chapter of his *The New Criticism* — "Wanted: an Ontological Critic" — and elaborated his theory in many subsequent essays. Blackmur early made his position clear in "A Critic's Job of Work" (1935, reprinted in *Language as Gesture*, 1952). Cleanth Brooks outlined his critical credo in "The Formalist Critic" (*Kenyon Review*, Winter, 1950-51). Tate answered in a bleak affirmative the question he raises in "Is Literary Criticism Possible?" (*The Forlorn Demon, Didactic and Critical Essays*, 1952).

By 1950 the "old" New Critics and their allies (one can instance Austin Warren, Richard Chase, Arthur Mizener, Francis Fergusson, and W. K. Wimsatt, Jr.) had seized the citadel. They continued to exert their influence through the journals they controlled. (New names seldom appeared.) In many universities they had compounded their quarrel with the literary historians. Most of them had become professors themselves — Ransom at Kenyon, Tate at Minnesota, Warren and Brooks at Yale, Blackmur at Princeton. They even had an academy of their own, the Kenyon

School of Letters (later transferred to Indiana University) where devoted students gathered every summer to undergo the desired indoctrination.

In the 1950's the only attack in force against the New Critics was undertaken by the so-called Chicago Critics, a group of professors of literature under the leadership of Professor Ronald S. Crane. After having practiced historical scholarship for many years, Professor Crane underwent conversion to literary criticism in 1935. During the next fifteen years he and his associates published a number of reviews and articles which set forth their conception of the nature of criticism and of its importance as one of the four humanistic disciplines, the others being linguistics, history, and the analysis of ideas. In 1952 Professor Crane collected fourteen of these articles, together with six new ones, in *Critics and Criticism, Ancient and Modern*. Here, in a massive volume of over 600 pages, was a philosophy of criticism based largely on Aristotle, a program for putting it to work, and an attack on the theories and the practice of the New Critics. Though there are many pejorative references to them throughout the volume, the direct attack was made in five essays: Crane's "I. A. Richards on the Art of Interpretation" and "The Critical Monism of Cleanth Brooks"; Elder Olson's "William Empson, Contemporary Criticism, and Poetic Diction" and "A Symbolic Reading of the *Ancient Mariner*" (the reading under attack was R. P. Warren's); and W. R. Keast's " 'The New Criticism' and *King Lear*." These essays in refutation fill only about one fourth of *Critics and Criticism* but the volume is more than the announcement of a program and a refutation. It is an attempt at dislodgement.

In his Introduction Crane states the basis for the quarrel the Chicago Critics have with the New Critics. Their criticism, he argued, had been qualitative and general, "concentrating on selected parts or aspects of poems and treating these in terms of wholes which are not concrete objects but compositions of qualities having their substrate in the poet or his tradition or age or in poetic language rather than in individual poetic works." They had attempted to distinguish poetry from other kinds of discourse (this is laudable) but they did this "by breaking down or neglecting distinctions of form and function as between different works." They are responsible for a great proliferation of different theories of poetry, "so that criticism itself seems constantly to be making new starts but never, as a discipline, getting anywhere in particular." At the same time there has been "an alarming kind of irresponsibility in the interpretation of individual works."

The New Critics were not provoked into offering the countercheck quarrelsome. Ransom answered patiently and suggested how a reconciliation could be effected ("Humanism at Chicago," *Kenyon Review*, Autumn, 1952). The severest cut was delivered by W. K. Wimsatt when in reviewing *Critics and Criticism* (*Comparative Literature*, Winter, 1953) he rebuked the "school" for the meagerness of its fruits in practical criticism. In their hundreds of pages of theory and the history of theory only two exemplifications of their method were offered: Maclean on *Lear* and Crane on *Tom Jones*. "The Chicago critics," he concluded, "are people who have a fine blueprint of an automobile and sit around complaining that Henry Ford got started on the wrong principles."

VI

Lecturing at the University of Minnesota in 1956 on "The Frontiers of Criticism," T. S. Eliot expressed some bewilderment at the fact that he had come to be regarded as one of the ancestors of modern criticism — "if too old to be a modern critic myself." He could not believe there was any critical movement which could be said to derive from him, though he hoped that as an editor he had given "the New Criticism, or some of it, encouragement and an exercise ground in *The Criterion*." Eliot's disclaimer was more modest than exact. More than anyone else he had been responsible for the movement. He was first in the field and his theories about literature and his methods of analyzing it had, by 1956, been persuasive for nearly forty years. In all the years between, his newest collection of essays was asked for in bookshops and libraries almost as eagerly as his poetry. In reviewing the 1950 edition of Eliot's *Selected Essays*, R. P. Blackmur described this long-continued influence as follows.

It is clear that what he wrote about Milton and Shelley and Swinburne had more effect than he intended, for certain classes of people quit reading these poets at all. . . . They also took Eliot neat, undiluted with other reading: as with [his essays on] Dryden, Samuel Johnson, and the 17th Century preachers. . . . Again, partly because of Eliot's quotations in his own poems from Dante and partly from the effects of his long essay on him, a "cult" for Dante spread through Bloomsbury and Cape Cod. No modern critic has had anything like the effect of Eliot on the literary people.

Those who object that Eliot's worldwide reputation as a poet is based on a slender output, might bring the same charge against his productivity as a critic. His essays are gathered in eight not very large volumes and these gatherings Eliot has winnowed further into two collections: *Selected Essays* (1932, revised 1950) and *On Poetry and Poets* (1957). But Eliot was actually one of the most prolific of critics. In the twenties and thirties, especially, he poured out a stream of reviews, review-articles, commentaries, introductions to anthologies, and prefatory notes to books. In 1927, for instance, there were forty-five such pieces. A *complete* collection of his critical writing would fill a shelf.

One can mark out roughly four stages in Eliot's course as a critic. In the first, represented by *The Sacred Wood* collection (1920) and a kind of supplement to it, *Homage to John Dryden, Three Essays on Poetry of the Seventeenth Century* (1924), he was concerned with fundamental critical problems ("Tradition and the Individual Talent" and "The Function of Criticism") and in establishing his critical method (the essays on the Elizabethan dramatists, Swinburne, Blake, Dante, Dryden, and Marvell). The ideas put forth in these essays are bold. He avoids abstract terms and long theoretical arguments. Already evident is the clarity which continued to characterize his prose. Though not announced as such, there is a program here, the items of which Eliot would return to again and again to elaborate and refine.

The second stage began soon after Eliot's reception into the Church of England. Almost immediately he became a much sought-after apologist for the Anglo-Catholic position and it was natural enough that his preoccupation with theology and the position of the Church in the modern world should have influenced his criticism. The most indicative essays of this period are those on two Anglican bishops of the seventeenth century, "Lancelot Andrewes" and "John Bramhall" (in *For Lancelot Andrewes*, 1928), the University of Virginia lectures on the relations between religious and literary orthodoxy and heresy (*After Strange Gods*, 1934), and "Religion and Literature" (in *Essays Ancient and Modern*, 1936). Of all the pronouncements in these essays none provoked more discussion than his statement that his general point of view might now be described "as classicist in literature, royalist in politics, and anglo-catholic in religion" (Preface to *For Lancelot Andrewes*). Admirers of Eliot's criticism agonized over this puzzling remark as much as did the admirers of his poetry who felt that he had let them down when he shed the despair of "The Hollow Men" and began to write religious verse. But the essays of this period raised questions about the relations between poetry and religion on which Eliot, first and last, said many contradictory things.

Eliot as the Sage was stage three. As his reputation as a man of letters increased, he was asked to speak before many learned societies and on many ceremonial occasions. (From the beginning he had been in request as a lecturer in the universities.) In this fashion many of his important later essays came into being. The first annual Yeats Lecture, delivered at the Abbey Theatre in 1940, appears as the essay on Yeats in *On Poetry and Poets*. The British-Norwegian Institute Address in 1943 became "The Social Function of Poetry." His Presidential Address to the Virgil Society in 1944 is one of the most learned of his later essays: "What is a Classic?" During the War Eliot was a kind of literary ambassador for his adopted country, the Dean of the cultural diplomatic corps, as it were. Next to the award of the Nobel Prize in 1948, the most signal event in this stage of his career was the presentation to him in 1954 of the Hanseatic Goethe Prize. The address he prepared for the occasion he called "Goethe as the Sage." (In it he made up rather handsomely for earlier derogatory remarks.) His epithet can be applied to the Eliot of this period. Audiences in America as well as England and Europe wanted to hear him because they expected treasurable words from Eliot the Sage. These lecture-essays are broad in scope, easy and witty in style, and filled with ideas which his audiences could readily grasp. Such a literate spell-binder had never been heard. When he spoke at the University of Minnesota in 1956 only the basketball arena could accommodate the thousands who came to listen.

In these years when Eliot the Sage was winning a remarkably large audience, he began to speak out about his own ambitions and difficulties as a poet and the connection between his poetry and his criticism. The essays which convey this information constitute a fourth stage in his career as a critic. This abandonment of his earlier reticence about his own work gratified the seekers of biographical fact. It had been possible to infer that Eliot had chosen to write in praise of poets whose idiom or ideas were useful to him and to condemn those he felt might exert a harmful influence on modern poetry. There was satisfaction in having these inferences confirmed by such essays as "The Music of Poetry" (1942), "Milton II" (1947), and the most detailed of these excursions into literary autobiography, "Poetry and Drama" (1951).

To Eliot, in the beginning, the proper activities of the critic and the limits of criticism seemed fairly easy to define, and his early views on the matter were condensed in "The Function of Criticism," published in *The Criterion* for October, 1923. The work of art itself is autotelic but criticism is not. The critic should "endeavor to discipline his personal prejudices and cranks." When he does not, we may suspect that he "owes his livelihood to the violence and extremity of his opposition to other critics." Most necessary in the equipment of the ideal critic is "a highly developed sense of fact." This is probably why the best critics of an art are its practitioners. They can make discussions of technique meaningful and thus concentrate attention on the object, the work of art itself.

Even earlier, in an essay published in 1919, Eliot had made his stand for pure aesthetic criticism. The critic "must not have any very pronounced theory or scheme and must not set out to prove anything very important." The same idea, only slightly altered, turns up in the Minnesota lecture in 1956. The proper activity of critics and readers alike is "to divest ourselves of the limitations of our own age, and the poet, whose work we are reading, of the limitations of *his* age, in order to get the direct experience, the immediate contact with his poetry."

In his early critical essays Eliot's method was comparative and analytical. John Ransom has described it as follows.

But what occurs to him most characteristically, and most makes him the powerful critic he is, is that it can never cease to be instructive to see a poem in the light of other comparable poems; and perhaps that a critic's fertility derives from his power and patience to observe the limits within which the like poems differentiate themselves and branch off from each other. Eliot has nothing like a formula ready in advance; he looks at the poem against its nearest background to see what sort of criticism it needs; he comes up presently with a set of judgments which are comparative in the first instance, but critical in the end.

Eliot's method of analysis might be termed a search for coordinates. Once these have been noted on the graph, we know exactly where the poem being discussed is to be placed. A flash of observation then follows, one of those shrewd though not ultimate generalizations for which Eliot became famous. Ransom calls them half-truths or gnomic truths and observes that there are enough of them to have stocked the mind of a generation.

One of Eliot's great assets as a critic was the abundance of his ideas. He was constantly throwing out new ones, some of which (the "gnomic truths" Ransom speaks of) he let stand without further elaboration. These were often seized on by his followers and were then so much debated that in time they became hypotheses or even laws in the New Criticism.[13] Other ideas Eliot continued to work over for many years. There is space here to discuss only two of them, but they are the most important ones: his conception of the relation between the modern poet and the European poetic tradition, and his "impersonal theory" of poetry. The first of these stood up well under repeated testings; the second gave Eliot considerable trouble as his poetic practice changed and his religious faith deepened.

The *locus classicus* for the first of these ideas is "Tradition and the Individual Talent" (1917), though elaborations of it occur as late as the long essay on Virgil — "What is a Classic?" (1944). This is the most significant passage:

No poet, no artist of any art, has his complete meaning alone. His significance, his appreciation is the appreciation of his relation to the dead poets and artists. You cannot value him alone; you must set him, for contrast and comparison, among the dead. I mean this as a principle of aesthetic, not merely historical criticism. The necessity that he shall conform, that he shall cohere, is not onesided; what happens when a new work of art is created is something that happens simultaneously to all the works of art which preceded it. The existing monuments form an ideal order among themselves, which is modified by the introduction of the new (the really new) work of art among them. The existing order is complete before the new work arrives; for order to persist after the supervention of novelty, the *whole* existing order must be, if ever so slightly, altered; and so the relations, proportions, values of each work of art toward the whole are readjusted; and this is conformity between the old and the new. Whoever has approved this idea of order, of the form of European, of English literature will not find it preposterous that the past should be altered by the present as much as the present is directed by the past.

Much of importance in modern criticism, and literary scholarship as well, followed from this generative paragraph. It was a stout bridge between contemporary literature and "the tradition." Here was the indisputable answer to Babbitt and More who wished to write off contemporary literature as anarchic and degenerate. There was nothing they could do about the situation, as Eliot had now proved. Writers like Joyce and Yeats (who had obeyed "the necessity to conform") were already "set among the dead." Further than that, the experiments of contemporary writers, if successful, were bound to alter, if ever so slightly, "the *whole* existing order." There could be no doubt that the transformation was actually taking place. Admirers of the work of Yeats, Eliot, Pound, Ransom, Tate, and Auden had already deserted the Romantics. Shelley was down; the metaphysical poets were up.

Tied to the conception of the poet's use of tradition and the eventual effect of his work on "the existing order" was Eliot's "impersonal theory" of poetry. (This theory is also discussed in "Tradition and the Individual Talent.") It was Eliot's belief thus early in his career that "the progress of an artist is a continual self-sacrifice, a continual extinction of the personality." The poet does not express or communicate his emotions. As poet he does not have a "personality" to express. But his mind is like a shred of platinum which acts as a catalyst in causing chemical transformation to take place. "The more perfect the artist, the more completely separate in him will be the man who suffers and the mind which creates; the more perfectly will the mind digest and transmute the passions which are its material." The poet need not seek for new human emotions to express. His business is to use "the ordinary ones and, in working them up into poetry, to express feelings which are not in actual emotions at all." The clinching argument comes in one sentence (and what debate would follow from it!): "Poetry is not a turning loose of emotion, but an escape from emotion; it is not the expression of personality, but an escape from personality."

The impersonal theory of poetry would not lie quiet. Eliot returned to it time after time, continuing in some essays to qualify it so that he might defend it; but the problem was one on which he never entirely satisfied himself. There seem to have been two hurdles which he could not leap over. His early poetry — "Prufrock," "The Waste Land" — squared with the theory; much of his later poetry did not. One could see that his personal experiences and strongly held beliefs had got into his verse. Was he destined to be, like Arnold, a poet whose practice did not accord with his theory?

The higher hurdle was the question of the relation between poetry and belief. If one holds to the catalyst theory of artistic creation, what can one say for those poets to whom ideas were important and who used their art as a medium for disseminating them, Dante, for example, whom Eliot greatly admired? But the question was even more involved than this. The critic who maintains the impersonal theory of art must be pleased with a poem in which the poet has satisfactorily "worked up" emotions and ideas whether they happen to be his own or not or whether he thinks them valid. This problem became acute for Eliot when he entered the Church. He now had a set of beliefs — about God, the nature of man, society, western culture, and the responsibilities of the artist — to which he was committed. Were readers to keep their religious and moral convictions in one compartment and read merely for entertainment "or on a higher plane for aesthetic pleasure"? When he published "Religion and Literature" (in *Essays Ancient and Modern*, 1936) Eliot had swung over to a view directly opposed to the impersonal theory of art. He declared flatly in this essay that "the author, whatever his conscious intentions in writing, in practice recognizes no such distinctions." Still, there was a wistful note (recalling what he may at this time have considered a youthful heresy) in this dictum.

It is our business, as readers of literature, to know what we like. It is our business, as Christians, *as well as* readers of literature, to know what we ought to like. It is our business as honest men not to assume that whatever we like is what we ought to like; and it is our business as honest Christians not to assume that we do like what we ought to like. And the last thing I would wish for would be the existence of two literatures, one for Christian consumption and the other for the pagan world. What I believe to be incumbent upon all Christians is the duty of maintaining consciously certain standards and criteria of criticism over and above those applied by the rest of the world; and that by these criteria and standards everything that we read must be tested.

Is it then permitted to the "rest of the world," to those who are not Christians, to believe, if they wish, in the "depersonalization of art"?

How does one account for Eliot's influence as a critic, so pervasive and extending over so many years? Does one answer the question, *en tout,* by agreeing with John Ransom (as the fact requires) "that his has been the most interesting literary personality we have had in these times"? If Ransom means by this what one thinks he means, then Eliot is, in his own field (or rather three fields, poetry, criticism, and drama) a Churchill, a Freud, a Bertrand Russell, one whose thoughts and acts were touched with flamboyance and kept one guessing what might be coming next. But this answer is not sufficient. One has to imagine an impossible thing: what Eliot's criticism might look like without the poetry. It *might* seem less weighty because the reader inevitably tries to find the poet hiding behind the critic. Also to be considered is Eliot's genius for apothegm. His critical dicta have a way of sticking just as his lines of verse do. As a poet he already stands up near Pope in the contribution he has made to Familiar Quotations. His criticism is just as quotable, though none of it has yet been heard on a Hollywood soundtrack, as the poetry has. The "dissociation of sensibility," the "objective correlative," the "impersonal theory" of poetry, "tradition and the individual talent," the "direct sensuous apprehension of thought" — where did these terms come from? the English major asks and then guesses that they originated with Aristotle or Coleridge. The essays from which they come are also now "standard." Professor H. J. C. Grierson edits a selection from the metaphysical poets and writes an able introduction to it. But Eliot reviews Grierson in 1921 and *his* essay — "The Metaphysical Poets" — is what one now reads first — to see if Grierson was right. Eliot on Donne, on Dante, Marvell, Milton, Swinburne, Shakespeare, Virgil, Goethe — what a nuisance he must be to professors who hold divergent views.

Finally, one must take into account the grave, measured, witty tone of Eliot's prose style, so like his conversation. His criticism never taxes or annoys the intelligent reader. Beside it the criticism of Burke seems tangled in superfine distinctions. Winters is too insistently moral. Tate, on occasion, is authoritarian and severe; Blackmur too fond of digressions; Ransom too philosophical and schematic. Elegance is all.

Acknowledgments

Bibliography

Notes

Index

Acknowledgments

The illustrative passages of prose cited in this book are reprinted by courtesy of the publishing houses listed below.

D. Appleton and Company:
Edith Wharton, *The Age of Innocence*, New York, 1920.

Albert & Charles Boni:
Ambrose Bierce, *The Devil's Dictionary*, New York, 1911.

George Braziller, Inc:
Joseph Wood Krutch, *The American Drama since 1918*, New York, 1957 (coypright Joseph Wood Krutch, 1939, 1957).

Jonathan Cape and Harrison Smith, Inc.:
William Faulkner, *As I Lay Dying*, New York, 1930 (copyright William Faulkner, 1930).

The University of California Press:
Blake Nevius, *Edith Wharton, A Study of her Fiction*, Berkeley and Los Angeles, 1953.

The University of Chicago Press:
Ronald S. Crane, *Critics and Criticism. Ancient and Modern*, Chicago, 1952.

The Citadel Press:
Gene Feldman, ed., *The Beat Generation and the Angry Young Men*, New York, 1958.

Columbia University Press:
Y. H. Krikorian, ed., *Naturalism and the Human Spirit*, New York, 1944.

Crown Publishers, Inc.:
John Gassner, ed., *Twenty-Five Best Plays of the Modern American Theatre*, Early Series, New York, 1949.

Doubleday, Page and Company:
Frank Norris, *The Responsibilities of the Novelist*, New York, 1903; Elmer Rice, *The Adding Machine*, New York, 1923; Booth Tarkington, *The Magnificent Ambersons*, New York, 1918.

Duffield and Company:
Lloyd Morris, *The Young Idea: An Anthology of Opinions Con-*

cerning the Spirit and Aims of Contemporary American Literature,
New York, 1917.
E. P. Dutton & Company, Inc.:
    Van Wyck Brooks, *Three Essays on America*, New York, 1934.
Farrar, Straus and Cudahy:
    T. S. Eliot, *On Poetry and Poets*, New York, 1957; Edmund
Wilson, *Classics and Commercials: A Literary Chronicle of the
Forties*, New York, 1950 (copyright 1950, Edmund Wilson);
Edmund Wilson, *The Shores of Light: A Literary Chronicle of
the Twenties and Thirties*, New York, 1952 (coypright 1952,
Edmund Wilson).
Harcourt, Brace & Company:
    E. E. Cummings, *Poems, 1923–1954*, New York, 1955; John Dos
Passos, *The Big Money*, New York, 1936; T. S. Eliot, *Essays An-
cient and Modern*, New York, 1936; T. S. Eliot, *Selected Essays,
1917–1932*, New York, 1932; Sinclair Lewis, *Babbitt*, New York,
1922; Sinclair Lewis, *Dodsworth*, New York, 1929; Sinclair Lewis,
Free Air, New York, 1919; Sinclair Lewis, *Main Street*, New York,
1920; Kenneth Macgowan, *Footlights across America, Towards a
National Theater*, New York, 1929 (copyright 1929, Kenneth
Macgowan); Joel Elias Spingarn, *Creative Criticism and Other
Essays*, New York, 1931 (copyright 1925, 1931, J. E. Spingarn);
Robert Penn Warren, *All the King's Men*, New York, 1946.
Harper & Brothers:
    A. H. Quinn, A *History of the American Drama from the Civil
War to the Present Day*, New York & London, 1927.
Houghton, Mifflin and Company:
    Irving Babbitt, *Literature and the American College*, New York
and Boston, 1908 (copyright, 1908, Irving Babbitt); Willa Cather,
My Ántonia, Boston and New York, 1918; Maxwell Geismar, *The
Last of the Provincials: The American Novel, 1915–1925*, Boston,
1947.
Alfred A. Knopf, Inc.:
    Malcolm Cowley, trans., André Gide, *Imaginary Interviews*, New
York, 1944 (copyright Jacques Schiffrin & Co., 1944); Stanley Edgar
Hyman, *The Armed Vision, a Study in the Methods of Modern
Literary Criticism*, New York, 1955; H. L. Mencken, *Prejudice,
Fourth Series*, New York, 1924; Dr. Karl A. Menninger, *The
Human Mind*, New York, 1949, (copyright Dr. Karl A. Menninger,
1930, 1937, 1945); Wallace Stevens, *The Necessary Angel. Essays
on Reality and the Imagination*, New York, 1951 (copyright 1942,
1944, 1947, 1948, 1949, 1951, Wallace Stevens).
Little, Brown and Company:
    Owen Davis, *Icebound*, Boston, 1923 (copyright 1922, 1923,

Owen Davis); George Kelly, *The Show-Off*, Boston, 1924 (copyright 1923, 1924, George Kelly).

Liveright, Inc.:
  Sherwood Anderson, *Death in the Woods, and Other Stories*, New York, 1933 (copyright, 1933, Sherwood Anderson); Eugene O'Neill, *Mourning Becomes Electra*, New York, 1931.

McClure, Phillips & Company:
  Willa Cather, *The Troll Garden*, New York, 1905.

The Macmillan Company:
  Frank Luther Mott, *Golden Multitudes: The Story of Best Sellers in the United States*, New York, 1947 (copyright 1947, Frank Luther Mott).

New Directions:
  Herbert J. Muller, *Thomas Wolfe*, Norfolk, Connecticut, 1947; John Crowe Ransom, *The New Criticism*, Norfolk, Connecticut, 1941.

San Pasqual Press:
  Lawrence Clark Powell, *Robinson Jeffers, The Man and His Work*, Pasadena, California, 1940 (copyright, 1934, 1940, Lawrence Clark Powell).

Random House:
  S. N. Behrman, *No Time for Comedy*, New York, 1939 (copyright 1939, S. N. Behrman); James Branch Cabell, *Jurgen*, New York, 1934 (copyright 1919, James Branch Cabell); William Faulkner, *Go Down, Moses*, New York, 1942 (copyright 1942, William Faulkner); Robert Frost, *Poems*, 1946 (New York, The Modern Library); Eugene O'Neill, *The Iceman Cometh*, New York, 1939 (copyright 1940, 1946, Eugene O'Neill); Robert Penn Warren, *Selected Essays*, New York, 1958.

Henry Regnery Company:
  Louise Bogan, *Achievement in American Poetry*, 1900–1950, Chicago, 1951; Alan Downer, *Fifty Years of American Drama*, 1900–1950, Chicago, 1951.

Charles Scribner's Sons:
  Conrad Aiken, *The Great Circle*, New York, 1933; Ernest Hemingway, *A Farewell to Arms*, New York, 1929; Ernest Hemingway, *For Whom the Bell Tolls*, New York, 1940, (copyright 1940, Ernest Hemingway); Ernest Hemingway, *The Old Man and the Sea*, New York, 1952 (copyright 1952, Ernest Hemingway); Ernest Hemingway, *The Sun also Rises*, New York, 1926; Stuart Pratt Sherman, *Critical Woodcuts*, New York and London, 1926; Robert Emmet Sherwood, *Abe Lincoln in Illinois*, New York and London, 1938 (copyright 1937, 1939, Robert Emmet Sherwood); Robert Emmet Sherwood, *The Road to Rome*, New York, 1927;

Edith Wharton, *The Custom of the Country*, New York, 1913; Thomas Wolfe, *The Story of a Novel*, New York, 1936.

Upton Sinclair:
  The Jungle, New York, 1906 (copyright 1905, 1906, 1920, Upton Sinclair).

Theatre Arts Books: Robert M. MacGregor:
  Rosamond Gilder, ed., *Theatre Arts Anthology. A Record and a Prophecy*, New York, 1950.

The Vanguard Press:
  James T. Farrell, *The League of Frightened Philistines and Other Papers*, New York, 1945.

The Viking Press:
  Richard Aldington, *Life for Life's Sake. A Book of Reminiscences*, New York, 1941 (copyright 1940, 1941, Richard Aldington); *The Portable Sherwood Anderson*, New York, 1949; *The Portable Faulkner*, New York, 1946; John Steinbeck, *The Grapes of Wrath*, New York, 1939 (copyright 1939, John Steinbeck).

The World Publishing Company:
  James T. Farrell, *Gas-House McGinty*, Cleveland and New York, 1933 (copyright 1933, The Vanguard Press).

The illustrative passages of poetry cited in this book are reprinted by permission of the individuals and the publishing houses listed below.

Harcourt, Brace and Company:
  E. E. Cummings, *Poems, 1923–1954*, New York, 1954; T. S. Eliot, *The Complete Poems and Plays, 1909–1950*, New York, 1952; Carl Sandburg, *The People, Yes*, New York, 1936.

Henry Holt and Company:
  From *A Witness Tree* by Robert Frost, copyright, 1942 by Robert Frost; Carl Sandburg, *Chicago Poems*, New York, 1916.

Houghton Mifflin Company:
  Archibald MacLeish, *Poems, 1924–1933*, Boston, 1933.

Alfred A. Knopf, Inc.:
  Wallace Stevens, *The Collected Poems of Wallace Stevens*, New York, 1955, copyright 1954 by Wallace Stevens.

The Macmillan Company:
  Vachel Lindsay, *Collected Poems*, New York, 1934; Marianne Moore, *Collected Poems*, New York, 1952, copyright 1951 by Marianne Moore; Edwin Arlington Robinson, *Collected Poems of Edwin Arlington Robinson*, New York, 1954, copyright 1935 and 1937, by The Macmillan Company.

Acknowledgments

New Directions:

Ezra Pound, *The Cantos of Ezra Pound*, Norfolk, Connecticut, 1948, copyright 1934, 1937, 1940, 1948 by Ezra Pound, reprinted by permission of New Directions; William Carlos Williams, *The Collected Earlier Poems of William Carlos Williams*, Norfolk, Connecticut, 1951, copyright 1938, 1951 by William Carlos Williams, reprinted by permission of New Directions.

Random House:

Robert Penn Warren, *Brother to Dragons*, New York, 1953.

Rinehart and Company:

Archibald MacLeish, *Public Speech*, New York, 1936.

Charles Scribner's Sons:

Allen Tate, *Poems, 1922–1947*, New York, 1953.

Irving Shepard:

Jack London, *Martin Eden*, New York, 1909.

Robert Penn Warren:

For "History," from *Selected Poems, 1923–1943* by Robert Penn Warren, copyright, 1944 by Robert Penn Warren.

Yale University Press:

Muriel Rukeyser, *Theory of Flight*, New Haven, Connecticut, 1935.

Bibliography

GENERAL

Joseph Warren Beach. *American Fiction, 1920–1940*, New York, The Macmillan Co., 1941.

Horace Gregory and Marya Zaturenska. A *History of American Poetry, 1900–1940*, New York, Harcourt, Brace and Co., 1942.

Harry Hartwick. *The Foreground of American Fiction*, New York, American Book Co., 1934.

Frederick J. Hoffman. *The Modern Novel in America, 1900–1950*, Henry Regnery Co., Chicago, 1951.

Alfred Kazin. *On Native Grounds: An Interpretation of Modern American Prose Literature*, New York, Reynal and Hitchcock, 1942.

S. J. Kunitz and H. Haycraft. *Twentieth Century Authors*, New York, The H. W. Wilson Co., 1942.

F. B. Millett. *Contemporary American Authors*, New York, Harcourt, Brace and Co., 1943.

Lloyd Morris. *Postscript to Yesterday, America: The Last Fifty Years*, New York, Random House, 1947.

William Van O'Connor. *Sense and Sensibility in Modern Poetry*, Chicago, University of Chicago Press, 1948.

R. E. Spiller, W. Thorp, T. H. Johnson, H. S. Canby, eds. *Literary History of the United States*, III (Bibliography), New York, The Macmillan Company, 1948; and IV (Bibliography Supplement), ed. Richard M. Ludwig, 1959.

Allen Tate. *Sixty American Poets, 1896–1944*. Selected, with Preface and Critical Notes by Allen Tate, Revised edition, Washington, D. C., The Library of Congress, Reference Department, 1954.

Hyatt Howe Waggoner. *The Heel of Elohim: Science and Values in Modern American Poetry*, Norman, University of Oklahoma Press, 1950.

Harry R. Warfel. *American Novelists of Today*, New York, American Book Company, 1951.

CHAPTER ONE
The Age of Innocence

Floyd Dell. *Upton Sinclair. A Study in Social Protest*, New York, Albert and Charles Boni, 1930.

James D. Hart. *The Popular Book: A History of America's Literary Taste*, New York, Oxford University Press, 1950.

Grant C. Knight. *James Lane Allen and the Genteel Tradition*, Chapel Hill, University of North Carolina Press, 1935.

Ernest E. Leisy. *The American Historical Novel*, Norman, University of Oklahoma Press, 1950.

Isaac F. Marcosson. *David Graham Phillips and his Times*, New York, Dodd, Mead and Co., 1932.

Frank Luther Mott. *Golden Multitudes: The Story of Best Sellers in the United States*, New York, The Macmillan Co., 1947.

Edith Wharton:

Percy Lubbock. *Portrait of Edith Wharton*, New York, D. Appleton-Century Co., 1947.

Blake Nevius. *Edith Wharton. A Study of her Fiction*, Berkeley and Los Angeles, University of California Press, 1953.

CHAPTER TWO
New Voices

S. Foster Damon. *Amy Lowell: A Chronicle*, Boston, Houghton Mifflin Co., 1935.

Karl Detzer. *Carl Sandburg: A Study in Personality and Background*, New York, Harcourt, Brace and Co., 1941.

Bernard Duffey. *The Chicago Renaissance in American Letters*, East Lansing, The Michigan State College Press, 1954.

Horace Gregory. *Amy Lowell: Portrait of the Poet in her Time*, New York, Thomas Nelson and Sons, 1958.

Irving Howe. *Sherwood Anderson*, New York, William Sloane Associates, 1951.

Glenn Hughes. *Imagism and the Imagists: A Study in Modern Poetry*, Stanford, Stanford University Press, 1931.

Edward G. Lueders. *Carl Van Vechten and the Twenties*, Albuquerque, University of New Mexico Press, 1935.

Edgar Lee Masters. *Vachel Lindsay: A Poet of America*, New York, Charles Scribner's Sons, 1935.

Carl Van Doren. *James Branch Cabell*, New York, Robert McBride and Co., 1932.

Edwin Arlington Robinson:

Ellsworth Barnard. *Edwin Arlington Robinson: A Critical Study*, New York, the Macmillan Co., 1952.

Edwin S. Fussell. *Edwin Arlington Robinson: The Literary Background of a Traditional Poet*, Berkeley, University of California Press, 1954.

Hermann Hagedorn. *Edwin Arlington Robinson*, New York, The Macmillan Co., 1938.

Emory Neff. *Edwin Arlington Robinson*, New York, William Sloane Associates, 1948.

Robert Frost:

Reginald L. Cook. *The Dimensions of Robert Frost*, New York, Rinehart and Co., 1958.

Lawrance Thompson. *Fire and Ice: The Art and Thought of Robert Frost*, New York, Henry Holt and Co., 1942.

Richard Thornton, ed. *Recognition of Robert Frost: Twenty-fifth Anniversary*, New York, Henry Holt and Co., 1957.

Willa Cather:

Mildred R. Bennett. *The World of Willa Cather*, New York, Dodd, Mead and Co., 1951.

E. K. Brown (and Leon Edel). *Willa Cather: A Critical Biography*, New York, Alfred A. Knopf, 1953.

David Daiches. *Willa Cather: A Critical Introduction*, Ithaca, Cornell University Press, 1951.

Edith Lewis. *Willa Cather Living: A Personal Record*, New York, Alfred A. Knopf, 1953.

CHAPTER THREE
Dramatic Interlude, 1915–1940

Anthologies of plays:

Bennett Cerf and Van H. Cartmell, eds. *Sixteen Famous American Plays*, New York, Garden City Publishing Co., 1941.

John Gassner, ed. *Twenty-five Best Plays of the Modern American Theatre*, Early Series, 1916–1929, New York, Crown Publishers, 1949.

———. *Twenty Best Plays of the Modern American Theatre*, 1930–1939, New York, Crown Publishers, 1939.

———. *Best Plays of the Modern American Theatre*, Second Series, 1939–1946, New York, Crown Publishers, 1947.

———. *Best American Plays*, Third Series, 1945–1951, New York, Crown Publishers, 1952.

———. *Best American Plays*, Fourth Series, 1951–1957, New York, Crown Publishers, 1958.

The Theatre Guild Anthology, New York, Random House, 1936.

Barrett H. Clark and George Freedley, eds. *A History of Modern Drama*, New York, D. Appleton-Century Co., 1947.

Alan S. Downer. *Fifty Years of American Drama, 1900–1950,* Chicago, Henry Regnery Co., 1951.

Hallie Flanagan. *Arena,* New York, Duell, Sloan and Pearce, 1940 (an account of the Federal Theatre).

Eleanor Flexner. *American Playwrights: 1918–1938, The Theatre Retreats from Reality,* New York, Simon and Schuster, 1938.

John Gassner. *The Theatre in Our Times: A Survey of the Men, Materials and Movements in the Modern Theatre,* New York, Crown Publishers, 1956.

Norris Houghton. *Advance from Broadway,* New York, Harcourt, Brace and Co., 1941.

Joseph Wood Krutch. *The American Drama Since 1918: An Informal History,* New York, George Braziller, Inc., 1957.

Eugene O'Neill:

Barrett H. Clark. *Eugene O'Neill: The Man and his Plays,* New York, Dover Publications, 1947.

Edwin A. Engel. *The Haunted Heroes of Eugene O'Neill,* Cambridge, Harvard University Press, 1953.

Doris V. Falk. *Eugene O'Neill and the Tragic Tension,* New Brunswick, Rutgers University Press, 1958.

Sophus Keith Winther. *Eugene O'Neill: A Critical Study,* New York, Random House, 1934.

CHAPTER FOUR
Caste and Class in the Novel, 1920–1950

Malcolm Cowley. *The Literary Situation,* New York, The Viking Press, 1955.

Maxwell Geismar. *Writers in Crisis: The American Novel between Two Wars,* Boston, Houghton Mifflin Co., 1942.

Kenneth S. Lynn. *The Dream of Success: A Study of the Modern American Imagination,* Boston, Little, Brown and Co., 1955.

Arthur Mizener. *The Far Side of Paradise: A Biography of F. Scott Fitzgerald,* Boston, Houghton Mifflin Co., 1951.

Walter B. Rideout. *The Radical Novel in the United States, 1900–1954,* Cambridge, Harvard University Press, 1956.

Harrison Smith, ed. *From Main Street to Stockholm: Letters of Sinclair Lewis, 1919–1930,* New York, Harcourt, Brace and Co., 1952.

Walter Fuller Taylor. *The Economic Novel in America,* Chapel Hill, University of North Carolina Press, 1942.

Willard Thorp, "American Writers on the Left," in *Socialism and American Life,* ed. D. D. Egbert and S. Persons, Princeton, Princeton University Press, 1952, I, 601–620.

John Dos Passos:

Maxwell Geismar. "John Dos Passos: Conversion of a Hero," Chapter Three in *Writers in Crisis*, Boston, Houghton Mifflin Co., 1942.

Blanche Housman Gelfant. "John Dos Passos: The Synoptic Novel," Chapter Five in *The American City Novel*, Norman, University of Oklahoma Press, 1954.

There is no full-length critical study of Dos Passos in English.

CHAPTER FIVE
The Persistence of Naturalism in America

Lars Åhnebrink. *The Beginnings of Naturalism in American Fiction*, Upsala, The American Institute in the University of Upsala, 1950.

John Berryman. *Stephen Crane*, New York, William Sloane Associates, 1950.

Robert H. Elias. *Theodore Dreiser: Apostle of Nature*, New York, Alfred A. Knopf, 1949.

Maxwell Geismar. *Rebels and Ancestors: The American Novel, 1890–1915*, Boston, Houghton Mifflin Co., 1953.

Richard Hofstadter. *Social Darwinism in American Thought, 1860–1915*, Philadelphia, University of Pennsylvania Press, 1944.

Seymour Lawrence, ed. *Wake 11, Conrad Aiken Number*, New York, Wake Editions, 1952.

Ernest Marchand. *Frank Norris: A Study*, Stanford, Stanford University Press, 1942.

F. O. Matthiessen. *Theodore Dreiser*, New York, William Sloane Associates, 1951.

Herbert J. Muller. *Thomas Wolfe*, Norfolk, New Directions, 1947.

Louis D. Rubin, Jr. *Thomas Wolfe: The Weather of his Youth*, Baton Rouge, Louisiana State University Press, 1955.

Charles Child Walcutt. *American Literary Naturalism, A Divided Stream*, Minneapolis, University of Minnesota Press, 1956.

Ernest Hemingway:

Carlos Baker. *Hemingway: The Writer as Artist*, Princeton, Princeton University Press, 1956.

Charles A. Fenton. *The Apprenticeship of Ernest Hemingway: The Early Years*, New York, Farrar, Straus and Young, 1954.

Robert Penn Warren. "Ernest Hemingway," in *Selected Essays*, New York, Random House, 1958, pp. 80–118.

Philip Young. *Ernest Hemingway*, New York, Rinehart and Co., 1952.

CHAPTER SIX
Make it New: Poetry, 1920–1950

Louise Bogan. *Achievement in American Poetry, 1900–1950,* Chicago, Henry Regnery Co., 1951.

Malcolm Cowley. *Exile's Return: A Literary Odyssey of the 1920's,* New York, The Viking Press, 1951.

Elizabeth Drew. *T. S. Eliot: The Design of his Poetry,* New York, Charles Scribner's Sons, 1940.

Frederick J. Hoffman. *The Twenties: American Writing in the Postwar Decade,* New York, The Viking Press, 1955.

F. J. Hoffman, Charles Allen, Caroline Ulrich. *The Little Magazine: A History and Bibliography,* Princeton, Princeton University Press, 1946.

Hugh Kenner. *The Poetry of Ezra Pound,* London, Faber and Faber, 1951.

Vivienne Koch. *William Carlos Williams,* Norfolk, New Directions, 1950.

F. O. Matthiessen. *The Achievement of T. S. Eliot: An Essay on the Nature of Poetry,* New York, Oxford University Press, 1947.

Charles Norman. *The Magic-Maker: E. E. Cummings,* New York, The Macmillan Co., 1958.

John Crowe Ransom, Delmore Schwartz, John Hall Wheelock. *American Poetry at Mid-Century,* Washington, D. C., Library of Congress, Reference Department, 1958.

Grover Smith, Jr. *T. S. Eliot's Poetry and Plays,* Chicago, The University of Chicago Press, 1956.

Harold H. Watts. *Ezra Pound and the Cantos,* London, Routledge and Kegan Paul, 1951.

Wallace Stevens:
Harvard Advocate (Wallace Stevens number), December, 1940.

Robert Pack. *Wallace Stevens: An Approach to his Poetry and Thought,* New Brunswick, Rutgers University Press, 1958.

CHAPTER SEVEN
Southern Renaissance

R. C. Beatty, F. C. Watkins, T. D. Young, R. Stewart, eds. *The Literature of the South,* Chicago, Scott, Foresman and Co., 1952.

John M. Bradbury. *The Fugitives: A Critical Account,* Chapel Hill, University of North Carolina Press, 1958.

W. T. Couch, ed. *Culture in the South,* Chapel Hill, University of North Carolina Press, 1935.

Hugh M. Gloster. *Negro Voices in American Fiction,* Chapel Hill, University of North Carolina Press, 1948.

Shields McIlwaine. *The Southern Poor-White from Lubberland to Tobacco Road*, Norman, University of Oklahoma Press, 1939.

Rob Roy Purdy, ed. *Fugitives' Reunion. Conversations at Vanderbilt*, Nashville, Vanderbilt University Press, 1959.

Louis D. Rubin and Robert D. Jacobs, eds. *Southern Renascence. The Literature of the Modern South*, Baltimore, The Johns Hopkins Press, 1953.

Sewanee Review (Homage to John Crowe Ransom). Summer, 1948.

Willard Thorp, ed. *A Southern Reader*, New York, Alfred A. Knopf, 1955.

William Faulkner:

Harry M. Campbell and Ruel E. Foster. *William Faulkner. A Critical Appraisal*, Norman, University of Oklahoma Press, 1951.

Malcolm Cowley. Introduction to *The Portable Faulkner*, New York, The Viking Press, 1946.

Frederick J. Hoffman and Olga W. Vickery, eds. *William Faulkner. Two Decades of Criticism*, East Lansing, Michigan State College Press, 1954.

Irving Howe. *William Faulkner. A Critical Study*, New York, Random House, 1952.

The Princeton University Library Chronicle (William Faulkner number), Spring, 1957.

Robert Penn Warren, "William Faulkner," in *Selected Essays*, New York, Random House, 1958, pp. 59–79.

CHAPTER EIGHT
Off to the Critical Wars

Anthologies of Criticism:

R. S. Crane, ed. *Critics and Criticism. Ancient and Modern*, Chicago, The University of Chicago Press, 1952.

Charles I. Glicksberg, ed. *American Literary Criticism, 1900–1950*, New York, Hendricks House, 1951.

John Crowe Ransom, ed. *The Kenyon Critics. Studies in Modern Literature from the Kenyon Review*, Cleveland and New York, The World Publishing Co., 1951.

Joel E. Spingarn, ed. *Criticism in America. Its Function and Status*, New York, Harcourt, Brace and Co., 1924.

Robert W. Stallman, ed. *Critiques and Essays in Criticism: 1920–1948*, New York, Ronald Press, 1949.

Ray B. West, Jr., ed. *Essays in Modern Literary Criticism*, New York, Rinehart and Co., 1952.

Morton D. Zabel, ed. *Literary Opinion in America*, New York, Harper and Brothers, 1951.

Gertrude H. Brownell. *William Crary Brownell: An Anthology of his Writings, Together with Biographical Notes and Impressions of the Later Years*, New York, Charles Scribner's Sons, 1933.

Norman Foerster. *American Criticism: A Study in Literary Theory from Poe to the Present*, Boston, Houghton Mifflin Co., 1928.

Stanley Edgar Hyman. *The Armed Vision: A Study in the Methods of Modern Literary Criticism*, New York, Alfred A. Knopf, 1948.

John Paul Pritchard. *Criticism in America*, Norman, University of Oklahoma Press, 1956.

Robert Shafer. *Paul Elmer More and American Criticism*, New Haven, Yale University Press, 1935.

Bernard Smith. *Forces in American Criticism*, New York, Harcourt, Brace and Co., 1939.

William K. Wimsatt, Jr., and Cleanth Brooks. *Literary Criticism: A Short History*, New York, Alfred A. Knopf, 1957.

T. S. Eliot:

M. C. Bradbrook. "Eliot's Critical Method," in B. Rajan, ed., *T. S. Eliot: A Study of his Writings by Several Hands*, London, Dennis Dobson, 1947.

Victor Brombert. *The Criticism of T. S. Eliot: Problems of an "Impersonal Theory" of Poetry*, New Haven, Yale University Press, 1949.

Kristian Smidt. *Poetry and Belief in the Work of T. S. Eliot*, Oslo, I Kommisjon Hos Jacob Dybwad, 1949.

Notes

CHAPTER ONE
The Age of Innocence

1. Jeanette Porter Meehan, *The Lady of the Limberlost: The Life and Letters of Gene Stratton-Porter;* quoted by Frank Luther Mott in *Golden Multitudes, The Story of Best Sellers in the United States* (1947), p. 220.
2. In 1955 *Richard Carvel, The Crisis, To Have and to Hold,* and *Janice Meredith* were still in print.
3. His *Passing of the Frontier* is in the Yale Chronicles of America Series, as is White's *The Forty-Niners.*
4. Roosevelt deplored the rise in the number of divorces in a special message to Congress in 1905. Three years later the Bureau of the Census published a study of the problem. Roosevelt was a leader in the crusade against "race suicide."
5. Actually the first muckraking work was Henry Demarest Lloyd's exposure of the tactics of Standard Oil in *Wealth against Commonwealth* (1894).
6. *Edith Wharton, A Study of Her Fiction* (1953), p. 33.
7. "A Memoir of Edith Wharton," in *Classics and Commercials* (1950), p. 417.

CHAPTER THREE
Dramatic Interlude

1. *Fifty Years of American Drama, 1900–1950* (1951), pp. 1–21.
2. "Little Theatre Backgrounds," in *Theatre Arts Anthology,* ed. Rosamond Gilder (1950), p. 473. Macgowan's *Footlights across America, Towards a National Theater* (1929) is the standard work on the little theater movement.
3. The materials for this section on the art theaters are derived largely from the Introduction to John Gassner's *Twenty-Five Best Plays of the Modern American Theatre,* Early Series (1949).
4. Op. cit., pp. xxii–xxiii.
5. See Owen Davis' interesting observations on how he came to

desert the writing of melodrama, at which he had been enormously successful: *My First Fifty Years in the Theatre* (1950),
pp. 33–34.
6. *The American Drama since 1918* (1957), p. 201.
7. A play based on Cabell's *The Rivet in Grandfather's Neck*.
It was never produced professionally.
8. Quoted in the article on the Federal Theatre in *The Oxford
Companion to the Theatre*, ed. Phyllis Hartnoll (1951).
9. Quoted by A. H. Quinn in *A History of the American Drama
from the Civil War to the Present Day* (1927), II, p. 199.

CHAPTER FOUR
Caste and Class in the Novel, 1920–1950

1. In June 1941 (two weeks before Germany invaded Russia) a
fourth Congress was held in New York under the auspices of
the League of American Writers, the American Artists Congress,
and the United American Artists. The names of the speakers
indicate that this was almost entirely a Communist affair.
2. The title symbolizes New York, the modern Babylon. Passengers
on the Pennsylvania Railroad who were bound for downtown
New York used to change at a way station — Manhattan Transfer — just beyond Newark. This station no longer exists.

CHAPTER FIVE
The Persistence of Naturalism in the Novel

1. This passage on the impact of Social Darwinism on America
draws heavily on Richard Hofstadter's *Social Darwinism in
American Thought, 1860–1915*, Philadelphia, University of
Pennsylvania Press, 1944.
2. Quoted by Horace Gregory in his Introduction to *The Portable
Sherwood Anderson*, p. 27.
3. Steinbeck's preoccupation with naturalistic themes, symbols,
and metaphors derives, in part, from his experiments as an
amateur of marine biology.
4. "How *Studs Lonigan* was Written," in *The League of Frightened
Philistines and other Papers* (1945), pp. 88–89.
5. A clarification of the modern philosophical naturalist's stand on
this question is given in Abraham Edel's "Naturalism and Ethical
Theory", Chapter 4 in *Naturalism and the Human Spirit*, ed.
Y. H. Krikorian (1944). Two passages relevant to this discussion
will be found on pages 93 and 94.
   The naturalistic tradition in philosophy has constantly
pointed to the need for causal examination of values and the

relation of ethical to non-ethical phenomena. It has sought the aid of the prevailing sciences and in turn mapped programs for them. As the sciences grew, naturalism had concomitant phases. It interpreted values on a physical analogy as special movements of the particles or internal movements. Nineteenth-century naturalism was to a great extent biological, under Darwin's influence. Marxian materialism was an exception, and it marked the beginning of a fuller naturalism, which recognized the causal role of social factors.

There is plenty of room for spontaneity in human affairs, but it is an empirical phenomenon that falls within the context of men who are striving to achieve their values, to redirect some and preserve others. It is not an explanation of their doings. The mere assumption of freedom tends to make men leave the direction of change of values to chance. Freedom, in a naturalistic ethics, is to be found in the widest understanding that may be attained of the conditions and causes of choice, so that choice may be a function of knowledge.

6. It scarcely needs to be said, in this connection, that Americans place a great value on the "things" they own. We are notably a consumer nation and we usually have the money to buy what we want. Professor Ralph Gabriel tells me there was a school of sociology some years ago which believed it could assess the status of an American family without going beyond an inventory of the furnishings of the principal rooms in its house or apartment.

7. The tradition of Homer and Eakins was carried on by John Sloan, George Bellows, Edward Hopper, Charles Burchfield, Paul Cadmus, Ben Shahn, and Peter Hurd. If permitted an undirected choice, possibly many visitors to the Museum of Modern Art might still prefer a Hopper to a Jackson Pollock. Certainly the favorite painter of the great American public is Norman Rockwell, whose realism is all surface.

CHAPTER SIX
Make it New: Poetry, 1920–1950

1. Louise Bogan, *Achievement in American Poetry, 1900–1950* (1951), p. 42.

CHAPTER SEVEN
Southern Renaissance

1. In Blanche Gelfant's *The American City Novel* (1954) there is no mention of a novel on southern urban life.
2. Several events in this novel are derived from Long's career. There

are two other novels which make some use of the Huey Long legend: John Dos Passos' *Number One* (1943) and Adria Locke Langley's *A Lion is in the Streets* (1945).

3. It is worth noting that many southern novelists have written biographies of historical figures: Basso on Beauregard; Tate on Lee and Stonewall Jackson; Lytle on General Forrest; Warren on John Brown.

4. A notable exception is Warren's *Band of Angels* (1955), which follows the tribulations of a southern girl, educated at Oberlin College, who discovers that she is the daughter of one of her father's slaves. Set in the period just before, during, and after the Civil War, this novel is in essence a modern "slave narrative," a literary genre which was popular in the 1850's.

5. Several successful Negro novelists — Ann Petry and Chester Himes, for instance — are beyond the scope of this chapter because they were born in the north and wrote about Negro life above Mason and Dixon's line.

6. *God's Little Acre*, the first of Caldwell's books to be issued in a paperback edition (1946), sold over 5,000,000 copies within four years.

7. In *The Paris Review*, Spring, 1956.

8. This analysis draws on R. P. Warren's essay on Faulkner in his *Selected Essays*, New York, 1958.

9. The novels which were put together this way are: *The Unvanquished* (1938); *The Hamlet* (1940); *Go Down, Moses* (1942); and *The Town* (1957).

CHAPTER EIGHT
Off to the Critical Wars

1. Vintage Books, 1955, pp. 7–8.

2. His essays on acting and the drama were not collected until 1948 when Allan Wade edited them under the title of *The Scenic Art*. John L. Sweeney collected his notes on the pictorial arts in 1956: *The Painter's Eye*.

3. Aside from his biographies of Chopin and Liszt, his autobiography *(Steeplejack*, 1920), and a novel *(Painted Veils*, 1920), Huneker's volumes are critical miscellanies. The subjects treated in *Ivory, Apes, and Peacocks* (1915) range, for instance, from Conrad and Lafcadio Hearn to Richard Strauss and Puvis de Chavannes.

4. Set forth in *The Opinions of Oliver Allston* and *On Literature Today*, both published in 1941.

5. This hypothesis is at the center of the two biographies Brooks wrote to demonstrate and account for the characteristic blight-

ing of the careers of American authors: *The Ordeal of Mark Twain* (1920) and *The Pilgrimage of Henry James* (1925).

6. This brief discussion of Mencken cannot suggest the extraordinary impact he had on his generation, for his social criticism was undoubtedly more impressive than his literary criticism. What he had to say about American "Puritanism", about prohibition, the Ku Klux Klan, American business ethics, the Scopes trial was listened to with immense respect by all young people who hoped they were emancipated from the mores of the "booboisie". Perhaps the best place to see Mencken laying about him is the essay "On Being an American" *(Prejudices: Third Series*, 1922), available in the Vintage Books Edition of *Prejudices, A Selection* (1958). The Mencken vogue came to an end very quickly in the depression years.

7. "Irving Babbitt," in *On Being Human*, New Shelburne Essays, Vol. III, 1936.

8. In tribute to this fructifying period of his life More's collected articles, issued almost yearly between 1904 and 1921, were published under the title of *Shelburne Essays*.

9. For an account of these disconcerting shifts in theory see Willard Thorp, "American Writers on the Left," in D. D. Egbert and Stow Persons, eds., *Socialism and American Life*, 1952, I, pp. 606–619.

10. This solidarity was notably in evidence at the time of the controversy over the award of the 1948 Bollingen Prize to Ezra Pound, made by the Fellows in American Letters of the Library of Congress. Among the many American writers who signed statements or wrote letters protesting Robert Hillyer's attack, in the *Saturday Review*, on Pound, T. S. Eliot, and the givers of the award were several of these critics, their friends and disciples.

11. *A Literary Chronicle: 1920–1950*, 1956, p. 135.

12. Elton's "A Glossary of the New Criticism," alluded to on p. 299, contains 114 entries. A study of these definitions will give the reader an excellent conspectus of New Critical theory.

13. A good example is his *obiter dictum* (in "The Metaphysical Poets") that "in the seventeenth century a dissociation of sensibility set in, from which we have never recovered; and this dissociation, as is natural, was aggravated by the influence of the two most powerful poets of the century, Milton and Dryden."

Index